e

||||| || ||||||||||||||||||||||||| |||
D1553284

7

STRATEGIES FOR SURVIVAL

Recent Titles in
Contributions in Ethnic Studies
Series Editor: Leonard W. Doob

STRATEGIES FOR SURVIVAL

American Indians in the Eastern United States

Edited by Frank W. Porter III

FOREWORD BY EUGENE CRAWFORD

CONTRIBUTIONS IN ETHNIC STUDIES, NUMBER 15

GREENWOOD PRESS
NEW YORK • WESTPORT, CONNECTICUT • LONDON

Library of Congress Cataloging-in-Publication Data

Main entry under title:

Strategies for survival.

(Contributions in ethnic studies, ISSN 0196-7088 ;
no. 15)
  Bibliography: p.
  Includes index.
  1. Indians of North America—Northeastern States—
Government relations—Case studies. 2. Woodland
Indians—Government relations—Case studies. 3. Indians
of North America—Northeastern States—Social
conditions—Case studies. 4. Woodland Indians—Social
conditions—Case studies. I. Porter, Frank W.,
1947-   . II. Series.
E78.E2S77 1986   974'.00497   85-30189
ISBN 0-313-25253-X (lib. bdg. : alk. paper).

Library of Congress Catalog Card Number: 85-30189
ISBN: 0-313-25253-X
ISSN: 0196-7088

First published in 1986

Greenwood Press, Inc.
88 Post Road West, Westport, Connecticut 06881

Printed in the United States of America

The paper used in this book complies with the
Permanent Paper Standard issued by the National
Information Standards Organization (Z39.48-1984).

10 9 8 7 6 5 4 3 2 1

CONTENTS

FIGURES

SERIES FOREWORD

"Contributions in Ethnic Studies" focuses upon the problems that arise when people with different cultures and goals come together and interact productively or tragically. The modes of adjustment or conflict are various, but usually one group dominates or attempts to dominate the other. Eventually some accommodation is reached, but the process is likely to be long and, for the weaker group, painful. No one scholarly discipline monopolizes the research necessary to comprehend these intergroup relations. The emerging analysis, consequently, inevitably is of interest to historians, social scientists, psychologists, and psychiatrists.

The original and undoubtedly the most appalling ethnic confrontation in the Americas has been between the early explorers or settlers and the many hundreds of recognized and unrecognized Indian societies they have sought to control, humiliate, evict, or exterminate. In this book, after the editor describes past colonial and current United States policies with respect to Indians, attention is concentrated upon unrecognized and therefore neglected Indian enclaves whose hunting grounds have been not on the plains or in the Southwest or the Wild West as depicted in films but in the Eastern sector of the United States. These Indians were not pushed westward; instead they have been compelled to abandon their precious lands and somehow to endure a sedentary existence.

Europeans and their descendants have identified Indians by their skin color, their facial features, and the alleged proportion of "native" blood. Over the years these Indian societies have lost many of their traditional ways, and perforce they have adopted some of the customs and modes of thinking associated with the intruders and conquerors. They have been assigned to reservations from which many of them have migrated. Although indigenous, they have been subject to similar pressures as the American Blacks with whom only a small number have intermarried and with whom they have occasionally been classified. They have been the target of ardent missionaries. They have been employed (or exploited) to serve the dominant group, for example, in the whaling industry off the coast or as tourist attractions.

This volume, as the editor also indicates, shatters "the myth of the vanished Indian" in the densely populated East. The original treaties with the "tribes" have played a fluctuating role, as have courts of law to which the Indians have referred their grievances and have claimed governmental recognition, especially during the legal changes introduced by the Roosevelt administration and then during the varied interpretations of succeeding administrations. Above all, the "persistence and survival" of these Indian cultures, however modified, must be attributed to the people themselves and their leaders. They have not completely lost their identity; they have retained family bonds and a sense of community; they have been able to adapt their lives, in spite of miseries, to the overpowering outsiders. Even now, a century or two later, they continue to claim their economic and civil rights from the federal government.

We have in this volume, therefore, case studies of Indians in involuntary transition in varying degrees from Indian to Indian-American modes of accommodation. Although prejudice, indifference, and carelessness have hindered the recording of past events and the preservation of the significant documents that we would wish to grace scholarly archives, the authors of each chapter have assembled the existing, relevant, and surprisingly abundant evidence, including interviews with survivors, to support their historical and anthropological accounts of what has transpired. The details enable us to comprehend how each of the five groups has fared in the regions of the East which they have had the misfortune or fortune to inhabit.

Leonard W. Doob

FOREWORD

My first real insight into the myriad problems faced by members of non-federally recognized American Indian tribes was in 1974. That year the chairman of the Pascua Yaqui tribe came to our National Indian Lutheran Board conference and explained the complications involved in obtaining any kind of services for his tribal members. They were Indians and the state said go to the federal government. The federal government said that it had no official relationship with the tribe and that its members were not eligible for services. They were in a Catch-22 situation. Our board was able to help them prepare the necessary documentation to petition for federal acknowledgment status. The Pascua Yaqui tribe won and, as a result, the Administration mandated certain criteria for any future petitioners.

The criteria, and the voluminous work they demand, led us to one of the most interesting and extensive efforts in our board's history. The criteria are legalistic and needed to be interpreted. After understanding what was required, professional expertise was necessary. Over a dozen seminars were held across the country, utilizing the expertise of anthropologists, ethno-historians, genealogists, and attorneys to help those tribal groups work through the seven requirements. Continuous help was necessary, not just a one-time consultation, and that is when our board elected to have full-time person, Dr. Frank W. Porter III, provide the necessary services to help petitioners with their arduous task.

When a tribal group spends many thousands of dollars to prepare petitions, one may ask what is the ultimate value of achieving this status. If the group meets all the criteria and the Secretary of the Interior approves its application, a whole new set of rules applies to the tribe and could dramatically change their lives. Are the monies now available from the federal government substantial enough to meet their needs? Probably not. To the tribal groups and their members federal acknowledgment means a distinct recognition of their culture and heritage. They are a nation. Through the course of history their identity, or lack of identity, has made them an ethnically and culturally disenfranchised segment of American Indian country. These criteria are the only recourse available to reestablish this distinction.

The intense desire of these tribal groups to be legally recognized as Native American people has had great influence on our board and me, both professionally and personally. To deny their appeal was tantamount to the historical rejection of their tribal status. The board listened, they understood and, with compassion and resources at hand, acted to express their support of these people in their quest for identity. We now have two board members from tribes that are in the petition preparation process.

Many have helped along the way. Without Dr. Porter our efforts would have been limited. His knowledge guided our involvement and helped to make this a significant contribution to American Indian people.

Eugene Crawford, Executive Director
National Indian Lutheran Board

PREFACE

The study of geographically defined communities of distinct ethnic origin throughout the United States has attracted the attention of social scientists for many years. Chinatown, Little Italy, Spanish Harlem, the Black ghetto—each invokes an image of a tightly knit, racially distinct, and ethnically similar community. Similarly, the presence of communities of American Indians has almost always been associated with reservations, usually located west of the Mississippi River. Tribes such as the Schaghticoke, Nanticoke, Poospatuck, Lumbee, Mattaponi, or Coharie, however, do not bring to mind such an image. The status of American Indian tribes in the eastern United States has been legally challenged, historically questioned, and anthropologically misunderstood.

Believing that the last stronghold of American Indian culture was to be found among tribes living on Federal reservations in the West, anthropologists were slow to recognize the possibility of obtaining ethnographic data from Indian survivals east of the Mississippi River. During the nineteenth century the Iroquois in New York and the Cherokee in North Carolina did attract the scholarly attention of Lewis H. Morgan and James Mooney. It is not surprising that there has been sustained public interest in and scholarly concern for these prominent tribes. The essays in this volume provide a specific focus on the successful strategies for survival which smaller but certainly not less significant tribal groups employed to adapt to European settlement in the eastern United States. Too many studies emphasize the failure of American Indians to adjust to and survive in White society. Actually, most tribes had devised successful strategies to cope with the intrusion of Whites into their traditional habitats. Despite the concerted efforts by Whites to make sure the Indians would vanish, many Indian communities throughout the eastern United States did withstand contact with White society. They did so by developing new communities during the nineteenth century which have survived to the present. Some were successful; others, such as the Okehocking band of Delaware, were not. This collection of essays examines the strategies for survival of the Okehocking band of Delaware Indians, the Nanticoke of Delaware, the Powhatan tribes of Virginia, the Wampanoag of Massachusetts, and the Poospatuck of Long Island.

1
NONRECOGNIZED AMERICAN INDIAN TRIBES IN THE EASTERN UNITED STATES: AN HISTORICAL OVERVIEW

Frank W. Porter III

INTRODUCTION

In 1932, Grant Foreman published *Indian Removal: The Emigration of the Five Civilized Tribes of Indians*. This study dramatically depicted the militarily enforced emigration of the Choctaw, Creek, Chickasaw, Cherokee, and Seminole to land west of the Mississippi River. Later studies, strongly influenced by Foreman's work, have added further documentation of and insight into the removal of these and other tribal groups (for example, Wilkins 1970, Young 1975, and Green 1982). Not all of the tribes and Indians, however, suffered removal. The treatment of those tribes, bands, families, and individuals who refused to leave their traditional homelands or who returned after being removed is a significant part of the history of the American Indian which is only beginning to be revealed and studied (Williams 1979).

For more than 350 years American Indians in the eastern United States have seen their way of life dramatically changed while still maintaining an Indian identity in an environment continuously dominated by a Euro-American culture. The imposition, and at times acceptance, of Euro-American land tenure practices necessitated changes in livelihood, settlement, mobility, and material culture. Having undergone the full range of acculturative processes with commensurate loss of traditional Indian traits, few American Indians in the eastern United States have been accorded the protection and rights of the Federal trust relationship. There are currently more than 400 tribes in the United States, but the Bureau of Indian Affairs provides services to only 290 (American Indian Policy Review Commission 1977:461). Approximately 115,000 Indians are members of "nonrecognized" tribes. Essentially, these are Indian people who have been denied services either because they have not been identified as *Indians* or as *tribes* as the terms are used in United States policy and law (ibid., Anderson 1978).

The history of American Indian policy and the development of the trust relationship have been exhaustively studied (Prucha 1962, 1976, 1977, and 1985; see also *Report on Terminated and Nonfederally Recognized Indians*). Nonrecognition of American Indian tribes by the Federal government, however, is an anomaly in American Indian policy (Swenson 1981). It is just as frustrating to attempt to find a consistent pattern and rationale for the administrative determination of a federally recognized Indian tribe, as it is to determine why over 100 tribes are not recognized. The results of nonrecognition, nevertheless, are far more tangible. Task Force Ten (1976:1695) succinctly described the effect of nonrecognition on American Indian communities:

The results of nonrecognition upon Indian communities and individuals have been devastating, and highly similar to the results of termination. The continued erosion of tribal lands, or the complete loss thereof; the deterioration of cohesive, effective tribal governments and social organization; and the elimination of special Federal services, through the continued denial of such services which Indian communities in general appear to need desperately. Further, the Indians are uniformly perplexed by the current usage of "Federal recognition" and cannot understand why the Federal Government has continually ignored their existence as Indians. Characteristically, Indians have viewed their lack of recognition as Indians by the Federal government in utter disbelief and complete dismay and feel the classification as "nonfederally recognized" is both degrading and wholly unjustifiable.

During the 1970s the Department of the Interior developed the Federal Acknowledgment Project and established specific criteria whereby these tribal groups could petition for recognition. The

Federal Acknowledgment Project, mandated to determine an Indian group's eligibility for recognition, was not in operation until 1978. In essence, this petition process requires the preparation of an historical narrative documenting the continuity of the group with a known historic tribe and the compilation of a thorough family history of each member of the tribe. Few of these tribes have members who possess the special training required to research, write, and prepare this document. Consequently, social scientists from the academic community and attorneys-at-law have an important and critical role to play in assisting these tribes in obtaining Federal recognition. Scholars will have taken an important step if they understand the diverse processes responsible for the presence of nonrecognized Indian communities throughout the United States and the problems they continue to face in a White-dominated society (Porter 1982:47).

There is no simple explanation as to why some tribes are not recognized. According to the American Indian Policy Review Commission (1977:462), the distinction the Department of the Interior draws between the status of recognized and nonrecognized tribes seems to be based merely on precedent—whether at some point in a tribe's history it established a formal political relationship with the government of the United States. The failure of the Federal government to recognize certain tribes has often been the product of long-forgotten historical accidents and the belief that many tribes became extinct. Whatever the reasons for their nonrecognized status, one thing is absolutely certain: They have not vanished!

BRIEF OVERVIEW OF AMERICAN INDIAN POLICY

Administrative refusal on the part of the Federal government to recognize certain tribes is a relatively recent phenomenon, in part a by-product of the Indian Reorganization Act and the termination policy of the 1950s. The neglect of most tribes, however, is the result of historical circumstances. For example, American officials, accepting jurisdiction over former colonial territories, also assumed responsibility for collecting, translating, and resolving the agreements that former European nations had made with individual Indian tribes. Yet, some tribes which had been familiar participants in colonial affairs were virtually unknown to the government of the United States. Other tribes had become so weakened and depopulated as a result of their dealings with colonial governments that they were overlooked. Other tribes understandably avoided any contact with the colonial governments, the Continental Congress, or the newly created Federal government.

Behind the Frontier

Several travelers who visited the American colonies and fortuitously recorded their observations and experiences, clearly conveyed the impression that the Indians were a vanishing people. Journeying through Maryland in 1679 and 1680, Jaspar Danckearts remarked: "There are few Indians in comparison with the extent of the country. When the English first discovered and settled in Virginia and Maryland, they did great [wrong] to these poor people, and almost exterminated them" (James and Jameson 1913:115). François Marie René de Chateaubriand observed that "the Piscataway of Maryland; the tribes who obeyed Powhatan in Virginia; the Paroutis in the Carolinas—all of these tribes have disappeared" (Chateaubriand 1969:175). In a thought-provoking monograph, D'Arcy McNickle (1962:2) has convincingly argued, however, that Indians in the eastern United States did survive ethnically and culturally.

The persistence and survival of Indians along the Atlantic seaboard and the states bordering the Gulf of Mexico during and after the colonial period occurred in part because certain groups of Indians refused to migrate west after their tribes signed treaties of land cession. Since the treaties frequently did provide land allotments, individual families, bands, or parts of bands remained behind on these tracts. Others simply would not abide by these agreements and severed themselves from the tribe. Occasionally, although the Indians had sold all or part of their land to Whites, they continued to reside within the immediate locale. Some tribes had been granted reservations by colonial authorities, yet only a few still maintained possession during the nineteenth century. Under such diverse circumstances these groups of Indians became remnant populations in their traditional habitats. In the course of time, many gradually were assimilated into the numerically superior White society, ultimately forgetting their native language and losing much—if not all—of their aboriginal culture.

During the greater part of the nineteenth century, little attention was paid to the possible existence of small enclaves of Indians remaining in the eastern United States. In 1889, James Mooney, then employed by the Smithsonian Institution, distributed a questionnaire about the possible existence of Indian communities to one thousand local physicians in certain counties of Maryland, Virginia, Delaware, and North Carolina. Mooney requested information about Indian local names, archaeological remains, and possible survivors of pure and mixed Indian origin. The replies to this circular letter indicate that a substantial number of local groups of Indian origin were present at that time in those states. Many of the respondents voiced the prevalent racial prejudice held by Whites toward these communities. Mooney was informed that on the Eastern Shore of Maryland and Virginia "the few who remained at the beginning of the last century had become so mixed with negro blood that in the general alarm occasioned by the Nat Turner slave rising in 1831 they had been classed as full negroes and driven from their homes, so that their identity was lost." Despite these conclusions, Mooney perceptively noted that several groups still claimed descent from the Nanticoke, Piscataway, and Wicocomoco and attributed their strong sense of being Indian, in spite of their small number, to their stated fear of losing their "identity by absorption into the black race, and against this they have struggled for a full century" (National Anthropological Archives MS. 2190; Mooney 1907:144-45).

Although in the 1930s a small group of scholars directed their attention to those population groups who claimed Indian descent, many of these communities in the eastern United States continued to be perceived by Whites as mulattoes, mestizos, mixed-bloods, or tri-racial isolates. The fact that some of these communities did not have a specific tribal identity partially explains this confusion. To date, there has been no general agreement about a generic term for these Indian groups, but B. Eugene Griessman's "The American Isolates" conveys the idea of apartness, whether genetic or social, that has characterized these communities (Griessman 1972). The consensus has been that many of these people are of intermingled Indian, Caucasian, and Negro ancestry. Invariably, these communities have been assigned a marginal social status, "sharing lot with neither white nor colored, and enjoying neither the governmental protection nor the tribal tie of the typical Indian descendants." Furthermore, argues Edward T. Price, "each is essentially a local phenomena, a unique demographic body defined only in its own terms and only by its own neighbors" (Price 1953).

In some cases the precise origin of these isolated communities of Indians is unknown and unlikely to ever be determined. Most of the so-called "American Isolates" originated along the Atlantic seaboard. Each group has to some degree come under the scrutiny of professional scholars. Brewton Berry surveyed these isolated communities and confirmed the general confusion that exists among the White and Black populations as to the origin of these people (Berry 1963). Consequently, any attempt to establish the origins of some of these Indian communities must contend with an unwieldy body of folk history and naive, often biased, interpretations of scanty historical evidence. Nevertheless, this is the task that confronts tribal groups seeking Federal acknowledgement.

COLONIAL PERIOD

> Spanish civilization crushed the Indian; English civilization scorned and neglected him; French civilization embraced and cherished him. (Parkman 1867, vol. 1:131)

The development of Indian policy reflected the fundamental challenge that Europeans had to meet when they first encountered men of different cultures and different religions in the New World.

Spanish Indian Policy

Spain had two major interests in colonizing the New World. The Spanish conquistador, dependent on the Indian as a source of labor, sought to extract wealth from the land, be it agriculture or mining. Jesuit missionaries, on the other hand, viewed the Indian as an object of conversion to Christianity. The land south of the Rio Grande possessed more than 12 million Indians. A large number of these Indians lived in established communities, had highly developed systems of agriculture and irrigation, and were superb artisans and craftsmen. This combination of factors determined, in large measure, the Spanish policy of dealing with the Indians.

As a result of the conquest of New Spain, the Spanish Crown made grants of land (*repartimientos*) and appointments of Indians (*encomiendas*) to the conquistadores in return for services rendered. The *encomendero* was entitled to collect a tribute, in money or labor, from the Indians assigned to him. In return, the *encomendero* was obligated to provide for the conversion of his charges, to reside in the same district, and to protect them from any outside danger (Zavala 1935; Simpson 1950). This feudal lord and serf system of colonization caused tremendous havoc among the Indian population. The Indian became a mere commodity to be sold to mines, sugar mills, and farms; furthermore, he was considered to be an expendable resource. The Indians, forced to accept fundamental elements of civilization, suffered a continued decline in population, a loss of morale, and devastating changes in their culture. In *Cycles of Conquest,* Edward H. Spicer states:

It was agreed that Spanish regal authority and law must be the framework of Indian life. It was also agreed that the setting for these primary elements of civilization must be in town life. In addition, the Indians must be made to dress in the Spanish manner at least to the extent of trousers and shirts for men and skirts and upper garments for women. They must also practice monogamy and employ formal marriage ceremonies, and they ought to live in adobe or stone houses. (Spicer 1962:282)

Through the strenuous efforts of the missionaries and the passage of "paternalistic" legislation by the Crown, the Indians in New Spain received the protected status of royal wards. The Crown clearly had ulterior motives. Perceiving that whoever was lord and master of the Indians was also lord and master of the land, the Crown declared the Indians to be direct vassals, like the colonists themselves (Wolf 1959:190). For many years ordinances were drawn up to protect the Indians by regulating the behavior of the Spaniards toward them. Yet, as many scholars have pointed out, these thousands of laws could not all be enforced throughout an empire that stretched from Patagonia to California (Hanke 1969:3). Spanish Indian policy depended upon the management and control of one resource: the indigenous population of the New World. As Eric Wolf (1959:195) has forcefully pointed out: "the conquerors wanted Indian labor, the crown Indian subjects, the friars Indian souls." Spanish presence in the New World also caused a biological catastrophe. By 1650, six-sevenths of the Indian population of Middle America had been wiped out (ibid.; Crosby 1972).

Dutch Indian Policy

Although the Dutch certainly believed that European culture was both materially and non-materially superior to that of the American Indian, they did recognize the Indians' prior right to the soil. The Dutch purchased land for settlements and for agricultural purposes. Nevertheless, the Dutch considered the Indians to be backward, ignorant, and superstitious and argued that the Indian had far more to learn from the Dutch than to teach them.

Consequently, the Dutch tended to maintain a physical and cultural gap with the Indians.

The Indians were generally unwilling to adopt most [of] the white man's ways until their own civilization had become eroded through sustained contact. The Dutch, for their part, did less than most powers to bridge the gap. Even more than the British, they appear to have followed a policy of live and let live so far as acculturation, assimilation, and religious conversion were concerned. (Trelease 1969:48)

Very little missionary work was done by the Dutch among the Indians, partly because of the austere Calvinism offered to them by the Dutch Reformed Church. Miscegenation between Dutch and Indian was quite rare, and intermarriage was virtually unknown. Predictably, the Dutch did not encourage conversion or cultural assimilation of the Indians.

The Dutch and the Indians treated each other as separate powers. The Dutch ventured to the New World strictly for trade and empire. Their policy toward the Indians reflected these goals. They viewed the Indians as possessors of the land to be acquired, as sources of trade and wealth, and as military and political powers to be negotiated with, either as enemies or allies (ibid.:51). The precedents set by the Dutch were essentially followed by the English when New Netherlands came under English control.

French Indian Policy

The French have been frequently acclaimed for their genius in securing the cooperation and retaining the good will of the Indians.

Unlike the Spanish, who sought to make the Indians slaves or dependent wards and the English, who disliked and distrusted the Indians, the French basically treated the Indians as younger brothers (Tyler 1973:25).

The development of the fur trade was the pivotal factor influencing the attitude of the French toward the Indians. The Company of New France, given an area of activity stretching from Florida to the Arctic Circle and as far as the sources of the rivers flowing into the Great Lakes, monopolized the fur trade. In return, the company promised to settle four thousand colonists in New France within fifteen years, ensure the conversion of the Indians, and preserve Catholicism among orthodox French colonists (Wade 1969:65). Significantly, the Company of New France and other fur trading companies failed miserably as colonization agents and barely tolerated missionary activity.

Under successive administrators and merchants more interested in the fur trade than in colonization and more eager for personal gain than for the welfare of the colony, the pattern of French relations with the Indians was set. Missionaries sought to convert the Indians. Colonial administrators found the Indians useful allies in their struggle with the English for control of North America. Fur traders, typified by the *coureurs de bois,* melded with the Indians in their quest for pelts.

English Indian Policy

With the successful conclusion of the French and Indian War in 1763, the English inherited New France. The English came to North America to occupy permanently the land. The Indians, while certainly useful to the early English settlers who exhibited little skill in adapting to the physical environment, were never viewed as a necessary component of colonial society. Like their European counterparts, the English legitimized acquisition of land through the "doctrine of discovery." In essence, the doctrine of discovery established the right of the discoverer of "unoccupied" lands to acquire these lands in the face of competing claims of discovery by other European nations (F. Cohen 1942:291-94). The doctrine of discovery was imposed on Indians occupying the "unoccupied" land.

The English, however, did acknowledge "aboriginal title."

Aboriginal title was an exclusive right of occupancy. According to this specific view of land rights, an individual European could secure land only through discovery. In actuality, the doctrine of discovery proved to be a rationale for taking land from the Indians (ibid.).

Among the English there appeared to be a general attitude of hostility toward the Indians. All too often, the English viewed the Indian as an obstacle to settlement. It is significant to note that while the Crown was nominally the source of agreements between Europeans and Indians, the colonial governors of the individual colonies were representatives of the Crown. They were frequently authorized to work out relationships with the Indians. The various colonies differed widely in the policies they adopted toward the Indians. During the eighteenth century, England, faced with rapidly developing independent commonwealths in North America, allowed greater colonial control over Indian affairs. "Muddle and strife were two of the main characteristics of British-Indian policy throughout most of the colonial period" (Jacobs 1969:94).

In regard to the English policy of dealing with the Indians' possessory rights, Charles Royce has argued that the Indian was overlooked and ignored in most of the original grants of territory to private companies and colonists (Royce 1899:549-551). While the Crown granted away title to land in the New World, it left to the discretion of the grantees how to deal with the inhabitants. In effect, actual contact with the Indians would create the need to develop a policy that recognized the Indians' right of occupancy and the responsibility of the grantees to extinguish this right by purchase or other proper methods. Three important spheres of activity throughout the English colonies would gradually lead to the formation of an Indian policy: development of missionary activities, establishment of trade relations with the Indians, and procurement of land from the Indians for the colonists.

The colony of Maryland offers one example of how this policy developed. The Indians were not completely excluded in the charter issued by Charles I in 1632 which granted Maryland to Lord Baltimore. Four phrases in the charter allude to the Indians, but fail either to stipulate the rights of the Indians, or to indicate any concern for their welfare or proper treatment. First, there is a simple recognition that the granted territory was occupied by Indians. Second, mention is made of a payment which required "two Indian arrows of those parts to be delivered at the said castle of Windsor." Third, "savages" are referred to as among the possible enemies the colonists might have to encounter. Finally, the fourth allusion to Indians is the twelfth section of the charter which authorized Lord Baltimore to collect troops and wage war on the "barbarians" and other enemies who might threaten the settlements, "to pursue them beyond the limits of their province," and "if God shall grant it, to vanquish and captivate them; and the captives to put to death, or according to their discretion, to save" (Royce 1899:549-51; Stottnero-Montero 1963).

In the Maryland charter the King transferred to Lord Baltimore absolute authority, without reservation in regard to the Indians, to deal with them in his own way as to their title to and possession of the land. In soliciting potential settlers to accompany him to Maryland, Lord Baltimore declared that his "chief intention" was "to plant Christianity there." In an early promotional tract about the colony, Lord Baltimore declared:

The first and most important design . . . is, not to think so much of Planting fruits and trees in a land so fruitful, as of sowing the seeds of Religion and piety. Surely a design worthy of Christians, worthy of *angels,* worthy of *Englishmen. (An Account of the Colony of Lord Baltimore,* p. 7)

Although Lord Baltimore had publicly announced his intent to Christianize the Indians, his primary objectives centered on securing land and establishing trade relations with the Indians. To further sway the interest of "noble Gentlemen" in colonizing Maryland, Lord Baltimore generously offered two thousand acres of good land to any person who would contribute £100 for the transportation of five able men and furnish them with arms, tools, clothes, utensils, and food for one year. In order to prevent any hostilities with the Indians, Lord Baltimore waived any question of right or superior power to the land and agreed to purchase outright the site for a town and a thirty-mile extent of land. Unfortunately for the Indians, a substantial inconsistency existed between Lord Baltimore's official interpretation of the legal status of Indian land titles and the voluntary purchase of them by the colonists. In a situation comparable to many of the other colonies, ambitious settlers (apparently unable to obtain grants of land from the proprietor) purchased land directly from the Indians and then produced their Indian deed as proof of title to the land (Porter 1979a:177). Large-scale encroachment of Indian land vastly exceeded the ability of the colonial authorities to control it.

On several occasions the Crown tried to implement a coordinated Indian policy, but was repeatedly frustrated by the individual colonies. In 1754, British authorities advised delegates from New England, Maryland, New York, and Pennsylvania to meet at Albany and to make a treaty with the Iroquois. The delegates, instead, drafted an amended version of Benjamin Franklin's earlier "plan of union," which called for a union of all the colonies (excluding Georgia and Nova Scotia) under a president general appointed and paid by the Crown. There was to be a grand council elected by the colonial assemblies. The president general and the grand council were to have jurisdiction over Indian affairs. The plan was rejected by both the colonies and the Crown. The French and Indian War illustrated the dismal failure of English Indian policy and the insecurity of the frontier settlements against Indian raids. The Proclamation of 1763 established that the tribes had a right to the peaceful protection of their lands and that definite borders should be created, and it called for the removal of non-Indians from Indian lands (McNickle 1957:6). In 1768, the Crown created a line running from the eastern end of Lake Ontario to the Gulf of Mexico, beyond which there could be no European settlements, but thousands of White settlers poured over this legal boundary line (DeVorsey 1966). In each of these instances, the Crown failed to provide the means of enforcing its agreements with the Indians.

Conclusion

The history of Indian policy during the colonial period is a "record of the interaction between the Crown or national governments, and the frontiersman or local government, in their relations with individual Indian tribes" (Tyler 1973:28). The Crown dealt with the Indians in such a way as to maintain their national credibility. The frontiersman treated the Indian in a way that was advantageous to him, often ignoring laws designed to protect the Indians and their land. For the Indians, it was a persistent struggle to preserve their lands and way of life. In theory, the individual European nations sought to implement a humane policy toward the Indians. In practice, it failed miserably.

One of the critical developments during the colonial period was the repeated attempts to establish a firm boundary between the various Indian tribes and the American colonies. The Proclamation of 1763, which created the boundary line, was only provisional, occasioned by continuing Indian hostilities. In reality, it was a means of regulating the acquisition of Indian land without hostility. The Proclamation of 1763 was the first delineation of "Indian Country." It set a precedent that Indian tribes existed only to the west of White settlements and that Indian title to land within the colonies had been extinguished. It should not be surprising that most Whites also believed that Indians along the Atlantic seaboard had disappeared. While clearly inaccurate, these beliefs and attitudes were carried over into the new nation.

EARLY NATIONAL PERIOD

With the creation of a new nation after the American Revolution, the formulation and control of Indian policy became the responsibility of the Congress. The immediate problem facing the United States was to establish peace with tribes who had been allies of Great Britain. There were other equally pressing problems. What was the nature of authority of the states and the Federal government in administering Indian affairs? What means were available to extinguish peacefully Indian title to the land to accommodate expanding settlement? How could Congress keep land-hungry pioneers from encroaching on Indian land? How could trade with the Indians be regulated? And how could Christian Whites meet the responsibility of bringing civilization to the Indians (Prucha 1962:2)? The basic Indian policy of the United States took shape as the Federal government sought a solution to these problems.

Given the fact that during the American Revolution Indians were used as important pawns between the rebelling colonies and England, it is surprising that the Constitution was ratified with very little discussion about Indian affairs. The Constitution gave the Federal government power to regulate commerce "with the Indian tribes." This would appear to be a limited and frail basis from which to build effective legislation. Nevertheless, in 1790 the

Congress of the United States passed a series of laws "to regulate trade and intercourse with the Indian tribes." These laws would become the essential features of Federal Indian policy. Chief Justice John Marshall, in *Worcester v. Georgia,* noted that the Constitution "confers on Congress the powers of war and peace; of making treaties, and of regulating commerce with foreign nations, and among the several states, and with the Indian tribes. These powers comprehend all that is required for the regulation of our intercourse with the Indians. They are not limited by any restrictions on their free actions; the shackles imposed on this power, in the confederation, are discarded" (quoted in Prucha 1962:43). The first trade and intercourse act was necessary to provide a framework for trade with the Indians. Yet, one of the most vital sections dealt with the tremendous unrest and hostility toward the Indians among the dispersed settlements in the back-country. Significantly, these laws were directed against the lawless Whites on the frontier who continued to violate treaties made with the Indians.

Between 1789 and 1820, the United States was neither strong enough militarily nor secure enough in her new role as a nation among nations to engage forcefully with the Indians. The Federal government pursued a policy virtually dictated by the military circumstances of the period: to make treaties with the Indian nations. Through the treaty process the United States not only acquired lands but also legal responsibilities to the Indians. Kirke Kickingbird and Karen Ducheneaux (1973:7) poignantly state that the Indian tribes "in effect parlayed their claims to land into claims for services from the new American government."

There was another important development during this period. The Louisiana Purchase of 1803 and the acquisition of Florida between 1812 and 1819 doubled the size of the United States. With the addition of new territory the problem of regulating trade with the Indians became even more difficult. Thomas Jefferson, ever aware of the deleterious effect of contact between White society and the Indians, proposed an amendment to the Constitution in 1803 to exchange Indian land east of the Mississippi River for land west of the river (Sheehan 1973). Although he was unsuccessful, the idea would soon become a modus vivendi in government circles: move the Indians to a permanent reservation west of the Mississippi River. The consolidation of military and political strength by the

Federal government and the emergence of the philosophy of manifest destiny made the removal of the Indians not only feasible but also the primary objective of Federal Indian policy.

THE REMOVAL ERA

Francis Paul Prucha (1962:224-25 and 1969) has persuasively argued that many of the proponents of Indian removal sincerely believed "that only if the Indians were removed beyond contact with whites could the slow process of education, civilization, and Christianization take place." Selfish economic motives, however, especially the insatiable desire of eastern Whites for Indian lands and the efforts of eastern States—most notably Georgia—to be rid of independent tribes within their borders, clearly dominated the euphemistic exchange of land with the Indians. Almost the entire Indian population of the southeastern United States was removed to territory west of the Mississippi River.

In 1830, Congress enacted the Removal Bill, which empowered the President of the United States to transfer any eastern tribe to trans-Mississippi River areas. Although the bill did not mention the use of coercion to remove the Indians, it was apparently understood that military force would be necessary. The first treaty to be made and ratified under the Indian Removal bill was the Treaty of Dancing Rabbit Creek, signed on September 27, 1830. The Choctaw Indians ceded to the United States all of their land east of the Mississippi River and agreed to remove within three years to land within the Indian territory which the Federal government promised to convey to them in fee simple (Foreman 1932: 28; DeRosier 1970:116-28). Arthur DeRosier, in his study of *The Removal of the Choctaw Indians* (1970:126), states: "It symbolized the evolution of the policy toward Indians from Thomas Jefferson's desire to move all eastern Indians across the Mississippi River, through John C. Calhoun's proposal for educating the Indians to accept the need for removal, to Andrew Jackson's policy of forcing the removal." For the Choctaws, the treaty symbolized the depressed spirit prevalent among many of the eastern tribes. Chief David Folsom sadly remarked: "We are exceedingly tired. We have just heard of the ratification of the Choctaw Treaty. Our doom is sealed. There is no other course for us but to turn our focus to our new homes toward the setting sun" (quoted in DeRosier 1970:128).

The Cherokee Indians in Georgia were not prepared to relinquish their land. Under a series of treaties beginning in 1791 made with the United States, the Cherokees inhabiting the state of Georgia were recognized as a nation with their own laws. Georgia, under a state law of December 19, 1829, declared the laws of the Cherokee Nation null and void after June 1, 1830. The Cherokees appealed to the Supreme Court. Chief Justice John Marshall dismissed the appeal on the grounds that the Cherokee Nation was not a foreign state within the meaning of the Constitution and therefore could not bring suit in the Supreme Court (*Cherokee Nation v. Georgia*, 5 Peters 1). Georgia quickly passed a law which ordered White residents among the Cherokee to obtain a license from the governor and to take an oath of allegiance to the state. Samuel A. Worcester and Elizur Butler, missionaries who had been working with the Cherokees, refused to obey the law and subsequently were convicted and sentenced to four years at hard labor (Bass 1936). Once again, the Cherokees appealed to the Supreme Court. This time, Chief Justice Marshall held that the Federal government had exclusive jurisdiction in the territory of the Cherokee nation (*Worcester v. Georgia,* 6 Peters 515) and that the Georgia law was unconstitutional.

Chief Justice Marshall had reasserted the existence of Indian tribes as independent nations. President Andrew Jackson refused to enforce Marshall's decision. Despite various attempts by the Federal government to induce the Cherokees to move willingly, the Cherokee families adamantly refused to depart. In 1835, Jackson addressed the Cherokees and stated his position:

I have no motive, my friends, to deceive you. I am sincerely desirous to promote your welfare. Listen to me therefore while I tell you you cannot remain where you are. Circumstances that cannot be controlled and which are beyond the reach of human laws render it impossible that you can flourish in the midst of a civilized community. You have but one remedy within your reach. And that is to remove to the west and join your countrymen who are already established there. And the sooner you do this the sooner will commence your career of improvement and prosperity. (Quoted in Prucha 1962:247)

The Cherokees could not withstand the tremendous pressure being exerted on them. The Appalachian Cherokees were allowed to avoid removal because of a special arrangement made on their behalf by their White legal counsel, William Thomas. In order to remain in their homeland, the Appalachian Cherokees had to separate themselves from the Cherokee Nation and to accept North Carolina's sovereignty over their villages. Many of the Cherokees believed such a decision would preserve their traditional way of life. Although many of the Cherokees in North Carolina elected to remain behind—doing so legally—other Cherokees managed to evade removal by hiding in the mountains or other remote areas. Many of the families who did remain were provided with small tracts of land; the rest of the Cherokees were removed to Indian Country. The tragic story of the "Trail of Tears" need not be recounted. During the remaining years of the 1830s, most of the tribes in the eastern United States were removed.

All but hopeless the Indians were as they approached their new home, forbidding and strange. And yet there was a wistful hope of a partial recompense—that in this remote country they would find surcease from the cruelty, sordidness, and rapacity of the frontier white man. Hope that in the country he did not covet and would not have, they would be allowed to live in peace to restore their broken health and homes, institutions and governments. (Foreman 1932:386)

But what of those who chose to remain in their ancestral land? Those who soon were forgotten? Those who became nonrecognized tribes?

INDIAN SURVIVALS IN THE EASTERN UNITED STATES

The removal of Indians east of the Mississippi River was not complete. Groups of Indians, who for several reasons remained behind, were scattered throughout the eastern United States. Communities seemed to have developed especially where environmental circumstances such as forbidding swamps or inaccesible barren country favored their growth. Calvin Beale (1957:188) asserts that it is difficult to locate an Indian community that is not associated with a swamp, a hollow, an inaccessible ridge, or the backcountry of a sandy flatwoods. Secrecy meant survival during these years of isolation. After long periods of exposure to the harsh inroads of Euro-American culture and the forced removal of many tribes, these remnant Indian groups would have inhabited sites that would afford them minimal contact with the outside world. These settlement sites would have been perceived by contemporary White standards as a marginal environment. These areas would have appeared to be unfit for large-scale commercial agriculture and to have lacked satisfactory transportation links with tidewater ports. They would, however, have offered the necessary resources to meet the basic needs of the Indians. Significantly, these remote and isolated settlements served to maintain enforced and self-imposed social distance between Indians, Whites, and Blacks.

Separate and Marginal Racial Status

Almost without exception these Indian communities in the eastern United States have been assigned a separate and marginal racial status, usually based on their distinct physiognomy. In his analysis of the mixed-blood Indian, Harry L. Shapiro has asserted that the process of miscegenation has not been seriously investigated nor considered as a method of absorbing the Indians into the general population (Shapiro 1942). Conversely, few scholars have considered the possibility that miscegenation, whether actually proven or not, served as a process whereby the Indians were able to maintain their identity. All too often, investigators have concluded that where the opportunity for miscegenation has been greatest and long practiced, tribes have become extinct. In part this can be explained by the relentless search for "full-blooded" Indians; those Indians identified as mixed-bloods frequently were assigned the classification of White or Black. Undeniably, the difficulty lies in defining the term "Indian" and identifying Indians. William C. Sturtevant and Samuel Stanley, while pointing out that certain communities fit the accepted criteria of Indianness, state that others suffer discrimination and are not accepted as being Indian by their neighbors because they fail to exhibit identifiable Indian biological characteristics (Sturtevant and Stanley 1968). Phenotypic variation of members of these Indian communities is present, with extremes of skin color from light to dark and of hair texture from very curly to straight. Clearly, the racial status of the members of these communities varies considerably, both as perceived in the minds of the Indians and in the eyes of their White and Black neighbors.

Racially and culturally, those Indians who remained in the eastern United States have been treated as a unique people. Rejected and scorned by Whites and refusing to associate with Blacks, the Indians consciously and purposely remained apart, caught between two cultures. A precise assessment of the forces operating to preserve their separate status and identity is essential to an understanding of the formation and persistence of these distinct Indian communities. Each group of Indian survivals in the eastern United States is unique with regard to the historical circumstances surrounding its origin and community development. The specific ways and means of the eventual integration of Indian survivals into the prevailing system of the dominant White society, however, appear to have certain common denominators. In their analysis of racially mixed minorities, Noel P. Gist and Anthony G. Dworkin argue that the development of community consciousness appears to depend on the relative size of the mixed-race population and the nature of their relationships with other groups (Gist and Dworkin 1972:1-23). A close examination of the process of community development reveals that other factors were also responsible for holding these Indian groups together during the nineteenth century as they were gradually adapting to their place and role in a plural society. Most important were the maintenance of family unity, the transition from an aboriginal to a Euro-American concept of land tenure, the effect of racial discrimination, and the adoption of specific American core institutions.

MAINTENANCE OF FAMILY UNITY

At the time of initial contact, the various tribes residing in the eastern United States had devised successful systems of land tenure that were adapted to particular combinations of ecological and social conditions. As the culture of the Indians and the ecology of their habitat were dramatically changed by contact with Europeans, their traditional form of land tenure gradually became nonfunctional (Linton 1942; Sutton 1975). With the loss of their land by one means or another, these dispossessed Indian groups were faced with several choices: amalgamation, assimilation, sexual unions (either in conventional marriages or in unconventional unions) with Europeans and Africans, and migration, to name just a few. Another option, which a large number clearly pursued, was to remain in their traditional habitat. These were small groups, in many cases family units, who would have been large enough to be relatively self-contained, yet small enough not to deplete the game within an ever dwindling hunting range.

Critical to the survival of many of these Indian groups who chose to remain in or near their traditional habitat was the continuance of the family hunting unit. Accustomed to dispersing to remote areas and to maintaining lengthy periods of isolation, the family hunting unit would have allowed some Indian families to subsist successfully in their traditional habitat even though much of their land had been preempted by Europeans. Similarly, the move of the remnant Indian groups to marginal environments would not have proven to be a severe hardship and would have partially reduced their contact and conflict with White settlers.

These Indian families gradually assumed the outward appearance of Euro-Americans through their acquisition of material culture traits. Frequently, the Indians became destitute and impoverished and were reduced to selling pottery, baskets, and furs to Whites. Lewis Evans, the Pennsylvania surveyor and cartographer, observed that the "Remnants of some Nations . . . wander here and There for the Sake of making ordinary wicker Baskets & Basons" (Gipson 1939:93). George H. Loskiel (1794:130), a Moravian missionary, lamented that these detached Indian families subsisted by making "baskets, brooms, wooden spoons, dishes &c. and sell them to the white people for victuals and clothes."

At this particular juncture these isolated Indian families became indistinguishable from the lower stratum of eighteenth century rural White society. Accustomed to fishing, trapping, and hunting for their White neighbors, as well as manufacturing various utensils to be sold, the Indians also had adopted many of the outward accoutrements of White society (Porter 1982). Andrew Burnaby (1775:40-41), another astute observer of colonial society, admitted mistaking these isolated Indian groups as rural Whites. Many other observers were similarly misled and identified comparable Indian groups as mixed-blood populations. The uncritical acceptance of these observations by many scholars and state and Federal government officials has confused immeasurably our understanding of how Indians in the eastern United States survived and maintained their sense of identity.

TRANSITION FROM ABORIGINAL TO EURO-AMERICAN CONCEPT OF LAND TENURE

Frontier expansion rapidly engulfed these isolated enclaves of Indian families, and they frequently lost contact with other tribes. It is a paradox that these Indians were often perceived as squatters on the land. The nineteenth century would bring many changes to these Indian families. Men, when so inclined, sought wage work on White-owned farms, lumber mills, or other light industries. Hunting and fishing remained an important activity. The women sold produce from small gardens and sold or bartered various handcrafted items to local merchants and peddlers. From these varied activities and experiences during the nineteenth century, the Indian survivals not only became fully acquainted with the rural White economy but also gained an intimate knowledge of the legal institutions and social customs of the Whites. Their repeated appeals to the county courts about land encroachment, destruction of private property, physical abuse, and murder strongly support this point.

One of the first steps on the part of the Indian survivals in their move toward participating in the Euro-American form of land tenure was to become tenants on the land. It is extremely difficult to ascertain the precise motives behind their decision to become tenants. A strong possibility exists that these Indians had worked for White farmers as sharecroppers, a pattern quite common in the rural South. As tenants, they gradually accumulated enough capital and material wealth to purchase their own property. This property would afford a land-base upon which the communities in time would develop.

In order to reconstruct the evolving system of land tenure in which the Indians participated, the researcher is totally dependent on the data contained in the early land records, wills, inventories of estates, and real and personal tax lists. Several factors account for the apparent paucity of documentary evidence concerning the land tenure of Indian survivals. During the nineteenth century no precise criteria existed for determining the racial status of Indians (Beale 1958). In most cases the records fail to indicate a designation for Indians. Instead, local tax assessors, census takers, and other public officials classified the Indians as being either mulattoes or "colored" people. In addition, many land transactions were oral agreements that were never recorded; presumably, most of the Indians at this date were illiterate, which explains the absence of private papers. Nevertheless, the growth and development of Indian communities in the eastern United States can be, and has been, thoroughly documented (Porter 1979b; Stern 1952; Williams 1979; and Griessman 1972).

PROCESS OF COMMUNITY DEVELOPMENT

The traditional habitats in which these small, isolated bands of Indians continued to reside during the eighteenth century became the locus of new communities which grew and developed throughout the nineteenth century. Significantly, the events surrounding their earlier relationship with Whites in the seventeenth and eighteenth centuries influenced, and in some cases determined, whether these new communities would be able to withstand the tremendous pressures exerted upon them by a hostile and racially biased White society.

The antecedents of the idea of placing Indians in communities patterned after the Euro-American settlements are to be found in the colonial period. Colonial authorities repeatedly relocated entire tribes to act as buffer zones between the tidewater settlements and the hostile tribes who resided in the interior. In 1713, Governor Alexander Spotswood of Virginia recommended a plan for securing the frontier with settlements of tributary Indians. Scattered tribes and bands would be consolidated in units at strategic points. In addition to being in a better position to resist attacks, the Indians would be more accessible to missionaries and teachers. Spotswood attempted to dispel any apprehension on the part of the Indians by explaining that they would have "a large tract of land to hunt in, a body of English to live among them and instruct their children in literature and the principles of Christianity, to bring them to a more civilized and plentiful manner of living, and to establish a constant intercourse of trade between them and the inhabitants of this colony" (McIlwaine 1928:363-64). The Indians acknowledged their dependency on the King of England and were to hold their land by confirmed patents under the seal of the colony (Robinson 1959:58).

In Maryland, the Piscataway Indians relinquished land to Governor Calvert and his settlers and agreed to move their settlements northwest along the Potomac River. In this way they would serve as a buffer between the Susquehannock Indians and the growing settlement of St. Mary's City. In return, they were to receive protection provided by Governor Calvert (Ferguson 1960; Merrell 1979; and Porter 1979a). Unfortunately, the practice of using tributary Indians for protection did not prove to be successful. The ultimate result of being tributary Indians was detrimental as traditional settlement systems were altered, subsistence activities were severely disrupted, and economic and political relationships with neighboring tribes were rearranged (Jennings 1982).

Using Indians as tributaries caused a major departure from the aboriginal system of land tenure. By the middle of the seventeenth century and continuing into the eighteenth century, many of the tribes had been placed on permanent reservations. These reservations—as administrative units—became a form of property which incorporated post-contact aspects of aboriginal land tenure and changes generated by colonial administrative practice and law. Significantly, permanent residence on reservations proved in many cases to be unsatisfactory for those tribes whose subsistence strategy reflected an economic adjustment to differing ecological zones. The success of their subsistence efforts depended entirely upon freedom of mobility and access to micro-environments within their habitat at critical seasons of the year. Two mutually related problems developed from permanent residence on reservations. Reservations had been created with the explicit understanding that the Indians would reside within specific boundaries. After relatively brief periods of time, food resources (both flora and fauna) became sorely depleted. Forced to seek game outside the reservation, the Indians temporarily abandoned their dwellings. White settlers, interpreting this act as a violation of the reservation agreements, took possession of the land.

Missionaries attempted to convert Indians and to bring them together in small settlements where they would receive an education and learn new skills. Two notable examples of missionary activity were the work of the Reverend David Brainerd among the remnant groups of Indians in New Jersey and the Reverend John Eliot among the "Praying Indians" in the town of Natick, Massachusetts. When Brainerd visited the Indians living at Crossweeksung in New Jersey, he found only a small number and "perceived the Indians in these Parts were very much scattered, there being not more than two or three Families in a Place, and these small Settlements six, ten, fifteen, twenty and thirty Miles and some more, from the Place I was then at." Brainerd's work among the Indians resulted in their gathering "together from all Quarters to this place, and have built them little Cottages, so that more than Twenty Families live within a Quarter of a Mile of me." Within a short time, Brainerd excitedly exclaimed: "My people [went] out this Day upon the Design of clearing some of their Lands above fifteen Miles distant from this Settlement, *in Order to Their Settling there in a compact form* [my italics], where they might be under Advantages of attending the public Worship of God, of having their Children Schooled, and at the same time a conveniency of Planting" (Brainerd 1746:1-2, 102-3, 135, 153). The Brotherton Indians, as residents of this community were called, remained "civilized" only as long as the Reverend David Brainerd and, upon his death, his brother John were present.

In the middle of the seventeenth century, a number of Massachusett Indians made a decision to adopt specific aspects of English culture. This move was prompted, in part, by the devastating impact of European diseases on the Massachusett. The tremendous breakdown within Massachusett society caused many Indians to lose faith in their traditional beliefs, institutions, and practices. Some of the leaders assigned their affliction to the wrath of the English God, a belief which was intensified and fostered by the missionary effort of John Eliot. Fourteen Praying Towns of Indians, established after 1650, attempted some degree of assimilation. The Indians of Nonanetum, the first Praying Indian community, sought to establish a town organized along English lines. They selected Natick as the site for the first Praying Town. Within a decade, the English town of Dedham filed suit against the Massachusett, claiming that the Indians had settled on the land illegally. John Eliot, representing the Indians, asserted that their claim to Natick was just and must be respected. Eliot presented the court with a detailed and carefully prepared brief, which defended the position of the Praying Indians. After several appeals the Massachusetts Court of Assistants, thoroughly impressed with Eliot's arguments, rendered their judgment in favor of Natick. The Praying Towns were quite successful until the outbreak of King Philip's War in 1675 when most of the Indians were interned on

Deer Island in Boston Harbor. Few would return to Natick (Morrison 1983; Mochow 1968).

Despite all of these efforts—tributary Indians, reservations, mission settlements—to bring the Indians together into compact settlements and teach them new skills, by the close of the eighteenth century there was a general consensus, as noted above, that the aboriginal population of the eastern United States had become extinct. Forgotten or neglected by Whites, they gradually began to reconstitute a form of social organization and land tenure, retained a sense of their Indian identity, and maintained a spatially defined presence on the landscape. I have identified three types of communities of Indian survivals which developed in the eastern United States during the eighteenth and nineteenth centuries: reservation communities, missionary communities, and folk communities.

Reservation communities were able to survive as long as they retained possession of their land. Maintaining a land-base was not an easy task. Of the reservations created in the eastern United States, the only ones existing today are in Connecticut, Florida, Maine, Michigan, Mississippi, New York, and North Carolina.

The continued success of the Brotherton community was entirely dependent upon the energy and devotion of David and John Brainerd. After their deaths there was no one to take their place, and the community's raison d'être was gone. Although it was assumed that after the departure of the Brothertons there were no Indians remaining in New Jersey, this was not the case. Inevitably, there were individuals or families who were unwilling to leave their homes. A consciousness of Indian identity was kept alive, yet no spatially defined Indian community existed in New Jersey during the nineteenth century. Instead, there were widely dispersed families who collectively embraced their varied Indian ancestry and recently have organized themselves as the Nanticoke-Lenni Lenape, Inc. and the Ramapough Mountain Indians, Inc. (Collins 1972; D. Cohen 1974; Larrabee 1976).

The Natick Indians, once the successful experiment in assimilation, were "practically extinct" by 1848. Since 1810, they had been under a guardian, who supervised the sale of the last of their land in 1828. The Stockbridge Indians, who were greatly influenced by the missionary work of John Sergeant, had also attempted an experiment in Indian-White town living. By 1789, the Whites had forced the Indians out of the town of Stockbridge, Massachusetts. This group of Stockbridge Indians moved to Wisconsin in the early nineteenth century, where they created a new and viable community (Mochow 1968:182).

Folk communities developed as these Indian survivals began gradually to participate in the Euro-American form of land tenure. In many respects a folk community is quite similar to a folk society. Following the lead of Robert Redfield (1947, 1955), I define a folk community as a group (1) small and both socially and spatially isolated from other groups, (2) composed of people much alike in physical appearance (at least as perceived in the minds of an outside group), (3) similar in customary modes of behavior, (4) possessing a strong sense of belonging together, (5) having tightly knit social structures and clearly distinguished family relationships, and (6) economically self-sufficient with little class distinction (Porter 1982). A folk community is, in effect, "a little world off by itself."

EFFECT OF RACIAL DISCRIMINATION

A large number of the nonrecognized tribes in the eastern United States are also folk communities. Given their unique historical circumstances, no two folk communities (the terms folk and Indian communities are used interchangeably here) will have had identical experiences in the process of their formation during the nineteenth century. Having secured a property base and having been held together by the bonds of kinship, the Indians were confronted with the problems of maintaining individual and community identity.

Simultaneous with their acquisition of land, the Indians were subjected to the racial prejudice, hostility, and segregation normally accorded to Negroes. This prejudicial attitude was based on skin color and physiognomy. After 1830, especially with the heightened racial fears caused by the Nat Turner slave rebellion in 1831, the White population came to regard the Indians in the same manner as they regarded the Negro in the deep South. During the 1800s, most Americans recognized only two groups of people: Whites and non-Whites. The non-White category included Blacks, mulattoes, "colored people," and Indians. This perception cemented the racial status and classification of the Indians well into the twentieth century. During these years of self-imposed and externally enforced segregation, the Indians forgot much of their history and culture. When they finally emerged from their remote habitats and began to establish their present folk communities, they usually retained only the knowledge that they were Indian and the social cohesion that had been forged by shared hardship.

Neither White nor Black, in the eyes of their neighbors, the Indians were commonly referred to as "those people," or by a more disparaging epithet (Dunlap and Weslager 1947). Significantly, this external pressure served to further strengthen the social bonds of these folk communities. Racial prejudice served the critical function of intensifying the self-imposed spatial isolation and cultural separation of the Indians in their relationship with the White and Black populations. In turn, the isolation of the Indians permitted culture change to proceed at a slow pace, allowing the Indians to integrate selected material and non-material Euro-American traits into their own emerging culture.

Charles Hudson (1976:478-501), in considering the presence of Indians in the southeastern United States, distinguished three categories of Indianness: (1) those who have retained parts of their aboriginal culture, (2) those who have lost their aboriginal culture but who retain strong genetic and social identities as Indians, and (3) those racially mixed peoples who have only a tenuous cultural and genetic Indian background but are establishing social identity as Indians. It should be noted that these categories merely reflect the degree of acculturation experienced by the individual Indian communities. It is significant that despite the degree of culture change, the members of these communities have consistently identified themselves as Indians. Nevertheless, most of these Indian communities have been, and continue to be, officially nonrecognized by the Federal government.

ADOPTION OF SPECIFIC AMERICAN CORE INSTITUTIONS

While these Indian communities had managed to preserve their identity despite years of subordination and hostility, they had also recognized the value of certain aspects of White culture and had borrowed and integrated specific core American institutions, most notably formal education and organized religion, into their own cultural framework. The controversy over the racial status of those individuals claiming Indian ancestry, however, created the need in many of the Indian communities to construct and maintain separate churches and schools to accommodate the White, Black, and Indian populations (Berry 1963; Porter 1978; Rountree 1972; Stern 1952).

INDIAN COMMUNITIES AS TRI-RACIAL ISOLATES

Scholars have long been aware of the presence of Indian communities in the eastern United States. Their research of these groups, however, has until quite recently been biased because of their interpretation of them as tri-racial isolates, not necessarily as descendants of Indians. In the past, the designation of these groups as tri-racial was often the conclusion of the investigator based on a reflection of public opinion in the area rather than from information obtained directly from the community under consideration. Investigations from this particular perspective have distorted our understanding of the essential processes involved in the persistence of the Indian communities to the present. The information obtained from such studies directs our attention to either surviving aboriginal culture traits (for example, Harrington 1908; Speck 1915), or to the presumed social qualities and ramifications associated with these groups as tri-racial isolates (for example, Pollitzer 1972; Elston 1971; Witkop, et al 1966). The crucial point to determine in this issue is the impact such perceptions have had on the development of social institutions and the emergence of distinct communities. Whether miscegenation can be biologically demonstrated or not, both the Indians and those individuals outside their communities have reacted in their own specific ways to this question.

More recently, we have admitted that the most important question to consider is not whether or to what extent these groups are Indian. Rather, the emphasis should be on the process of acculturation, the reconstruction of tribal histories, the economic and social integration into White society, and the problems of maintaining tribal identity and achieving Federal recognition.

PRE-1978 RECOGNITION EFFORTS

Prior to the creation of the Federal Acknowledgment Project in the Bureau of Indian Affairs in 1978, several individual tribes discovered disparate means to achieve recognition from the Federal government. Each case clearly illustrates the complete lack of understanding of the phenomenon of nonrecognition, the absence of any formal procedure to establish Federal recognition, and the isolated nature through time of those tribes who successfully achieved Federal recognition.

The Indian Reorganization Act of 1934, which set forth specific rules for tribes seeking to incorporate under that legislation, also extended the fundamental right of self-government to Indian tribes. It was recommended that the Indians would be allowed to vote whether they would choose to accept the legislation on behalf of their tribes or not. A series of "congresses of Indians" were held in areas where Indian population was concentrated (Tyler 1973:131). In calling for these elections, however, it became necessary for the Secretary of the Department of the Interior to make determinations which, in effect, gave Federal recognition to a particular group of Indians as constituting a tribe. Consequently, the Federal government, because of Section 16 of the Indian Reorganization Act, has been forced in several instances to make administrative decisions about the question of what groups actually constitute a tribe.

Significantly, nonrecognized tribes were investigated by the Bureau of Indian Affairs to determine their eligibility under the Indian Reorganization Act. The Indian Organization Division was established in 1934 within the Bureau of Indian Affairs to carry out the organization of tribal governments. An "Applied Anthropology Unit" was also created to ensure that the organization established by each tribe be suited to its particular needs and that it reflected the tribe's traditional way of governing itself (Anderson 1978:10). Several anthropologists were sent to gather information about these tribes. In particular, a physical anthropologist was temporarily employed to assist in determining the degree of blood of certain Indians who had petitioned to organize under the Indian Reorganization Act. One example will suffice to demonstrate the "scientific" nature of the investigations of these physical anthropologists. Carl Seltzer was sent to North Carolina to determine the racial ancestry of the people now known as the Lumbee Indians. Seltzer used physical features, measurements, and blood type to demonstrate that only twenty-two out of more than 200 persons could qualify as having half or more Indian blood. Family relationships were blatantly ignored. In one case, the full brother of a man who qualified was excluded (ibid.; Blu 1980:72).

Federal recognition became a "vicious myth" (Anderson 1978). In response to an inquiry from Henry M. Jackson, Chairman of the Committee on Interior and Insular Affairs, concerning Federal recognition of Indian tribes, Commissioner of Indian Affairs LaFollette Butler responded:

In cases of special difficulty, a ruling has generally been obtained from the Solicitor for the Interior Department as to the tribal status of the group seeking to organize. The considerations which, singly or jointly, have been particularly relied upon in reaching the conclusion that a group constitutes a 'tribe' or 'band' have been:

(1) That the group has had treaty relations with the United States.

(2) That the group has been denominated a tribe by act of Congress or Executive Order.

(3) That the group has been treated as having collective rights in tribal land or funds, even though not expressly designated a tribe.

(4) That the group has been treated as a tribe or band by other Indian tribes.

(5) That the group has exercised political authority over its members, through a tribal council or other governmental forms.

Other factors considered, though not conclusive, are the existence of special appropriation items for the groups and the social solidarity of the group. The remaining question from your and Mr. Sigo's letters is whether Federal recognition can be extended to a tribe that does not have a land base. A land base is not a requirement for Federal recognition. (LaFollette Butler to the Honorable Henry M. Jackson, January 7, 1974, Washington, D.C.)

Butler also provided Senator Jackson with a partial list of tribes that had been granted recognition and the specific authority for such recognition:

Tribe	Authority Used
1. Menominee Indian tribe of Wisconsin	P.L. 93-197, 93rd Congress 1st Session, Approved December 22, 1973 (87 Stat. 770).
2. Original Band of Sault St. Marie Chippewa Indians (Michigan)	Commissioner's letter of September 7, 1972, and Solicitor's Opinion of February 7, 1974
3. Yavapai-Tonto Apache Tribe (Arizona)	P.L. 92-470 (86 Stat. 783) Approved October 6, 1972
4. Nooksack Indian Tribe of Washington	Solicitor's Opinion M-36833, August 13, 1971
5. Burns Paiute Indian Colony (Oregon)	Solicitor's Opinion M-36759, November 16, 1967
6. Upper Skagit Indian Tribe (Washington)	Act of June 30, 1913 (38 Stat. 101) Deputy Commissioner's letter of June 9, 1972
7. Sauk-Suiattle Indian Tribe (Washington)	Same as above. These two groups have common ownership in land purchased pursuant to the 1913 Act
8. Coushatta Indians of Louisiana	Letter of June 27, 1973, from Marvin L. Franklin, Assistant to the Secretary of the Interior, and June 13, 1973, supporting memorandum of Acting Director, Office of Indian Services
9. Miccosukee Tribe of Indians of Florida	Indian Reorganization Act of June 18, 1934 (48 Stat. 984), as amended. Approved by John A. Carver, Assistant Secretary of the Interior, January 11, 1962, and November 17, 1961, Order by Assistant Secretary of the Interior

It is estimated that at least twenty-one tribes were recognized by one means or another in the years between the passage of the Indian Reorganization Act and World War II (DeLoria 1977:19-20).

It should come as no surprise that achieving Federal recognition under the Indian Reorganization Act became so confusing that, by the 1970s, few could agree on who was eligible. In 1971, President Richard M. Nixon stated that nonrecognized tribes did not come under the responsibility of the Federal government. The Federal courts were of a different opinion. In 1972, the Passamaquoddy Indians of Maine sued to compel the United States to file suit against the state for the loss of approximately twelve million acres of tribal land under a 1794 treaty between the tribe and Massachusetts. The Passamaquoddy claimed that the transfer of land under the treaty violated the Nonintercourse Act of 1790. The Nonintercourse Act voids any attempt by a state or a private individual to obtain Indian land without the participation and consent of the Federal government (O'Toole and Tureen 1971:1-39). The Bureau of Indian Affairs recommended filing suit on behalf of the tribe, but the Department of the Interior rejected the recommendation on the premise that the Passamaquoddy were not Federally recognized. Ray Coulter, Acting Solicitor of the Department of the Interior, informed the Department of Justice that it would not request the bringing of a suit. Coulter presented two major points:

No treaty exists between the United States and the Tribe and, except for isolated and inexplicable instances in the past, this Department, in its trust capacity, has had no dealings with the Tribe. On the contrary, it is the States of Massachusetts and Maine which have acted as trustees for the tribal property for almost 200 years. . . . [Because] there is no trust responsibility between the United States and this Tribe, we are led inescapably to conclude that the Tribe's proper legal remedy should be sought elsewhere (Acting Solicitor Ray Coulter to Assistant Attorney General Kent Frizzell, June 20, 1972, quoted in *Passamaquoddy v. Morton,* 388F. Supp. at 653)

The district court, and later the Court of Appeals of the First District, held that the Passamaquoddy were included in the Nonintercourse Act's reference to "any . . . tribe of Indians."

The Court of Appeals also refuted the argument of nonrecognition simply because a tribe had not entered into a Federal treaty or had not been named in a statute. The Court of Appeals declared:

No one in this proceeding has challenged the Tribe's identity as a tribe in the ordinary sense. Moreover, there is no evidence that the absence of federal dealings was or is based on doubts as to the genuineness of the Passamaquoddies' tribal status, apart, that is, from the simple lack of recognition. Under such circumstances, the absence of specific federal recognition in and of itself provides little basis for concluding that the Passamaquoddies are not a "tribe" within the Act. (Ibid.)

After years of negotiations, a jurisdictional arrangement and an out-of-court settlement were reached and signed into law by President Carter on October 11, 1980.

In *Stillaquamish Tribe of Indians v. Kleppe*, the court further ruled that the Department of the Interior must respond in thirty days to a tribe's request for recognition. These decisions challenged the basic notion of nonrecognition and served as a catalyst to reform the recognition policy. The new regulations, 25 C.F.R. 83, embody the principle that the Federal government has a responsibility toward nonrecognized tribes. Nevertheless, we must bear in mind that this new policy came into existence only after earlier positions had proven to be untenable in light of recent court decisions and their effect on nonrecognized tribes (Swenson 1981:84). After the Passamaquoddy decision, petitions for recognition flooded the Bureau of Indian Affairs.

At first, the Bureau of Indian Affairs appeared to be very reluctant to initiate any actions that would bring new tribes under Federal jurisdiction. While attempting to incorporate the Passamaquoddy and other relevant court decisions into Indian policy, the Bureau of Indian Affairs rejected any broad implications about Federal responsibilities. The Department of the Interior adhered to two positions. First, nonrecognition did not exist because there were actually various types of recognition. Second, the Secretary of the Interior possessed no authority to recognize a previously unrecognized tribe. Such had been the case with the Ione Band of Miwok Indians in California. These positions clearly lacked legal justification. Furthermore, the increasing number of petitions for recognition held the threat of judicial review over their processing. The publication in 1976 of the American Indian Policy Review Commission's *Report on Terminated and NonFederally Recognized Indians* brought to the attention of the general public the social, economic, and political plight of the estimated 133 nonrecognized tribes.

The stage was set for the establishment and promulgation of a new procedure for tribes to achieve Federal recognition. John Shapard, the principal author of "The Procedures for Establishing That an American Indian Group Exists as a Tribe," spent a year consulting with tribal representatives, attorneys, anthropologists, historians, federal agencies, state government officials, and Congressional staff members. As a result, the Federal Acknowledgment Project was created, and the following seven criteria that must be satisfied by each tribe were delineated:

1. A statement of facts establishing that the petitioner has been identified from historical times until the present on a substantially continuous basis, as "American Indian" or "aboriginal." Fluctuations of tribal activity during various years cannot justify failing to satisfy any of the criteria.

2. Evidence that a substantial portion of the petitioning group inhabits a specific area or lives in a community viewed as American Indian and distinct from other populations in the area and that its members are descendants of an Indian tribe which historically inhabited a specific area.

3. A statement of facts which establishes that the petitioner has maintained tribal political influence or other authority over its members as an autonomous entity throughout history until the present.

4. A copy of the group's present governing document or, in the absence of a written document, a statement describing in full the membership criteria and the procedures through which the group currently governs its affairs and its members.

5. A list of all known current members of the group and a copy of each available former list of members based on the tribe's own defined criteria. The membership must consist of individuals who have established, using evidence acceptable to the Secretary of the Interior, descendancy from a tribe which existed historically or from historical tribes which combined and functioned as a single autonomous entity.

6. The membership of the petitioning group is composed principally of persons who are not members of any other North American tribe.

7. The petitioner is not, nor are its members, the subject of congressional legislation which has expressly terminated or forbidden the Federal relationship.

The formal burden of proof rests with the petitioning tribes. The research necessary to prepare a petition is an extremely expensive and time-consuming endeavor. Most of the nonrecognized tribes lack the legal, historical, and anthropological expertise required to prepare the petition. This has presented an overwhelming problem to many of these tribes because the Federal government has denied any responsibility for the petitioning groups, despite strong recommendations from the American Indian Policy Review Commission and the House Subcommittee on Indian Affairs and Public Lands that financial support be provided.

Nonrecognition of certain American Indian tribes has been a negative aspect of Federal Indian policy. Because these nonrecognized tribes presented no real threat to White society, they easily became a "forgotten people." The successful land claims case of the Passamaquoddy shattered this myth of the vanished Indian in the eastern United States. The approximate one hundred letters of intent to petition the Federal government for recognition clearly demonstrate that many of these tribes did indeed survive more than three centuries of disintegrative attacks. The Federal Acknowledgment Project has become one more obstacle to be overcome as these nonrecognized tribes seek to establish their legal trust relationship with the Federal government.

REFERENCES

American Indian Policy Review Commission.
            Final Report: Report on Terminated and NonFederally Recognized Indians (Task Force 10).
    1976   Washington: Government Printing Office.
An Account of the Colony of the Lord Baltimore, 1633. In *Narratives of Early Maryland.* Edited by Clayton C. Hall.
    1910   New York: Charles Scribners.
Anderson, Terry.
    1978   "Federal Recognition: The Vicious Myth." *American Indian Journal* 4: 7-19.
Bass, Althea.
    1936   *Cherokee Messenger.* Norman: University of Oklahoma Press.
Beale, Calvin.
    1957   "American Triracial Isolates." *Eugenics Quarterly* 4: 187-96.
    1958   "Census Problems of Racial Enumeration." In *Race: Individual and Collective Behavior,* pp. 537-40. Edited

by Edgar T. Thompson and Everett C. Hughes. New York: The Free Press.

Berry, Brewton.
1963   *Almost White: A Study of Certain Racial Hybrids in Eastern United States.* New York: MacMillan Company.

Blu, Karen I.
1980   *The Lumbee Problem. The Making of an American Indian People.* New York: Cambridge University Press.

Brainerd, David.
1746   *Mirabilia Dei inter Indicos, or the Rise and Progress of Grace Amongst a Number of the Indians of the Provinces of New Jersey and Pennsylvania.* Philadelphia: William Bradford.

Burnaby, Andrew.
1775   *Travels Through the Middle Settlements in North-America.* London: T. Payne.

Chateaubriand, François A. R.
1969   *Travels in America.* Translated by Richard Switzer. Lexington: University of Kentucky Press. (Original edition: Paris, 1827; 2 volumes.)

Cohen, David S.
1974   *The Ramapo Mountain People.* New Brunswick: Rutgers University Press.

Cohen, Felix S.
1942   *Handbook of Federal Indian Law, With Reference Tables and Index.* Washington: Government Printing Office.

Collins, Daniel.
1972   "The Racially-mixed People of the Ramapos: Undoing the Jackson White Legends." *American Anthropologist* 74: 1276-85.

Crosby, Alfred W., Jr.
1972   *The Columbian Exchange: Biological and Cultural Consequences of 1492.* Westport: Greenwood Press.

DeLoria, Vine.
1977   *A Better Day for Indians.* New York: The Field Foundation.

DeRosier, Arthur H.
1970   *The Removal of the Choctaw Indians.* Knoxville: University of Tennessee Press.

DeVorsey, Louis.
1966   *The Indian Boundary in the Southern Colonies, 1763-1775.* Chapel Hill: University of North Carolina Press.

Dunlap, Arthur R., and Clinton A. Weslager.
    1947   "Trends in the Naming of Tri-Racial Mixed-Blood Groups in the Eastern United States." *American Speech* 22: 81-87.

Elston, R. C.
    1971   "The Estimation of Admixture in Racial Hybrids." *Annals of Human Genetics* 35: 9-17.

Ferguson, Alice L. L., and Henry G. Ferguson.
    1960   *The Piscataway Indians of Southern Maryland.* Accokeek, Md: Alice Ferguson Foundation.

Foreman, Grant.
    1932   *Indian Removal: The Emigration of the Five Civilized Tribes of Indians.* Norman: University of Oklahoma Press.

Gipson, Lawrence H.
    1939   *Lewis Evans.* Philadelphia: Historical Society of Pennsylvania.

Gist, Noel P., and Anthony G. Dworkin, eds.
    1972   *The Blending of Races: Marginality and Identity in World Perspective.* New York: Wiley-Interscience.

Green, Michael D.
    1982   *The Politics of Indian Removal: Creek Government and Society in Crisis.* Lincoln: University of Nebraska Press.

Griessman, B. Eugene.
    1972   "The American Isolates." *American Anthropologist* 74: 693-94.

Hanke, Lewis.
    1969   "Indians and Spaniards in the New World: A Personal View." In *Attitudes of Colonial Powers Toward the American Indian,* pp. 1-18. Edited by Howard Peckham and Charles Gibson. Salt Lake City: University of Utah Press.

Harrington, Mark.
    1908   "Vestiges of Material Culture among the Canadian Delaware." *American Anthropologist* 10: 408-18.

Hudson, Charles.
    1976   *The Southeastern Indians.* Knoxville: University of Tennessee Press.

Jacobs, Wilbur R.
    1969   "British-Colonial Attitudes and Policies Toward the Indian in the American Colonies." In *Attitudes of Colonial Powers Toward the American Indian,* pp. 81-106. Edited by Howard Peckham and Charles Gibson. Salt Lake City: University of Utah Press.

James, Bartlett B., and J. Franklin Jameson, eds.
    1913   *Original Narratives of Early American History.* New York: Charles Scribner's Sons.
Jennings, Francis.
    1982   "Indians and Frontiers in Seventeenth-Century Maryland." In *Early Maryland in a Wider World,* pp. 216-41. Edited by David B. Quinn. Detroit: Wayne State University Press.
Kickingbird, Kirke, and Karen Ducheneaux.
    1973   *One Hundred Million Acres.* New York: Macmillan Publishing Company.
Larrabee, Edward Mc M.
    1976   "Recurrent Themes and Sequences in North American Indian-European Culture Contact." *Transactions of the American Philosophical Society,* vol. 66.
Linton, Ralph.
    1942   "Land Tenure in Aboriginal America." In *The Changing Indian,* pp. 42-54. Edited by Oliver La Farge. Norman: University of Oklahoma Press.
Loskiel, George.
    1794   *The History of the Mission of the United Brethren Among the Indians in North America.* London: Brethren Society for the Furtherance of the Gospel.
McIlwaine, H. R., ed.
    1928   *Executive Journals of the Council of Colonial Virginia, Vol. 3 (May 1, 1705-October 23, 1721).* Richmond: The Virginia State Library.
McNickle, D'Arcy.
    1957   "Indian and European: Indian-White Relations from Discovery to 1887." *The Annals of the American Academy of Political and Social Science* 311: 1-11.
    1962   *The Indian Tribes of the United States: Ethnic and Cultural Survival.* New York and London: University of Oxford Press.

Merrell, James H.
    1979   "Cultural Continuity among the Piscataway Indians of Colonial Maryland." *William and Mary Quarterly* 36: 548-70.
Mochow, Marion J.
    1968   "Stockbridge-Munsee Cultural Adaptations: Assimilated Indians." *Proceedings of the American Philosophical Society* 112: 182-219.

Mooney, James.
    1907   "The Powhatan Confederacy: Past and Present."
             American Anthropologist 9: 129-52.
Morrison, Dane.
    1983   "Law and Assimilation in a Seventeenth Century
             Praying Indian Town." Paper presented at the annual
             meeting of the American Society for Ethnohistory,
             Nashville, Tenneessee, October 13-16.
O'Toole, Francis J., and Thomas N. Tureen.
    1971   "State Power and the Passomaquoddy Tribe: 'A Gross
             National Hypocrisy'?" *Maine Law Review* 23: 1-39.
Parkman, Francis.
    1867   *The Jesuits in North America.* Boston: Little, Brown.
Pollitzer, William S.
    1972   "The Physical Anthropology and Genetics of Marginal
             People of the Southeastern United States." *American
             Anthropologist* 74: 719-34.
Porter, Frank W.
    1978   "Anthropologists at Work: A Case Study of the
             Nanticoke Indian Community." *American Indian
             Quarterly* 4: 1-18.
    1979a   "A Century of Accommodation: The Nanticoke
             Indians in Colonial Maryland." *Maryland Historical
             Magazine* 74: 175-92.
    1979b   "Strategies for Survival: The Nanticoke in a Hostile
             World." *Ethnohistory* 26: 325-45.
    1982   "Backyard Ethnohistory: Understanding Indian
             Survivals in the Middle Atlantic Region." *Virginia
             Social Science Journal* 17: 41-48.
Price, Edward T.
    1953   "A Geographic Analysis of White-Indian-Negro Racial
             Mixtures in the Eastern United States." *Annals of the
             Association of American Geographers* 43: 138-55.
Prucha, Francis Paul.
    1962   *American Indian Policy in the Formative Years: The
             Indian Trade and Intercourse Acts, 1790-1834.*
             Cambridge: Harvard University Press.
    1969   "Andrew Jackson's Indian Policy: A Reassessment."
             Journal of America History, 56: 527-39.
    1976   *American Indian Policy in Crisis: Christian Reformers
             and the Indian, 1865-1900.* Norman: University of
             Oklahoma Press.

1977   *A Bibliographical Guide to the History of Indian-White Relations in the United States.* Chicago: University of Chicago Press.

1985   *The Great Father: The United States Government and the American Indians.* Lincoln: University of Nebraska Press.

Redfield, Robert.

1947   "The Folk Society." *American Journal of Sociology* 52: 293-308.

1955   *The Little Community.* Chicago: University of Chicago Press.

Robinson, W. Stitt.

1959   "Tributory Indians in Colonial Virginia." *Virginia Magazine of History and Biography* 67: 49-64.

Rountree, Helen C.

1972   "Powhatan's Descendants in the Modern World: Community Studies of the Two Virginia Indian Reservations, with Notes on Five Non-Reservation Enclaves." *The Chesopiean* 10: 62-69.

Royce, Charles C., comp.

1899   *Indian Land Cessions in the United States.* Eighteenth Annual Report of the Bureau of American Ethnology, 1896-1897, part 2. Washington: Government Printing Office.

Shapiro, Harry L.

1942   "The Mixed-Blood Indian." In *The Changing Indian,* pp. 19-27. Edited by Oliver La Farge. Norman: University of Oklahoma Press.

Sheehan, Bernard W.

1973   *Seeds of Extinction: Jeffersonian Philanthropy and the American Indian.* Chapel Hill: University of North Carolina Press.

Simpson, Lesley B.

1950   *The Encomienda in New Spain. The Beginning of Spanish Mexico.* Berkeley: University of California Press.

Speck, Frank G.

1915   "The Nanticoke Community of Delaware." *Contributions from the Museum of the American Indian, Heye Foundation* 2. New York.

Spicer, Edward H.

1962   *Cycles of Conquest: The Impact of Spain, Mexico, and* the United States on the Indians of the Southwest, 1533-1960. Tucson: University of Arizona Press.

Stern, Theodore.
    1952   "Chickahominy: The Changing Culture of a Virginia Indian Community." *Proceedings of the American Philosophical Society* 96: 157-225.

Stottnero-Montero, Myriam.
    1963   "The Rights of the Indians in America and the English Land Policies in the 17th Century Colonies in America." Master's thesis, University of Virginia.

Sturtevant, William C., and Samuel Stanley.
    1968   "Indian Communities in the Eastern United States." *The Indian Historian* 1: 15-19.

Sutton, Imre.
    1975   *Indian Land Tenure: Bibliographical Essays and a Guide to the Literature.* New York: Clearwater Publishing Company.

Swenson, Sally.
    1981   "Nonrecognition: The Other Side of American Indian Policy." Senior thesis, Princeton University.

Trelease, Allan W.
    1969   "Dutch Treatment of the American Indian, with Particular Reference to New Netherland." In *Attitudes of Colonial Powers Toward the American Indian,* pp. 47-60. Edited by Howard Peckham and Charles Gibson. Salt Lake City: University of Utah Press.

Tyler, S. Lyman.
    1973   *A History of Indian Policy.* Washington: United States Department of the Interior, Bureau of Indian Affairs.

Wade, Mason.
    1969   "The French and the Indians." In *Attitudes of Colonial Powers Toward the American Indian*, pp. 61-80. Edited by Howard Peckham and Charles Gibson. Salt Lake City: University of Utah Press.

Wilkins, Thurman.
    1970   *Cherokee Tragedy: The Story of the Ridge Family and the Decimation of a People.* New York: MacMillan Company.

Williams, Walter L., ed.
    1979   *Southeastern Indians Since the Removal Era.* Athens: University of Georgia Press.

Witkop, C. J., et al.
1966   "Medical and Dental Findings in the Brandywine Isolate." *Alabama Journal of Medical Science* 3: 382-403.

Wolf, Eric R.
1959   *Sons of the Shaking Earth.* Chicago: University of Chicago Press.

Young, Mary.
1975   "Indian Removal and the Attack on Tribal Autonomy: The Cherokee Case." In *Indians of the Lower South: Past and Present,* pp. 125-42. Edited by John K. Mahon. Pensacola: Gulf Coast History and Humanities Conference.

Zavala, Silvio A.
1935   *La Encomienda Indiana.* Madrid: Imprenta Helenica.

2
THE OKEHOCKING BAND OF LENAPE: CULTURAL CONTINUITIES AND ACCOMMODATIONS IN SOUTHEASTERN PENNSYLVANIA

Marshall Becker

INTRODUCTION

The collections of documents dating from the colonial period of the Swedish colony and Philadelphia in the lower Delaware Valley have provided invaluable records for reconstructing the lives of the European immigrants. Although the Lenape, the native people of this area, are richly recorded in these same accounts, we have just begun the task of extracting information about them in ways which permit a detailed reconstruction of their lives. The ways in which this information can be organized are numerous, but two approaches appear well suited to learning about Lenape culture and culture change.

One approach is to trace the movements of individual Lenape during the critical eighteenth century when these people were moving west. The high degree of independence and individualism of these people, which would be expected in a foraging society, seems to have provided the flexibility needed to maintain cultural integrity through change and trials of all kinds. The individualistic Lenape were, in effect, well-adjusted to the hard life on the frontier. A second approach involves "upstreaming" from the historic data to reconstruct Lenape life back into the prehistoric period. This technique enables us to complement the archaeology of that period, just as archaeology can be used to interpret what is known of the historic period Lenape.

The volume of data which has been located creates an organizational problem for researchers of the early history of the Lenape. Studies of other peoples in the northeastern region of the United States have been successful and provide yet another dimension to this research. The variety of cultural processes used by these people, and by individual groups, has reversed our ideas about similarities among the Woodland populations. We now recognize a wide range of behaviors among people leading them to make a wide range of responses to European contacts. Ethnographies from other parts of the world suggest that foragers use organized variation in order to maintain flexibility in dealing with resources. Binford (1980) suggests that foragers organize themselves primarily around resources. However, Wiessner (1982) observed that foragers show a kind of organized variation (flexibility) which reflects a focus on resources as well as on other people, who provide the social relationships of production.

From what we know of the Lenape after 1650, their bands became much more oriented toward the colonists, and attention was paid to "cultivating" these relationships for the economic advantages which they brought. By 1700 the variations among the Lenape bands had increased, and some appear to have left the Delaware Valley to maintain a more traditional lifestyle. By 1740 all of the remaining bands had left, but various Lenape individuals remained. Those Lenape, who after 1740 continued to live in the area of their homeland, were entirely oriented toward the colonists as a source of all economic support. Our ability to see the variations among Lenape bands and changes from 1640 to 1740 enables us to answer certain questions which archaeological techniques alone can never answer. This research has great potential for understanding the Lenape as a varied and complex people, and not simply as a foraging population homogeneous in behavior and easily predictable in their responses to the all-important process of European colonization.

The focus of this research is on a single band of Lenape known as the Okehocking. They are documented clearly in the historic record only from 1700 to 1737, but their origins and their fate can be inferred from indirect evidence. A narrative history of the Okehocking, as far as it can be constructed, provides us with evidence for the response made by one Lenape band during one segment of their long history of contact with Europeans. The behavior of these people, therefore, does not describe a general pattern but offers insights into many ways in which various Lenape groups responded. There does not appear to be a single model which covers all Lenape culture change and accommodation, but rather a number of possible modes of response which will be discussed in the final section of this chapter.

POSSIBLE ORIGINS OF THE OKEHOCKING

The point in time from which the Okehocking are known clearly (1700) is over seventy years after the establishment of the first European trade stations, and probably a century after regular contacts first were made with Europeans. The Lenape had been dislodged by the Susquehannock (Minquas), allied to the Swedes and Dutch (1640-1650), joined the Susquehannock against the English (1650-1660), and regained power after 1660 (Becker: Ms. C) before selling all of their lands to William Penn after 1680. This century of change does not seem to have altered the socio-political structure of these egalitarian bands, but may have emphasized the value of flexibility in Lenape culture as a whole.

Each of the native bands inhabiting the Delaware Valley probably occupied a single tributary valley (such as along Ridley Creek) and the surrounding hills, as well as a section fronting the main river. Each band also may have had a fishing station on the coast (Barnes 1968:20). The size of each of these residential units may have been much smaller than the several hundred suggested by Lindestrom (1925), although individual band size may have varied considerably. Each group probably consisted of a small extended family, numbering perhaps twenty-five or thirty individuals. More accurately, such a group might be called a sib (or clan) and would include spouses who had married into the group. The "villages" along the major Pennsylvania waterways seem to have been summer encampments inhabited by those hunters and gatherers who practiced limited horticulture during the summer season. Just how much maize was actually grown is difficult to estimate, although it rarely appears to have been in sizable quantities.

Of considerable interest to historians studying the Lenape is a tract of land, located in Willistown Township, Chester County, Pennsylvania, commonly but erroneously called the "Okehocking Reservation." Information regarding this parcel of land was collected in an attempt to understand what happened to the local Lenape population during the colonial period.

One task to be undertaken was to determine the attitudes of this band of Lenape toward land holdings and how their concept would influence the utilization of a guaranteed (warranted) tract of land. The Okehocking concept of their relationship to the land might serve as an example of these behaviors in general, which, in turn, might be useful in evaluating land claims of a more general nature. The information regarding Lenape land use derived from this study might provide information that could be used to direct archaeological research. The excavation of a settlement area belonging to Lenape who lived in the early eighteenth century would provide direct evidence bearing on the history of the entire culture.

The first known specific reference to this Lenape group (Minutes, Commissioners of Property December 7 and 8, 1702) identifies these people as "Ockanickon or Crum Creek Indians. . . ." Only later (warrant of survey December 15, 1702) are they called Okehocking, a name which appears to be the actual referent they used. Nora Thompson Dean, a native speaker of Lenape, suggests that the locative "Okehocking" might be translated as "the place surrounded," perhaps referring to a piece of land which was bounded by the bends of a stream. Since these people lived along Ridley and Crum Creeks in Chester County, Pennsylvania, and since the name Crum Creek derived from the Dutch, meaning crooked or bent creek, we may infer that the native and the Dutch names have a similar origin. Any one of the many bends in this creek may have formed an area that was nearly surrounded by water. Both terms may derive from the same situation of a meandering course to this creek, or the Dutch term "crum" may have been derived as a translation from an original Lenape term. The use of the name "Ockanickon" to designate these people may have resulted from a confusion on the part of the recorder resulting from a similarity in the sound of this band's name and that of a well-known Jersey Lenape. The name of the Lenape elder, Ockanickon, was familiar to the colonists through the publication in 1682 of his dying words (Ockanickon 1682; Becker 1976:54). The possibility that the Okehocking may in some way be related to the well-known individual named Ockanickon is remote.

PROVIDING FOR LENAPE LAND RIGHTS:
THE OKEHOCKING CASE

William Penn's attempts to protect native land rights took several forms. The major protection was in his guarantee that all natives could continue to reside on any piece of ground that was a traditional place of habitation. The limited success of this policy was met, some scholars believe, by directing the natives to settle on the manors of Pennsylvania. A third, and equally unsuccessful attempt to provide for one group of Lenape in Chester County, was made through the direct grant of a tract of land to the band using the Ridley and Crum Creek area—a group who have come to be known as the Okehocking Indians. This parcel, sometimes called the Okehocking Indian Town, was given to a small band of Lenape in what appears to be a unique case in the history of Pennsylvania. In 1703 the Ockanickon, or Okehocking, were deeded a "settlement," or a parcel of nearly 500 acres of land within a larger tract of 1,920 acres on which they previously had been invited to settle. This was not a reservation, in the modern sense of the word, but only in the sense that it was a parcel of public land warranted to a small group of Lenape collectively for their exclusive use. These land owners were free to come and go as they pleased since they were the lawful proprietors of this tract.

The history of this land is intricately tied to the history of Penn's colonial land development. The larger parcel of 1,920 acres originally had been allotted to Griffith Jones, an important Quaker of the early settlement period. The tract had been surveyed by Charles Ashcam, on January 8, 1684, and the land had been granted to Jones in 1686, but, for unknown reasons, he never asserted his claim to this land. This large parcel appears to have been within the Welsh tract, a sector of 40,000 acres that was to have been settled by Welsh Friends and wherein Welsh was to have been the language used. Many of the original Welsh purchasers appear to have left this tract by 1690, and Jones simply may have decided against settling there. In any event, the 1,920 acres laid out for Griffith Jones reverted to the Proprietor.

In about 1700 the small group of Lenape who occupied the area near Ridley and Crum Creeks resettled on the vacant 1,920 acres originally allotted to Griffith Jones. This is known because these Lenape were there in 1701 when Abraham Beaks and other colonists petitioned for parts of the original Jones plot. Later references to this Lenape group also provide clues to indicate that by 1701 they were resident in the area of the Jones grant. These Lenape probably abandoned land farther down the creeks, closer to Upland (modern Chester) on the Delaware, and built new shelters farther up the river. Their decision to move probably was based on expanding colonial activity, and they wished to live beyond the area in which the colonists had already built houses by 1700.

The former territory of this band, as noted in the colonial documents referring to their petition for land, had been in the area by the Delaware River. From what we know of Lenape foraging patterns, the pre-contact extent of their land probably included an area along the Delaware River, the entire zone along the valleys of Ridley and Crum Creeks, and possibly a portion of the considerable area in the interior of the state far beyond the upper reaches of these creeks (fig. 1). Their summer station must have been on or near the Delaware River until the Swedish settlers moved into this area.

After 1680 English colonists created a considerable disturbance in the southern portion of this region, as they did all along the Delaware River. Of importance to the Okehocking was the activity along Ridley and Crum Creeks. Tracts of land in what is now Edgemont Township, due south of Willistown, were laid out as early as 1681. In keeping with Penn's policy of respect for lands occupied by the natives, however, the area between Ridley and Crum Creeks in Edgemont Township was not settled so long as there were native occupants in the area. Julia Colflesh (1974) has pointed out that research in the colonial settlement of Edgemont Township shows scattered taxable inhabitants occupying the western portion in 1693, and many more in the same section in 1696. However, even as late as 1696 not one taxable was located between the creeks in these valuable areas adjacent to good water resources. By 1705, however, the tax lists indicate that the entire township was settled by colonists. The interval between 1696 and 1705 coincides with the period during which the Okehocking appear to have relocated their summer station to an area within the

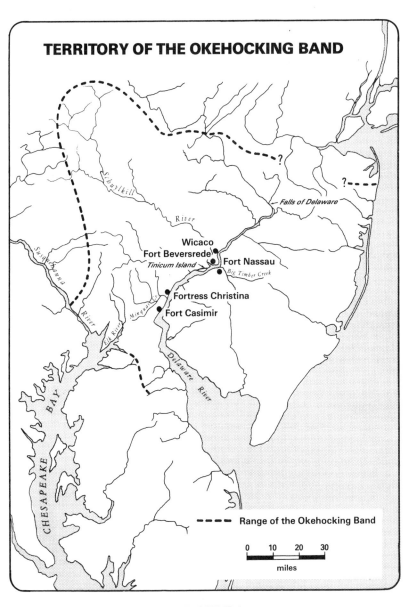

TERRITORY OF THE OKEHOCKING BAND

Schuylkill

River

Falls of Delaware

Wicaco
Fort Beversrede
Tinicum Island
Fort Nassau
Big Timber Creek

Fortress Christina

Fort Casimir

Susquehanna

River

Elk River

Minqua Cr.

Delaware River

CHESAPEAKE

BAY

- - - - Range of the Okehocking Band

0   10   20   30
miles

FIGURE 1

1,920 acres which became Willistown Township. Only after this shift in summer residence to an area somewhat to the north of their previous rendezvous point for summer activities was the land that they had occupied between the creeks granted to Whites, who seem to have jumped at this opportunity to petition for these tracts.

Although these early settlers appear to have had no policy of disrupting the native occupants or of actively dislodging the bands in the area, the rapidly expanding numbers of Europeans, due to a phenomenal birth rate, put considerable pressure on the Brandywine, Crum Creek, and other Lenape bands. The expanding colonial settlements along the Delaware and up the tributary rivers made the Okehocking quite eager to relocate to an area away from the forest-clearing settlers. Thus the Okehocking were probably pleased to relocate up the creeks to the tract that formerly had been allotted to Griffith Jones, but upon which there were no colonials. How they actually came to settle there is not specifically known. They may have initiated the move, or they may have been told by the Proprietors that they could settle on the Jones tract because it was not "seated" by the legitimate claimant and therefore was available to be assigned. The evidence for this relocation derives from the document described below.

The Commissioners of Property had issued a Warrant of Survey on "11th 12mo 1701" to Abraham Beaks and John and Moses Musgrove to survey the vacant tract between Edgemont and Willistown and "to survey as Caleb Pusey, Nicholas Pile & Nathaniel Newland shall direct so much of the said Tract as by them shall be thought sufficient to accommodate the Indians lately settled there." (Taylor 1682-1716:Warrant 71). This warrant bears the note: "Never executed nor likely to be."

Pusey, Newlin, and Pile were designated as having been charged by the Proprietary on "11th 12mo 1701" with determining the land needs of these Lenape, who were already resident on the tract of land in Willistown by the winter of 1701. The actual relocation of these Lenape prior to this date is clearly indicated in Minute Book G (Egle 1890, XIX:266-67):

[Abraham] Beaks for himself and some others, of the County of Chester, his Neighbors request a grant of that large tact of Vacant Land in the said County, formerly designed for Gr. Jones and laid out for 1,500 Acres for which they agree to pay 25 p'r 100, . . . and to leave out so much upon the

Creek as shall be Sufficient for a Settlem't for the Indians, lately removed thither, which quantity Shall be adjudged as also the place allotted by Caleb Pusey and Natha'l Newlin to whom the care of Settling the said Indians was committed by the Propr'y. Granted on the Terms aforesaid, the whole to be Survey'd first.

Although Pusey and others (Weslager 1972:171-72) suggested that this relocation took place by force, this interpretation probably derives from their understanding of colonial word use. Consistent with Lenape avoidance of settled and cleared areas, this band of Lenape appears to have decided to relocate themselves to an area within their traditional range between Ridley and Crum Creeks, but an area which, in 1700, remained free of colonial inhabitants. Possibly these Lenape already had requested a secure area for their settlement and had been offered a portion of the old Jones tract, with Pusey and Newlin helping to identify a specific area. Abraham Beaks' request does not appear to have been granted, but the survey of the area seems to have derived from his request. Perhaps the Proprietors wanted to be certain that the Lenape were settled before selling land in the area. Jonathan Bowater was granted 400 acres on November 24, 1702, but at the far western edge of the Jones tract and some distance from the area of the two main creeks which were the core of the natives' range. Even more significantly, the 400 acres granted to Bowater appear to be the very same which in 1692 had been granted by patent to Mary Sibthorp; the Bowater patent dates from 1697 (Cope 1901:22). Since the ultimate grant to Bowater was not made until 1702, ten years after the Sibthorp patent, a specific concern with protecting native land rights is indicated. By this I do not mean the prevailing concern with native rights in general, but a specific concern for the members of this band and for their use of the area of the Ridley and Crum Creek drainages. Conversely, no colonist wished to settle a tract of land which might later be lost to a native claim.

The records concerning the Bowater tract appear in the abstracts of the Warrants of Survey (Taylor 1682-1716:vol. 1). Reference number 99 lists two tracts (250 and 150 acres) and the following description for this grant of "24th of 9th 1702":

Jno. Bowater in lieu of 250 acres situate in Westtown and within the confines of the Welsh Tract where it hath been laid out to others, surrendered on that account to the present Welsh possessors or claimers. Grant the rt to take up like quantity in tract formerly laid out to Griffith Jones but by him quitted and now left vacant and to add thereto 150 Acres now purchased in the whole 400 A. next adjoyning or nearest the land by him quitted Not Interfering with the present Settlem'ts of the Indians thereupon.

Note the use of the plural "settlements," probably reflecting the scattered housing pattern traditionally used by Lenape. Perhaps Bowater applied for his patent in 1697 but had it granted in 1702. After this grant of 400 acres had been made to Bowater, within the original Jones parcel of 1,920 acres, only 1,520 acres remained. Since these Lenape had recently begun to move into this area, possibly during the previous year, and since nearby sections of land were being sold, the Okehocking had good reason to fear that other lands around them, if not the very land on which they were seated, might be sold.

Although Bowater's 400 acres was on the extreme western edge of the tract, in no way directly interfering with their settlement, and probably deliberately selected there to avoid all possible contact with the Lenape, these natives still felt cause for concern. On December 7 and 8, 1702, only two weeks after the Bowater grant, the Okehocking made the following petition (Minute Book G: Property: December 7 and 8, 1702, vol. 9:341):

The Ockanickon or Crum Creek Indians having removed from their old habitation before the Prop'rs Departure, by his Order seated, by Caleb Pusey, Nicholas Pyle, Nat'll Newlin and Jos. Baker on the Tract in Chester County, formerly laid out to Griff. Jones, but now vacant. But the said Indians expressing great uneasiness at the uncertainty of their Settlem'ts, pressed and Several times urged the Neighbouring Friends that they might be confirmed in some particular place under certain metes and bounds, that they might no more (be) driven like Dogs, as they expressed themselves. (Weslager 1953:140)

This record suggests that even within this tract, reduced to 1,520 acres by the grant to Bowater, these Lenape did not feel secure since they had no clear title to the land but only de facto rights. Their insecurity could only have resulted from the constant colonial expansion into those areas where the Lenape bands formerly had spent their summers. Having sold all of their land, the Lenape bands south of Philadelphia had no specific areas assigned to their use. Their periodic relocations plus winter dispersal left them feeling dependent on good will for their use of summer encampments. Although they now had been told that they could settle on the Jones tract, no grant or survey had been made. They had no "writing" granting them the use of a specific tract such as their colonial neighbors owned. One should note that the first reference to this group by name (Ockanickon or Crum Creek Indians) occurs on this petition of December 7 and 8, 1702.

Only one week later, on December 15, 1702, Edward Shippen, Griffith Owen, Thomas Storey, and James Logan, acting for the Proprietary, issued a Warrant of Survey to Isaac Taylor, surveyor of Chester County. This warrant to survey a tract for these people may demonstrate that the colonists recognized this Lenape problem and rapidly took steps to rectify the situation. On the other hand, the petition made by the Okehocking may have been welcomed by the Proprietors as a solution to one of their problems. As long as Lenape land rights were recognized as applying to any place where they were seated, the native holdings could grow if native population increased and would continue to shift as the Lenape relocated their settlements. Even the land in the general vicinity of Lenape habitation was unsaleable since the vague peripheries of land held by the Indians might be violated by the surveyed boundaries of measured tracts. Such an overlap, by law, would have to be decided in the favor of the native claimant.

The decision of a group of Lenape to accept the European system of metes and bounds put everyone on the same footing. This enabled proprietary land sales to be conducted right up to the margins of the native-held lands without fear of making errors that would be costly to both the purchasers and the Proprietors.

The warrant of December 10, 1702, noted that Pokais, Sepopawny, and Muttagooppa and others of the "Okehocking" together with their families, who were lately settled lower on Ridley and Crum Creeks (prior to 1701), were to be settled on "five hundred acres of land in one square tract in such place within the aforesaid tract as the said Indians shall desire. . . ." This grant was made at the behest of the Proprietors to provide a secure piece of land, but only to the members of this group and their descendants, to have and to hold provided that they never give, grant, or attempt to sell or dispose of this land. This clause reflects a subtle paternalism which in later years became a major problem in native relations. In this warrant a provision also was made that if they quit or left this tract it would "be surrendered to ye Proprietary without any further claim of the sd Indians. . . ." In every way, this Warrant appears to be a sincere attempt to provide a parcel of land for the well-being of this group, and not a land grab.

The actual survey of land for the Okehocking proved to be another matter. The interval between issuing the Warrant for survey and the actual survey itself was ten months. Measurement of the 500-acre tract involved in this grant was made on "10th 8th Month 1703." The survey (Document Book A-9:212) is entitled "The Oakhockney Indians 500 acres" on the obverse, and written on the actual map is "The Okehockeny Indians Land Containing 500 A." The marginal notes by Taylor, the surveyor, calculate that there were 500 acres and eighty-nine perches along Ridley Creek encompassed by the square plat which he had charted (figs. 2 and 3).

From an inspection of this document in the context described above, an inference on Lenape band size may be made. Lenape bands, like all foraging bands, were probably small. Since only three names were mentioned (Pokais, Sepopawny, and Muttaguppa) and since generally all adult males participated in band activities, this may have been an unusually small group. The references made to "others," who may have been adult males of the group, might bring the band size up; but probably, at most, only one or two other men may have headed families. The three men are not referred to as chiefs or by any title. It may be inferred, therefore, that this group included at most from fifteen to twenty-five individuals, on the basis of the maximum numbers of adult males possible (Becker Ms. D).

These data suggest that the Okehocking may not have numbered more than twenty-five persons. In 1700 the purchase of 500 acres by a White man heading a large family (ten children) would have provided more than adequate land for a farm. Grants and purchases of 200 or 300 acres were common at a time when colonial families often included ten or more children. However, multiple families in a single household do not become common until much later when land in this area became relatively scarce. Thus a grant of 500 acres might have appeared to the colonists as being quite adequate for a group of as many as twenty-five people, but would

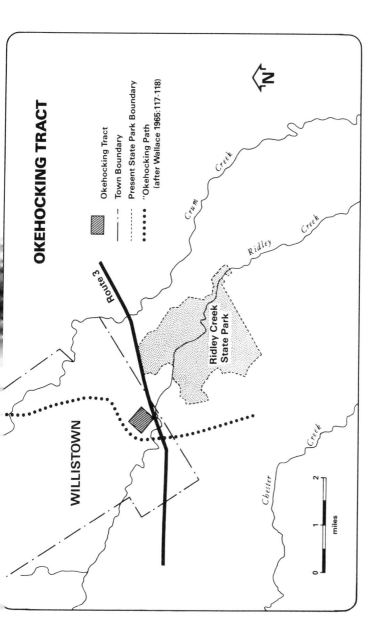

OKEHOCKING TRACT

Okehocking Tract

Town Boundary

Present State Park Boundary

"Okehocking Path
(after Wallace 1965:117-118)

N

Route 3

WILLISTOWN

Ridley Creek
State Park

Crum Creek

Ridley Creek

Chester Creek

miles
0   1   2

FIGURE 2

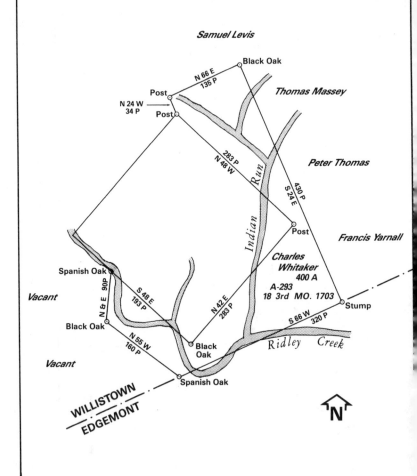

PLAN OF THE OKEHOCKING TRACT
(Traced from the Original Land Patent)

Samuel Levis

Black Oak

N 66 E
135 P

Post

Thomas Massey

N 24 W
34 P

Post

283 P
N 48 W

Indian Run

430 P
S 24 E

Peter Thomas

Post

Francis Yarnall

*Charles
Whitaker
400 A
A-293
18 3rd MO. 1703*

Spanish Oak

N 8 E
90P

S 48 E
193 P

N 42 E
283 P

Stump

Vacant

S 66 W
320 P

Black Oak

N 55 W
160 P

Black
Oak

Ridley Creek

Vacant

Spanish Oak

WILLISTOWN

EDGEMONT

N

FIGURE 3

probably have been considered too small for a larger number. Since every attempt at fairness on the part of the Proprietors seems to be evident during this period, there was probably no attempt to crowd these people on a restricted tract. One can only assume that the total number in the Okehocking band must have been small.

One might also note that Lenape land use did not require large central tracts of land. Their concern appears to have been to secure a clear title to a piece of land for annual summer encampments. Their location on the "frontier" provided easy access to the wilderness, which provided a hunting territory. The Lenape utilized the large runs of anadromous fish, including shad, to provide foodstuffs, and the women did summer planting; however, the concept of a totally sedentary life was foreign to them. Pastorious (in Myers 1912) notes that Lenape males would do no manual labor (farming), a trait Pastorius found to be disgraceful. But this lifestyle allowed the Lenape the flexibility to utilize forest resources very effectively as long as the access to these resources was not curtailed.

A glance at the tract of 500 acres within the 1,920 acres originally surveyed for Griffith Jones suggests that there may have been some discrimination against these Lenape, probably by surveyors and local residents rather than by the Proprietors. What we do not know is to what extent the survey reflects the actual habitation selected by the Okehocking and how much of the 500 acres chosen within the Jones tract actually were "in such place within the aforesaid tract as the said Indians shall desire. . . ." If the Okehocking selected this tract, then we might comment on some peculiarities of the bounds, which do not conform to the pattern in general use by the colonists. The Okehocking tract forms an oddly tilted square within an area where most tracts were surveyed as long rectangles with boundaries parallel to the township lines. Furthermore, the request of Abraham Beaks stipulates that land for the Lenape would be left out along the creek, yet only a short stretch of Crum Creek and only one possible stretch of Ridley Creek ultimately were included in the native land. Beaks' request certainly reflects a farmer's desire to have water for livestock and wetlands, but this may not have been a priority of the Lenape. The rough terrain of the largely waterless tract laid out for the Okehocking is the antithesis of the colonial farmer's ideal, but it may have suited the recipients, and may even have been selected by them.

Still other details may lead one to question the fairness of the treatment of these Lenape, and how closely this land conformed to their "desire" as the instructions to Isaac Taylor stated. The actual acreage in this tract turned out to be but 484 acres, an error of sixteen acres (under 4 percent), but well within the margin of error general at that time. Yet the tract surveyed for N. Newlin, which has become modern Newlin Township, erred in favor of the purchaser. The Proprietors may have recognized that if the Lenape were not content with this tract they might have refused the offer and taken up residence elsewhere, creating the same kind of difficulty which had existed previously. Despite a sincere effort to resolve the problem on the part of the Proprietors, we can say very little about Isaac Taylor's attitudes or those of any of the colonists who were living in close proximity to these people with drastically different life styles.

The survey of October 10, 1703 provided formal boundaries to a tract of land which appears to have been seated by the Okehocking since the beginning of the century nearly three years earlier. This appears to have been the first piece of land formally warranted to a native American group as a corporate community and the only such grant made to a Lenape band in the traditional Lenape range within Pennsylvania. One may note that the Jersey Lenape, meeting with the colonials nearly fifty years later (New Jersey 1756:6-7), suggested that the English help them "to purchase a Peice [sic] of Land sufficient for us all to settle together. . . ." This resulted in the formation of the Brotherton reservation in a procedure quite similar to that which led to the grant of the Okehocking tract (Larrabee 1976).

Some question exists regarding the actual date of the final survey for the Okehocking tract. The date often noted is March 1703. This appears most logical in light of other surveys which followed that of the Okehocking tract. The survey of firm boundaries for the Lenape's land was a boon to colonists interested in purchasing land in the vicinity of native areas. When these areas were vague, the prudent Pennsylvanian avoided them. A purchase of land which had Lenape seated on it was subject to being declared void, with another plot of land to be provided by the Proprietors. Any work that had gone into the original tract would be lost. With secure boundaries around the Okehocking, the colonists could make clear and unchallenged purchases, which they hastened to do with alacrity.

The records actually documenting the presence or tenure of these Lenape on this tract after 1703 are few in number and most elusive. One of the few references to them comes from the Charles Whitacre warrant, located in Minute Book G of the Commissioners of Property for 1703 (Egle 1890, XIX:370-71). Now that the Lenape were settled within definite bounds, Whitacre hastened to make his purchase. On April 19-20, 1703;

Charles Whitacre having requested to Purchase 300 a's in the tract in West Town, Chest'r Granted him the 2 Corners next Brassey's tract, by the two side Lines of the Indians' Land, reputed about 300 acres, and what Else may Accomodate him without Injuring the rest of the tract, be it More or Less, for 35 p'r C't, 5 to be abated on the first 300 A's to be Paid in 3 m'ths with Interest after 1, 3 mo. next. Rectifye this by 1st, 9 ber Next.

In fact, Whitacre ultimately purchased 400 acres of land (Deedbook A, p. 293) completing the arrangements on "18 3rd mo. 1703." His parcel flanked the Lenape land along more than two and a half sides and just happened to include most of the water-courses in the area (fig. 3) including Ridley Creek. Whitacre's parcel abutted the 1,500 acres held by Thomas Brassey, which lay northeast of Whitacre's land (Cope 1901:facing 22). Warrant 117 (Taylor Papers, Historical Society of Pennsylvania) was granted on May 18, 1703 to Charles Whitacre as follows:

Charles Whitacre for a certain parcel of Land within ye bounds of that tract formerly laid out to Griffith Jones in Westtown in ye County of Chester adjoyning on ye Lines of ye Indian Land and taken in ye two upper corners of ye sd Tract as cutt off by ye sd Lines and Extending ye hithermost Corner of ye sd Indian Tract till it take in Sufficient for a Convenient Settlemt to ye Quantity of abot 3 or 400 acres for which he hath agreed to pay Thirty five pounds for Every hundred.

The configuration of the Whitacre land enclosing their tract, like the direction of its bounds, suggests that the Okehocking may have been treated badly by the gentlemen in charge of the survey. The peculiarities of the boundaries of the Okehocking tract suggests that Mr. Whitacre may have had shady dealings with the surveyor,

Isaac Taylor, or someone directing Taylor's work. Whatever the reason, the Okehocking were allotted some of the most hilly land along the creeks and little of the fertile flood plain and bottom lands which were preferred by the Whites and Lenape alike. The actual configuration of the land allotted to them may have had little meaning for these Lenape, but that is unlikely. Anadromous fish runs had always been an important food resource for the Lenape. Unless dams had been built on the lower reaches of Crum and Ridley Creeks prior to 1700, disrupting these fish runs, the Okehocking would have wanted access to streams to harvest these fish. The Brandywine Lenape, neighbors to the south, had registered formal complaints to the government concerning the construction of dams after 1700.

By 1700, the Okehocking had long since been disrupted in most of their traditional activities and were probably highly dependent on the colonists for more than just tools and cloth. Changes in colonial technology were to create unsurmountable difficulties for these people. Whereas both Lenape and Whites had entered the seventeenth century with different but somewhat comparable technologies, the European agriculturalists, with their craft specialization, ultimately carried the tide. The colonists began the eighteenth century with skills and resources transplanted from Europe, while the Lenape had become increasingly dependent on these skills for their daily operations (Becker 1979, 1980). The changes and improvements in colonial technology permitted rapid development of resources. These developments left the simple hunting and gathering societies without an independent role. The increasing control by Whites over the environment and, especially, over animal husbandry is well documented.

The rapidly expanding colonial population, requirements for more land, and the thriving local economy all wrought important changes. On August 29, 1710 Daniel Hoops, Aaron James, Joseph Phips, Evan Lewis, Randal Malin, and George Smedly made "Return of a Road" which by "vertue of an Order of ye Last Court Layed out for ffrancis Yarnall and a Township of Indians . . ." (Cope 1901:22). The court ordered this road be not confirmed, and held to the next court. "Return" in this context means "to render an account," as by survey, to show where the road lay in relationship to the land. The court's request to halt the building of the road may reflect the Okehocking's concern that the planned road ran directly through their land, rather than along a boundary line as was always the case with roads laid out on land owned by Whites. This is a second land-related activity that suggests that the colonists were taking advantage of these Lenape.

Despite the court-ordered delay, a road was charted through the center of the Okehocking tract on November 28, 1710 (Cope 1901:22), running from the central part of Willistown Township to the Edgemont Road. This road, now the Delchester Road, at that time not only split this tract but also caused these Lenape, and not their English neighbors, to lose a good percentage of their land to the roadway. Quite obviously, only the colonists would benefit from this decision. However, if one considers the colonists' point of view, the Lenape could well afford the land taken by the road. The Okehocking were not farming the land and left most of their tract in forest. Furthermore, the Lenape had been free to cross the settlers' land in areas where roads were absent, which, prior to 1710, included most of the colony. Since Lenape bands traditionally moved inland to winter hunting areas, they did not need to cross colonial lands until their tracts, such as this, were surrounded by properties sold to settlers. Once surrounded, the Lenape had to cross private lands. One may be certain that the colonists believed that this road would give the Okehocking better access, free of trespass, to the places they wished to go. The positioning of the road, however, appears to have been a deliberate infringement on the rights of these Indian landholders.

The period from 1700 to 1720 was a major era of road building in Chester County. The Quaker colonists had finally gained effective control of the land, perfected animal husbandry, and begun to build large stone houses and substantial outbuildings such as spring houses, wagon barns, and barns. At that point, they needed to develop a system of roads to transport surplus produce to the rapidly expanding city and to bring back specialized goods (Browning 1967). Road building had become so common in the new townships that almost every property survey after 1720 made allowances for roads that had been built or might be built along the borders of each tract. When the Okehocking tract had been surveyed, no mention had been made of roads, nor had any of the neighboring tracts been surveyed with future roads in mind. However, the 1737 survey of the Okehocking tract to provide for its division and real-location states that Amos Yarnall's piece contained "196 acres and the Customary Allowance for Roads." The original warrant to Yarnall (Commissioners Book AI: 227) stated "and the allowance of six acres [per] cent for Roads and Highways. . . ."

George Smith (1862:124) commented on early road and highway building during the beginning of the eighteenth century and cautioned against assuming that they were for wheeled vehicles. Many were hardly footpaths, and others were so steeply graded that wheeled vehicles could not be pulled over them. Smith believed that these roads were to provide free access to places by all individuals without requiring that the traveler trespass or be forced to ask numerous landholders for permission to cross their property. Even those roads that were cut and graded for vehicular traffic did not necessarily allow passage of flocks. Dorothy Lapp (MS.:142) noted that in the deed transferring land from Amos Yarnall to Caleb Yarnall a road twelve-feet wide is mentioned, but its use was restricted to carts and it was not to be used by animals who could injure the grass or grain. Regardless of these early restrictions, the road system ultimately made additional problems for the Lenape by opening up distant land to further settlement and commerce.

Just prior to the development of the road that split the Okehock-ing tract, its owners hosted a gathering of Lenape from throughout the area. A letter from a Mr. Yeates, Caleb Pusey, and Thomas Powell (April 14, 1710) to the Governor of New Jersey noted that on the following day a great concourse of Indians, including Conestoga and Jersey, was to be held about two miles from "Jno. Warraws at Edgmond." Searching the historic documents pertaining to land allocations in Edgemont in 1710, one finds that John Worrall had held a considerable parcel of land along the southern border of Edgemont since February 11, 1695. This ground, just two miles from the Okehocking land, was adjacent to land formerly owned by Thomas Powell, one of the authors of the letter to the governor of New Jersey. One may assume that John Worrall must have been the person referred to in the letter, and that the tract some two miles away on which the Lenape were holding their meeting is an accurate location of the 500 acres held by the Okehocking.

References to the Indians' land appear in all of the surveys of the adjoining tracts up until 1737. Thus, in the abstract of warrants of survey (Taylor 1682-1716:No. 157), William Garrett arranged to forgo his original warrant for forty-two acres in favor of a warrant for 100 acres "taken out of the late vacant tract in Willistown in Chester County on part whereof the Indians are seated. . . ." This warrant, dated "16th 7mo 1713," provided William Garrett with 100 acres in the tract vacated by Griffith Jones "joining on the one side by his son Thomas Garrett's land and on the tract laid out to the Indians on the other." Similarly, a warrant for survey for 150 acres to be granted Francis Yarnall was issued on "the 18th of 9 mo. 1713," and the patent was granted on January 1, 1713. This land adjoined the Okehocking tract on the west, adjacent to land already owned by Yarnall (Fig. 3).

Another indirect mention of the Indians can be found in the deed (D-362) for 100 acres, from William Garrett to George Garrett (March 6, 1720), which reads in part as follows:

Beginning at the post at the corner of the Indians land thence North 24 degrees Westerly by Thomas James's land 34 perches to a corner post thence by Samuel Levis' land and Thomas Garratt's land, South 66 degrees West 211 perches to a corner black oak thence South 24 degrees Easterly 127 perches to a black oak then by the Indians land north 42 degrees east 231 perches to the place at the beginning containing one hundred acres with the allowance of six percent.

This text clearly refers to the Okehocking's land. However, two other transactions within the Garrett family (D2-210, 1726; G3-252, 1731) do not relate to the land held by the Indians and appear to represent changes in the ownership of plots that were not contiguous with the land in question.

Thomas James purchased 150 acres of land from John Cadwallader in 1711, but the purchase of the land was not recorded until 1726 (D-404). This plot, lying northeast of the Okehocking lands, had been sold to Cadwallader in about 1708. The deed to James, dated June 13, 1726 (D-404), notes "south 42 degrees Westerly by the said Francis Yarnalls land 24 perches to a post being a corner of the Indian's land, thence by the same land north 48 degrees Westerly 283 perches to a post, thence north . . ." (Deed D-404; see fig. 3). This indicates that as late as 1726 the land belonging to the Okehocking was intact. The wills of Thomas James, April 30, 1752 (B3-344), Charles Whitacre, April 8, 1720 (1-453), and Samuel Levis, April 13, 1734 (1-411) make no mention of native lands.

THE LENAPE DEPART

Individual members of various Lenape bands had been relocating, probably with their families, at Conestoga and other places to the west at least as early as 1694. This migration continued to accelerate a process which led to the formation of a reorganized and politically more unified people who were Lenape but who presented themselves to the colonists as members of the Delaware nation. William Hunter (1954b:341-44) designates the period from 1701 until 1757 as the era of growth in political unity among these people, leading to the formation of a united body which truly could be called the Delaware Nation. Perhaps the conclave of Lenape from New Jersey and elsewhere on the Okehocking tract on April 15, 1710 was part of an attempt to reaffirm ties to the groups with whom the Okehocking were most closely related and an attempt by the Okehocking group to bring themselves into concert with other traditional Lenape. Hunter (1978) suggests that by 1715 members of several bands previously identifiable in southeastern Pennsylvania had achieved a measure of coherence under the designation of Schuylkill Indians, but I believe that the Schuylkill band had always been a major Lenape unit. In any case, by 1718 the Lenape had sold all their Pennsylvania lands, except perhaps part of present Berks County, which was occupied and claimed by the Schuylkill band.

The treaty signed by Sasoonan and his followers on September 17, 1718 confirmed the release of all Lenape land to the colonists except for a small portion. This group then took up residence at Tulpehocken, where they remained for some years before moving to Shamokin. Quite clearly, the Okehocking and Brandywine bands continued to occupy the areas which they are known to have held until after 1730. The Okehocking, like the Brandywine band, probably left Chester County between 1730 and 1735.

Only a single small clue permits us to follow the Okehocking after their departure from Chester County. It is now known that Lenape individuals had been leaving this area since about 1690, if not before, but the departure of those remaining intact bands seems to mark the ultimate acknowledgement of their problems of trying to maintain their cultural traditions after colonial expansion had inundated them with more than just European-made goods. Over the forty years of gradual migration (circa 1700-1740), various Lenape individuals and small groups took up residence at or near Shamokin, where Sasoonan and his followers had gone, and at many other places scattered across the area along and beyond the Susquehanna River (see Kent, Rice, Ota 1981). Many of the Schuylkill River Lenape, having sold their land in Berks County, settled at Shamokin, and perhaps some Okehocking joined them (Smith 1862:209; Lapp MS.:139). Weslager (1972:175) believes that the Okehocking went to Tulpehocken, a settlement in the Tulpehocken Valley of the upper Schuylkill drainage. Tulpehocken Creek flows between the South Mountains and the Blue or Kittatiny Mountains, down to the Schuylkill at Reading. Quite possibly some of the Okehocking went to Tulpehocken, but there is no evidence to support this hypothesis. Only one obscure reference after 1736 notes the existence of the Okehocking as a distinct group; this is discussed later.

The movements of individual Lenape of this period have been traced through the appearance of the person's name on specific documents, which generally provide a date and location at which specific people can be found. These records often give information on the locations of the various Lenape "villages" or hamlets, clearly reflecting the settlement patterns used by these people. In the literature, the more vague references to the movement of groups of Lenape from a settlement recently abandoned to those settlements located on the frontier often are of little real value in tracing the activities of specific individuals, but they reflect the wide range of choices available to these people in regard to locations where they could take up residence.

As just noted, the area to which the Okehocking (or a group of them) removed after abandoning their Crum Creek land had been subject to just such speculation. The answer has been discovered only recently, hidden in the massive collections of documents published as the *Pennsylvania Archives*. Earlier reference was made to the patents for the Okehocking tract drawn up on August 1, 1737 and to the long interval which followed before the surveys were returned. This newly located reference, from Minute Book K, not only indicates where these Lenape had relocated, but also suggests that some effort had been made to contact them and to determine whether their claim to their old tract had been abandoned. This reflects colonial recognition of Indian rights to this land, as described in the warrant granted to the Okehocking, if not recognition of their basic rights to a secure tract.

1st 6 mo: 1737
Upon the Application of Mordecai Yarnal for the Grant of 500 Acres of Land joyning on his Plantation in Willistown which ws heretofore surveyed for the Crum Creek Indians who formerly settled and dwelt on the same but have for some Years past deserted their Habitations there and now (those Indians that are living) dwell about Swahatara Creek in Lancaster.

The Prop'r is pleased to Consent that Mordecai shall have the Priveledge of Purchasing the same when the claim of those Indians is further examined and cleared. (Egle 1894:89)

From this document, we can be certain that in 1737 there was a Lenape "settlement" somewhere on Swatara Creek and that some of the Okehocking were in residence there. Swatara Creek, the upper drainage of which is located nearly entirely in modern Lebanon County, is about seventy-five kilometers from the Oke-hocking tract. The only seventeenth century "village" now known to have existed along the complex Swatara Creek drainage system is Quittaphilla, located where Quittaphilla Creek meets the Swatara or where the present town of Lebanon is situated (Kent et al. 1981:No. 99). The ethnic composition of this native settlement is undocumented, and it is believed to have been abandoned in 1748. Quittaphilla lies about eleven kilometers southwest of the better known Tulpehocken, a Lenape settlement which was being used as early as 1705.[1] Quite possibly, the Okehocking went to Quittaphilla or to a satellite location elsewhere along Swatara Creek or its feeder streams.

Note also should be given to the account of September 5, 1730 sent by Joshua Lowe to James Logan (Hazard 1852, 1:268-69) re-garding the murder of three Lenape. Lowe went to the head of Swatara Creek where he received a full account of the affair. Oppenella, a Lenape, his daughter (about fourteen) by a previous marriage "and his Squaws and his sone a yong man" had been on a trading trip when one of the wives killed the other three members of the party. The murderess later told another man that she had killed her husband and his kin in order to be free to marry the man to whom she had confessed. Oppenella had come from ". . . Augaluta

a toune near Opessa . . ."; the inquest was made in the newly
formed (1729) Lancaster County. This all suggests that by 1730
there were several hamlets, in the Lenape style of scattered settlement, in addition to Quittaphilla along the Swatara Creek drainage
and that Lenape, and possibly others, were occupying these areas.
Augaluta and Opessa are two previously unnoted towns for which
we now have references.[2]

One further but very indirect bit of evidence suggests that Lenape
settlements were in this area of Swatara Creek. Some scholars
suggest that many of the manors of Pennsylvania were set up not
only as a land speculation scheme but also as a means by which
lands could be held open for Lenape use. The Manor of Fell on
Tulpehocken Creek, then in a part of Lancaster County which is
now in Berks County, may have been set up surrounding the settlement of Tulpehocken Creek (Egle 1895, IV:no. 19). The Manor of
Freame, established by Warrant in 1733, covered the entire core
area of the northeast branch of Swatara Creek in what is now
Lebanon and part of Dauphin counties (Egle 1895, IV:no. 23).
Again, no reference is made to native inhabitants, but part of the
land "speculation" may have been with regard to the Lenape settlements. As long as Lenape lived on the land, it could not be sold
legally. But Quaker experience for fifty years showed that the
Lenape would eventually move away, and then the land could be
sold at a profit.

The Schuylkill River Lenape appear to have relocated to
Shamokin[3] in about 1732, the year before the Brandywine band left
the Delaware River drainage. The last of the Okehocking must have
left soon after, having spent at least thirty years in residence on
their Willistown tact.[4] This period reflects a span of occupation not
significantly different from the period of use known for horticultural villages of the Susquehannock. This is not to suggest that these
Lenape had adopted a more settled lifestyle, but that the Lenape
emphasis on food production may have increased by 1700. The
horticultural Susquehannock had lived at the Washington Boro
Village from approximately 1600 to 1625, the Strickler Site (in
present Lancaster County) from 1635 to 1675, and Conoy Town
from 1718 to 1734 (P. Wallace 1981:108). The reasons for departure in each case vary, but lengthy occupations were common. The
gap between the years 1675 and 1718 reflects the destruction of the
Susquehannock and the subsequent scattering of the survivors,

some of whom resettled along the river at Conoy Town many years later.

No name of an individual Lenape associated with the Okehocking tract has ever been found associated with Shamokin. Hunter (1978) notes that, at a general treaty held at Philadelphia in 1742, a distinction was made between the "Delaware of Shamokin" and the "Delawares from the Forks" (all of whom this author believes to have been originally Jersey Lenape and that several other such groups were indicated). An interesting note is that Hannah Freeman, reputed to have been the last living Lenape in the Chester County area, died in 1802. She is believed to have been born near the Delaware border in 1730 or 1731 and may have been the last Lenape born and remaining in the area (Volkman 1949). The gathering of these remnant populations at Shamokin afforded a measure of protection from their respective enemies and enabled each culture to continue the old ways and to participate in the fur trade. The new circumstances and the multiethnic populations at areas such as Shamokin and Wyoming led to many kinds of change among these people. The various bands of Lenape developed greater political solidarity after their westward movement. Although the Lenape-Delaware were now more united in a political sense, they generally continued to occupy separate and distinct towns and may have used these new settlements to maintain consanguineous ties and old traditions. Although it cannot be demonstrated that the Okehocking actually became part of this process, there is every reason to suspect that their settlement on Swatara Creek had been a significant site in the 1730s.

THE OKEHOCKING: ONE MODE OF
ACCOMMODATION TO COLONIAL OCCUPATION

Numerous problems are involved in the ethnohistoric study of foragers. The primary difficulty lies in the tendency to view all of the bands of a single "culture" as if they behaved in ways similar to all the others. This leads the researcher to use data from one band to make inferences about others which may be removed in time and space. For the Okehocking in the first third of the eighteenth century there are a number of documents which reflect their unusual response to colonial expansion. Documents relating to other bands at this same time may reflect similar problems, but it can be demonstrated that the responses were different in each case.

In comparing the known data relating to the Okehocking with those pertinent to other Lenape bands, considerably different responses are found to the challenge or changes brought about by European settlement and expansion. For each group, and possibly for each individual, there is a separate pattern of culture change. This is to say that the acculturation process does not occur according to a uniform schedule or by any consistent mode, but rather that these patterns form a continuum within which at least five distinct areas can be differentiated.

Quite important in this study is the recognition that all change in a native population does not form one line or direction of acculturation. The various modes of change may lead toward cultural systems other than "White," and there even may be reversals of this "directional" movement. There is no single model to describe how the several members of a culture, or even of one band, change their lifestyles through time. Furthermore, the direction of change is not inexorably toward the "White agrarian" tradition. Reversals may alter the acculturation process or may place it on another course which the participants perceive as either reversing the process of change or altering the course of change toward that of perceived origins (e.g., Lenape wearing Plains Indians' headdresses to indicate "Indian" origins in the absence of having knowledge of traditional elements of Lenape culture). These processes are best described by theories of revitalization (see A. Wallace 1956). Although I know of no examples of such revitalization among the Lenape prior to 1750, instances may exist.

A further note regarding the modes discussed below concerns the possible existence of parallel courses of behavior. Within the diverse range of cultural processes, some behaviors which seem the same to the observer are actually the results of very different motivations or discreet origins. Only the results are parallel (or even congruent). This is particularly the case with the first mode discussed below.

Before describing the five modes of accommodation recognized among the Lenape, consideration should be given to the two orienting factors of change among the Lenape of the eighteenth century. These factors are "pushes and pulls" of their situation. The "pushes," or compelling reasons for incorporating change, reflect the flexible nature of a cultural system. Diversity of response enabled the Lenape to adjust to the many stresses involved in European contact. The invasion of their territory by the Susquehannock (circa 1600), followed by the establishment of European outposts and then colonial expansion after 1670, was met by the several responses described below. The great flexibility of these responses enabled the Lenape to adjust in various ways at separate locations and thereby to survive through time.

The "pulls," or attractions leading to culture change among the Lenape, reflect the opening of new avenues or alternatives to traditional life-styles due to the presence of colonial settlers. These societies created a demand for individual culture brokers (e.g., Teedyuscung), created an opportunity for native hangers-on, and even allowed individuals, over generations, to become White or Black or confused. These directions may be seen as "deculturizing" in the sense that they lead away from traditional values and beliefs.

MODES OF ACCOMMODATION

The five modes of accommodation suggested for the Lenape of the lower Delaware Valley are presented to indicate that there was a wide range of diversity in the responses of the various Lenape bands. Not only did the Lenape *not* act in concert (which reflects the autonomy of bands and individuals in foraging societies), but quite possibly no two groups may have followed the same course. The "titles" or descriptive labels placed on these "modes" are meant to reflect characteristic responses and in no way are conclusive statements of content (fig. 4).

I. Ultraconservatives: Resistance to Change

The ultraconservative mode encompasses those Lenape responses to European settlement and contact that were intended to minimize accommodation to change. These people were disturbed by the presence of Europeans and foresaw changes in material culture (and perhaps accompanying changes in social interactions within and beyond the Lenape system). They withdrew from close contact. This process may have begun in the early 1600s when Dutch and Swedish traders and some Scandinavian settlers made their appearance on the South (Delaware) River. Certainly, there was an ultra-

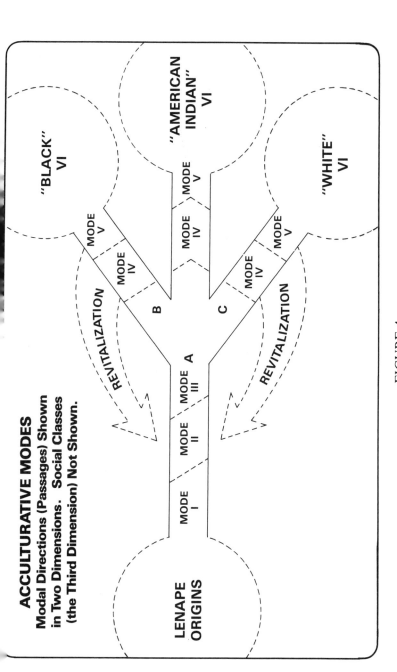

ACCULTURATIVE MODES
Modal Directions (Passages) Shown
in Two Dimensions. Social Classes
(the Third Dimension) Not Shown.

LENAPE
ORIGINS

MODE
I

MODE
II

MODE
III

A

MODE
IV

B

MODE
V

C

MODE
IV

MODE
V

MODE
IV

MODE
V

REVITALIZATION

REVITALIZATION

"BLACK"
VI

"AMERICAN
INDIAN"
VI

"WHITE"
VI

FIGURE 4

conservative withdrawal from the Delaware Valley after 1675 when the dispersal of the Susquehannock left the central Susquehanna River drainage open to penetration.

Although there may be aspects of revitalization in this activity, the wish to continue the old ways and to avoid accommodation appears to be the principal motivation. Economic enticement and resumption of traditional cultural roles in the form of hunting opportunities cannot be underestimated. These Lenape assumed a significant role in the fur trade, taking up various positions in the network left open by the dispersed Susquehannocks. Obviously, the participation in the fur trade reflects some change from the pre-contact Lenape situation, but within Lenape tradition the relative distance from European population centers and the ability to operate in large areas without colonial competition replicated the situation that had existed in the recent past.

If this mode can be designated IA, then a IB category can be identified. The IB slot is occupied by deviants, generally on an individual basis, distinct from mode IV and possibly mode V as described below. These people neither functioned well on the fringe of colonial society nor operated successfully within the wide range of acceptable Lenape behavior. These people may have been more commonly found well beyond the frontier, actively involved in the trapping aspects of the fur trade rather than acting as buyers/sellers in the system.

The next result is that people in the IB mode resisted change de facto, and individuals who conformed to this developed an active pattern of activity spatially removed from the direct influence of the colonists. Individuals conforming to this mode constantly emerged from among members of groups who conformed to the mainstream of Lenape culture, which I believe to be characterized by mode II.

II. Conservatives

Several Lenape bands, including the Okehocking as well as the nearby Brandywine band, continued into the 1730s to occupy the area of the lower Delaware drainage traditionally utilized by these people. Each group appears to have been associated with a specific river system or systems flowing into the Delaware, at least during the period after 1680 and possibly back into the pre-contact period.

These bands can be studied as specific units, although there is every possibility that others besides these two may have shifted their activity areas from place to place, and even these two best known examples may have their pre-1680 origins in other drainage zones of the Delaware.

Band membership appears to have been based on kinship, with the matriline forming the core members and adult males marrying (band exogamy) into the unit (becoming co-resident). Remarriage explains the shifting residence among certain males for whom we have data on band affiliation through time. Land rights were in the territory utilized by an individual's matriline, not in the area of residence. Thus, Teedyuscung's participation in a land sale in the Tom's River area of New Jersey in 1734 reflects his rights by kinship in an area where he and his kin rarely resided.

The members of the Okehocking band continued to reside in the Delaware Valley until colonial settlement density restricted direct access to some resources, provided competition for others, and generally impeded movement through expanding fenced areas. The last area of occupation for the Okehocking was a unique tract of 500 acres ceded to the band for their exclusive and collective use. The Brandywine band survived intact by locating within Springton Manor in about 1720. This technique for preserving Lenape group integrity appears to have been quite common, leading some individuals to suggest that Penn's manorial system was established, in part, to provide for these bands (John Witthoft, pers. com.). In fact, the manor system in Pennsylvania allowed the Proprietors to grant large tracts of land to individuals or groups. With these tracts exempted for sale to land-hungry purchasers, the owners could hold the property until the surrounding area had been subdivided and developed. This caused the value of these reserved tracts to increase greatly. However, during periods of dormancy such large tracts became inviting places for Indian bands to take up residence. Since some of these manors appear to have been established in areas already occupied by Indians, there is a valid question regarding the legitimacy of such sales by the Proprietary government.

III. Accommodations: Becoming non-Lenape

Three possible modes of change led away from Lenape traditions and lifeways. The documentation of these processes is greater among groups other than the Lenape, but these aspects of this third mode are noted here for clarity.

Mode IIIA. This submode includes families and individuals who were in the process of becoming "White." Moses Tatamy, a Jersey Indian, and his family are an example of this process. This transformation results from adoption of agrarian technology and acceptance, in some way, of Christianity. Along the frontier, such people would be enveloped by expanding settlement and absorbed into the developing community. This pattern is the variant in which the male or both partners in a couple are Lenape. Unions of European males and Lenape women appear to have been common among Scandinavian colonists after 1638, and probably continued to increase in frequency. The children of these couples, while not easily accepted, were on the road to being recognized as White. Although certain resistance by Whites to accepting these people may have existed for several generations, the process of change was in effect. Note should be made that this process must have become increasingly common after 1800 when Lenape bands, then forming loose "town" aggregates, began to practice some agriculture. This transformation had not yet taken place when Loskiel made his observations, but by the end of the nineteenth century even the "conservative" Lenape appear to have become agrarian.

Mode IIIB. A second path of Lenape accommodation involves a process parallel to that of IIIA, but was directed toward becoming identified with the African descent population. Although Whites often infer that this process was easier, this assumption may reflect ethnocentric ideas regarding racial status differentials. Black colonists may have resisted Indian "intrusion" in a pattern similar to that of White colonists. However, this mode is one which continues to attract attention by scholars who assume that Lenape physiognomy differed from the Europeans to a degree easily detectable by the casual observer. Portraits of early Lenape, as well as all other native people on the east coast, show individuals indistinct from Europeans except in costume.

Mode IIIC. A third variant of Mode III is postulated, but not documented. It is quite possible that some Lenape may have drifted away from their cultural traditions and toward those of other Native American people. If this did occur, the incidence was probably low, and the directions of change were probably varied. One might also consider that the mission Indians were making this choice—they adopted European lifeways while remaining a restricted Indian ethnic population. The rate of marriage between members of different cultures (e.g., Munsee and Lenape) increased, but the children were identified with their matrilineal kin. These people ultimately could continue as "Indian" affiliates or could depart toward either of the other "racial" modes indicated above.

IV. Peripherals

These individuals or clusters of Lenape continued to operate as Lenape within the native tradition but resident within the context of colonial society. Hannah Freeman, called "Indian Hannah," and some of her kin fall into this category (Becker MS. A). Hannah Freeman is generally recognized to have been the last Lenape in Chester County, Pennsylvania. Each of the counties in this region appears to be able to recognize as a "folk character" the last living Native American who maintained some vestiges of the old ways, but more important, who maintained an Indian identity. The majority of these peripherals appear to have been female, using role-defined skills (basketmaking, sewing) to provide services to colonial families in a form of cultural synchretism. Less clearly defined roles may have been performed by Teedyuscung's mother, who lived on the fringe of White society. Few males, if any, seem to be identified in this kind of relationship. Hannah Freeman's male kin appear to have gone off to the frontier or beyond to continue their roles in the traditional fashion—roles not available within settled colonial society.

Among the south Jersey Indians, some may have gone to sea (A. Paredes, pers. com.), although maritime trading along the Jersey shore may not have been using the same kinds of skills required by the whaling industry. Along the south Jersey shore, natives involved in activities aboard ship may have been part of Mode V, depending on the status of their sea duties.

V. Dropouts: Life on the Urban Fringe

At present, no clear example of a Lenape in this category can be identified, although some possible cases are suggested in the records. These people were not functioning with or in relationship to any Indian group, but were recognized by the colonials as

"Indian" as distinct from Whites or Blacks manifesting the same behavior. Most of the individuals occupying these very low status positions may have been males. Day laborers, short-term seamen, drunks, and derelicts all may fall into this category, and some female trades of similar status may have been assumed by Lenape women. The colonists' concern for the identification of these people was minimal, if any interest in them did appear in writing. A correct evaluation of the ethnic origins of any one of these individuals would be of relevance only for the purposes of presenting hard data to demonstrate that this mode was a possible choice for the Lenape.

Note should be made that during the eighteenth century, and certainly before and after, large numbers of children and adults were indigent drifters who provided labor at low rates. These people, generally but not exclusively of European descent, seldom receive mention, but are often known from attempts to channel this labor source into workhouses or other public institutions. Blacks or persons of color were subject to "appropriation," which may have limited their participation in this group. In 1717, Governor Hunter of New Jersey referred to some colonial petitioners as being "loose, vagrant and . . . real Inhabitants in no fixed place" (New Jersey Archives IV:312). These colonials appear to have been indigents occupying a category which was open to the Lenape as well as to members of any of the numerous ethnic groups already present in this part of the New World.

SUMMARY

These modes of accommodation available to the Lenape cannot be seen as discrete categories, but must be viewed as part of a complex system which reflects a continuum of behavioral change. Along these major avenues there may be many side streets and alleys by which individuals and groups may seek traditional identities or new identities associated with peoples of other cultural (ethnic) traditions. The possible changes available to these people are not meant to suggest that these people either sought or were forced to change. The majority seem to have wished to continue the old ways, but change inevitably affects all systems; the Lenape have changed no more over the past 400 years than any other American group.

Why the Okehocking selected the particular adjustment described above we do not know. What is important is that they took a relatively conservative course similar to that taken by other Lenape bands with one exception: They requested a bounded plot of ground for their own use and received it. No other Lenape band used this variation of the conservative mode of adjustment. We may speculate that simple ecological factors led the Okehocking to make this unusual request. In 1700 the Okehocking were nearing the headwaters of the streams along which they foraged. The Brandywine and Schuylkill bands of Lenape were both far from exhausting their potential for withdrawing from colonial settlement. Since the Okehocking were already at the limits of territory available in their traditional range, because both Crum and Ridley Creeks are short, their next voluntary move inland would cause them to encroach on their neighbors' lands. This was not a viable possibility. The Okehocking could have left the Delaware River drainage, as they ultimately did, or else petition for colonial aid in securing boundaries. In 1700 they chose the latter, but by 1737 they had no choice but to resort to the former.

At some point in the modern (post-contact) history of the Lenape, membership in traditional and recognizable units ceased to include the biological majority of people descended from these proud people. Today the numbers of people genetically related to the known members of Lenape bands is far greater than those few traditionalists who recognize their Lenape heritage. For these "lost" descendants, the recognition of their ancestry may confirm family stories, or the discovery may provide an unexpected linkage with the American past. For all of us, the knowledge of this heritage demonstrates the incredible mixture of our backgrounds and the importance of the genetic contribution made by the Lenape as well as other Native American peoples to today's society.

NOTES

1. The settlement of "Turpyhocken" appears in the 1707 narrative of Governor Evan's trip in this area (Colonial Records 1852, II:405). The Warrant of Survey of 1723 calls it Talpahockin (Penna. Bureau of Land Records BB 23-96). This appears to be the site noted along Tulpehocken Creek near Myerstown in present Lebanon County (Kent et al. 1981:no. 120). This site (36LE198/1) is represented by the Faver Collection in the

William Penn Memorial Museum, Harrisburg. Note the R-L variance, a common dialectical shift.

2. A probable Lenape site of this period (ca 1725) is located west of Kutztown in Berks County, Pennsylvania (36BK450: Ingefeld Site). This site, which may be on a feeder stream leading to Maiden Creek, is probably the source of artifacts from the Deisher Collection at the William Penn Memorial Museum (Cat. Nos. D.843-D.857). A reference to this site is provided by Brunner (1897:113-14), but the data are unclear (Becker 1980a). There is a remote possibility that this site or nearby hamlets of that period may be the Augaluta or Opessa mentioned in 1730.

3. Shamokin, or Shahamoking, the area or district around the junction of the west and north branches of the Susquehanna River, where Sunbury is located today (see Newcomb 1956:84-85; Kent 1966:May 10, 1728; Kent et al. 1981:no. 106), was a strategic location for controlling the fur trade and other commerce along the waterway. A number of "plantations" or settlements were established in this region during the second quarter of the 1700s, but, by that time, these lands were nominally controlled by the Six Nations (see Hunter 1954a:72). This area had been controlled by the Susquehannock until 1674, but, after their defeat and dispersal, numerous displaced peoples representing several cultures took up residence at Shamokin as well as at Conestoga and other places in former Susquehannock territory. The Six Nations were eager to have these members of other cultures settle here to provide a buffer between themselves and the colonists. Thus, the area along the river was settled by a polyglot assemblage, consisting mostly of Lenape but also Shawnee, Munsee, Conestoga (Susquehannock), Conoy, Tutelo, and even representative members of the Six Nations.

4. This deed is summarized as No. 29 in a list of 43 native sales of land in Pennsylvania (Colonial Records 1852, XIII:462-69). The reference indicates that this is ". . . recorded in book A, Vol. 6 page 59 and 60, 13th of May, 1728." The order in which the names are listed in this summary does not agree with the sequence presented in the earlier volume of the Colonial Record (III:320-21).

REFERENCES

Barnes, Carol.
      1968   "Subsistence and Social Organization of the Delaware Indians: 1600 A.D." *Bulletin of the Philadelphia Anthropological Society* 20(1):15-29.

Becker, Marshall Joseph.
      1976   "The Okehocking: A Remnant Band of Delaware

Indians in Chester County, Pennsylvania during the Colonial Period." *Pennsylvania Archaeologist* 46 (September):25-63.

1979 "Ethnohistory and Archaeology in Search of the Printzhof; The 17th Century Residence of Swedish Colonial Governor Johan Printz." *Ethnohistory* 26(1):15-44.

1980 "Lenape Archaeology: Archaeological and Ethnohistoric Considerations in Light of Recent Excavations." *Pennsylvania Archaeologist* 4:19-30.

1982 "Pre-Penn Settlements of the Delaware Valley: Lenape, Dutch, and Swedes in the Delaware Valley in the Seventeenth Century." *Pennsylvania Genealogical Magazine* 32:227-34.

1983 "The Boundary between the Lenape and Munsee: Indications That the Forks of Delaware Was a Buffer Zone during the Early Historic Period." *Man in the Northeast* 26 (Fall):1-20.

In press "The Lenape Bands Prior to 1740 A.D.: The Identification of Boundaries and Processes of Culture Change Leading to the Formation of the 'Delaware.'" Papers of the Lenape Indian Symposium held at Seton Hall University, March 28, 1981. H. C. Kraft, editor.

MS. A "Hannah Freeman, 1730?-1802: The Last Identified Lenape Resident of Chester County, Pennsylvania."

MS. B "Changing Lenape Mortuary Programs: Evidence of Culture Change and Cultural Conservation, and Indicators of Burial Practices as a Guide to Archaeological Interpretation."

MS. C Lenape Political Power Restored: The Period 1660-1680. Copy on file, Anthropology Program, West Chester University of Pennsylvania.

MS. D "Lenape Population, Technology, and Settlement Pattern: Ethnohistoric Clues to Archaeological Riddles." Copy on file, Anthropology Program, West Chester University of Pennsylvania.

Binford, Lewis.

1980 "Willow Smoke and Dogs Tails: Hunter-Gatherer Settlement Systems Archaeological Site Formation." *American Antiquity* 45:4-20.

Bokonyi, S.

1972 "Zoological Evidence for Seasonal or Permanent Occupation of Pre-historic Settlements." In *Man, Settlement and Urbanism,* pp. 121-126. Edited by Peter J. Ucko, Ruth Tringham, and G. W. Dimbleby. Cambridge: Schenkman Publishing Company.

Browning, Charles H.
1967   *The Welsh Settlement of Pennsylvania.* (Reprint of the 1912 edition). Baltimore: Genealogical Publishing Company.

Brunner, David B.
1897   *The Indians of Berks County, Pennsylvania.* 2d rev. ed. Reading, Pennsylvania: Eagle Book.

Colflesh, Julia.
1974   "A Report on Findings to Date on the Original Settlers of Edgemont Township." (November). Manuscript on file, Bishop's Mill Historical Institute, Edgemont, Pennsylvania.

Colonial Records (binders title).
1852   *Minutes of the Provincial Council of Pennsylvania.* vol. I-IV, Philadelphia: Jo. Severns; vol. VIII, Harrisburg: Theo Fenn.

Cope, Gilbert.
1901   *Genealogy of the Smedley Family.* Lancaster, Pa.: Wickersham Printing Company.

Egle, William H., ed./comp.
1890   *Pennsylvania Archives:* 2d ser., vol. XIX. Harrisburg: E. K. Meyers.
1894   *Pennsylvania Archives:* 3d ser., vol. I. Harrisburg, Clarence M. Busch.
1895   *Pennsylvania Archives:* 3d ser., vol. IV. Harrisburg: Clarence M. Busch.

Hazard, Samuel, ed.
1852-1856   *Pennsylvania Archives:* 1st ser., vol. 1-12. Philadelphia: Joseph Severns and Company.
1970   *Annals of Pennsylvania from the Discovery of the Delaware, 1609-1682.* (Reissued). Port Washington, N.Y.: Kennikat Press.

Hunter, William A.
1954a   "John Hays' Diary and Journal of 1760." Editor. *Pennsylvania Archaeologist* 24(2):62-83.
1954b   "The Ohio, the Indian's Land." *Pennsylvania History* 21(4):338-50.
1978   "Documented Subdivisions of the Delaware Indians."

Bulletin of the Archaeological Society of New Jersey 35:20-39.

Jennings, Francis.
  1966   "The Indian Trade of the Susquehanna Valley." *Proceedings of the American Philosophical Society* 110(6):406-24.
  1968   "Glory, Death and Transfiguration. The Susquehannock Indians in the Seventeenth Century." *Proceedings of the American Philosophical Society* 112:15-33.

Kent, Barry C., Janet Rice, and Kakuto Ota.
  1981   "A Map of 18th Century Indian Towns in Pennsylvania." *Pennsylvania Archaeologist* 51(4):1-18.

Kent, Donald H., project director.
  1966   *Guide to the Microfilm of the Records of the Provincial Council, 1682-1776.* Commonwealth of Pennsylvania, Pennsylvania Historical and Museum Commission.
  1974   *History of Pennsylvania Purchases from the Indians.* Iroquois Indians I, of the American Indian Ethnohistory Series. (Reprint of report for the Department of Justice). New York: Garland Publishing Company, Inc.

Lapp, Dorothy B.
  n.d.   "The Indian Reservation in Willistown." Manuscript in *Chester County Collections: 1936-1937.* 138-42.

Larrabee, Edward Mc M.
  1976   "Recurrent Themes and Sequences in North American Indian-European Culture Contact." *Transactions of the American Philosophical Society,* vol. 66.

Lindestrom, Peter.
  1925   *Geographia Americae with an Account of the Delaware Indians Based on Surveys and Notes Made in 1654-1656 by Peter Lindestrom.* Translated and edited by Amandus Johnson. Philadelphia: The Swedish Colonial Society.

Myers, Albert Cook, ed.
  1912   *Narratives of Early Pennsylvania, West New Jersey, and Delaware, 1630-1707.* New York: Charles Scribner's Sons.

Newcomb, William W.
  1956   *The Culture and Acculturation of the Delaware Indians.* Anthropological papers. Museum of Anthropology, University of Michigan, No. 10. Ann Arbor.

82   Strategies for Survival

New Jersey Archives. New Jersey, Government of (Croswicks Treaty).
    1756   *A treaty between the Government of New Jersey and the Indians, inhabiting the several parts of said Province, held at Croswicks, in the County of Burlington, 8 and 9 January.* Philadelphia: William Bradford.

Ockanickon.
    1682   "A True Account of the Dying Words of Ockanickon, an Indian King." Spoken to Jahkursoe, His Brother's Son, whom he appointed King after him. London: Benjamin Clark (1683). Reprinted in 1912 in *The Journal of the Friends Historical Society* IX:164-66.

Smith, George.
    1862   *History of Delaware County, Pennsylvania.* Philadelphia: Henry B. Ashmead.

Taylor, Jacob.
    1682-1716   *Abstracts of Warrants of Survey.* Taylor Papers, Historical Society of Pennsylvania.

Volkman, Arthur G.
    1949   "Lenape Basketry in Delaware." *Bulletin of the Archaeological Society of Delaware* 4:15-18.

Wallace, Anthony F. C.
    1947   "Women, Land and Society: Three Aspects of Aboriginal Delaware Life." *Pennsylvania Archaeologist* 17(1-4):1-35.
    1949   *King of the Delawares: Teedyuscung 1700-1763.* Philadelphia: University of Pennsylvania Press.
    1950   "Some Psychological Characteristics of the Delaware Indians during the 17th and 18th Centuries." *Pennsylvania Archaeologist* 20:33-39.
    1956   "Revitalization Movements." *American Anthropologist* 58:264-81.

Wallace, Paul A. W.
    1965   *Indian Paths of Pennsylvania.* Harrisburg: Pennsylvania Historical and Museum Commission.
    1981   *Indians in Pennsylvania.* 2d ed. Harrisburg: Pennsylvania Historical and Museum Commission.

Weslager, Clinton A.
    1953   *Red Men on the Brandywine.* Wilmington, Del.: Hambleton Company.
    1972   *The Delaware Indians: A History.* New Brunswick, N.J.: Rutgers University Press.

Wiessner, Polly.
    1982   ''Beyond Willow Smoke and Dogs' Tails: A Comment
            on Binford's Analysis of Hunter-Gatherer Settlement
            Systems.'' *American Antiquity* 47:171-78.

3
"WE'RE STILL LIVING ON OUR TRADITIONAL HOMELAND": THE WAMPANOAG LEGACY IN NEW ENGLAND

Laurie Weinstein

INTRODUCTION

Many individuals believe that there are no longer any "real" Indians living in New England. It is widely believed that since King Philip's War of 1675 New England Indians have vanished and that only mixed-bloods remain today. Such biases have even been expressed by some of the so-called "real" Indians of the North American Plains. However, as the Wampanoag Supreme Medicine Man, John Peters counters, "We're still on our traditional homelands" (Peters 1984: personal communication). All of these beliefs are erroneous. One need only to attend one of the powwows at the Wampanoag village of Mashpee, Massachusetts today to realize that native identity is indeed real and that today's identity is an expression of its ancient roots.

This chapter explores the mainland-dwelling Wampanoag since the seventeenth century.[1] I will try to prove, regardless of Federal recognition, that the Wampanoag are and have always been a bona fide Indian group.

The research is based upon ethnohistorical investigations of seventeenth- to twentieth-century documents, including state and local archives, and the diaries and letters of missionaries to the

Indians. Interviews with the contemporary Wampanoag formed a large portion of the research into the Indians' current expressions of cultural identity.

BACKGROUND INFORMATION

The mainland Wampanoag inhabited the southeastern portion of present-day Massachusetts and eastern Rhode Island.[2] Their territorial bounds were also those of the seventeenth-century Plymouth Colony. They spoke the Massachusett language—one of the five eastern Algonkian languages spoken in southern New England (Salwen 1978:168; Goddard 1978:70).

Prior to a devastating series of European-introduced epidemics which hit New England hard in the early seventeenth century, the Wampanoag had an estimated population of from 21,000 to 24,000 (Salisbury 1982:105, 191, 209; Snow 1980:34 suggest an average of 36,000 for all Massachusett speakers). Their population, like that of their Algonkian-speaking neighbors, declined 90 percent or more during the seventeenth century (Jennings 1975:26; Cook 1976:36).

The Wampanoag were principally farmers, and they grew the common American Indian triad of corn, beans, and squashes. Their other economic activities of hunting, gathering, and fishing were attuned to the agricultural cycle.

During the seventeenth century, the Wampanoag were forced to share their native lands with the Plymouth colonists who ventured to America in search of both religious and economic freedom. Some historians have viewed the ensuing Indian-White relationship as a friendly one (Vaughan 1980, 1965), while others (Leach 1966; Jennings 1975; Weinstein 1983a, 1983b) have pointed to a variety of tensions and conflicts (particularly land controversies) that ultimately led to King Philip's War in 1675. The war was the Indians' "last stand" against the colonists; however, the Wampanoag sachem King Philip and his confederated southern New England Indians were unsuccessful in their bid to drive away the colonists from Indian lands.[3]

The colonists recognized only two statuses for the Indians after the war as evidenced by the laws of the Massachusetts Bay Colony. Indians were either enemies or they were conquered and pacified subjects of the colonies. The Massachusetts Bay Colony defined enemies and subjects according to an imaginary frontier line which ran from Boston to Rehoboth in 1694 (Acts and Resolves 1869 [1694]:175) and was subsequently moved to the Connecticut River in 1695 (Acts and Resolves 1869 [1694]:224-25). The movements of the conquered Indians on the east side of the line were closely monitored. If Indians went beyond the bounds of their respective counties (where they resided), they had to forfeit three months of service to "whomsoever shall apprehend and convict them" (Acts and Resolves 1869 [1694]:175).

Most of the mainland Wampanoag were dispersed; others were either sold into slavery in the West Indies or into local servitude (MHC 1982:62; Conkey et al. 1978:177; Leach 1966:224).

The Cape and island-dwelling Indians were left relatively unscathed since these areas were on the periphery of the battles (see Leach 1966; Campisi 1985: personal communication). The Cape, particularly the Mashpee area, became both a "dumping ground" and a refuge area for the Wampanoag during and after King Philip's War. Indians who had surrendered to the English were moved to Mashpee and Sandwich (Leach 1966:216).

Mashpee's significance as a cultural center for many of the Wampanoag grew throughout the centuries, from the end of the seventeenth century to the present time.[4] Today it shares the heart of the Wampanoag Nation with the Gay Head Indians.

THE EIGHTEENTH CENTURY

"In many localities in southern New England, starting even before the War [King Philip's War], white officials assigned lands to local Indian groups . . ." stated Conkey (1978:178). "Some reservations were founded and supported by the colonies and later he states; some were organized by missionary societies; and some technically not reservations, consisted of lands retained and owned by Indian groups. . . ." Reservation assignment to Indians was increased during the late seventeenth and eighteenth centuries; this was followed by a series of state laws which were designed to both monitor and protect the Indians. One of the first of these laws, "An Act for the Better Rule and Government of the Indians on their Several Places and Plantations" (Acts and Resolves 1869 [1693-1694]:150-51), was passed in 1693-1694. This legislation called for the colony to appoint "one or more discreet persons within several parts of this province, to have the inspection and more particular care and government of the Indians in their respective plantations." The individuals were responsible for mitigating "all matters civil and criminal" for the Indians.

A more comprehensive act for regulating the Indians was passed in 1746-1747 (Acts and Resolves 1878 [1746-1747]:306-7). This law required that guardians be appointed for all plantations, and that such guardians would make yearly reports to the General Court of the colony. In spite of the insistence on yearly accounts, few were actually filed (Speck 1928:83, for example, discussed this problem for the Fall River Indian reservation). Inadequate reporting reflects other problems associated with the eighteenth-century ethnohistory of the Wampanoag. As one goes back in time, information about the Wampanoag is clearer in some respects but more vague in others relative to the succeeding centuries. Indian petitions and the letters and diaries of missionaries all offer glimpses into eighteenth-century Indian culture. However, there is little data concerning either the population size or the locations of the eighteenth-century Wampanoag—no Commissioners' reports enumerated Indian groups—and the non-Mashpee groups are underrepresented in the documents.

The records of Josiah Cotton offer some clues to the locations and numbers of the faithful Indians at the turn of the eighteenth century.[5] He recorded his "Services Among the Indians 1716-1717" as he preached to from twenty to fifty individuals at the following areas: Monument Pond (nine miles from Plymouth), Salt Water Ponds (twelve miles from Plymouth), Mattakees or Pembroke, Eel River, and Marshfield. He also visited the Indian homes of Ester Cunnitt, James Symond, Daniel Attaquin, and Francis Ned to deliver the gospel. All of these individuals reportedly lived within five miles north and west of Plymouth. Cotton's diary is particularly useful because it indicates that there were sizable numbers of Christian Wampanoag living in Plymouth in 1716-1717. Some of these Indians probably belonged to the Namatakeeset, Tumpum, and Middleboro reservations cited by the nineteenth-century Commissioners since the boundaries of Cotton's groups and the reservations overlap. The Massachusetts State Archives contain supplemental information on the Plymouth area groups, including Titicut and Mattakeeset. These brief, scattered records document numerous land problems in Titicut where certain Indians wished to rent either their timber or their lands in order to repay debts to Whites (Massachusetts State Archives 1715:21; 1754:494). Other Indians, however, opposed further resource and land sales, and they frequently petitioned the court against them (1741:319, 321-22).

Indian versus European land squabbles were also reported from Titicut. At one point, Indians claimed they were not fully acquainted with English law; consequently, the English took unfair "advantage of them" (Massachusetts State Archives 1715:21). Other records concern colony laws regulating Indians, such as an early curfew law imposed on Indian servants (Massachusetts State Archives 1703:243-44), or one designed to prevent the free passage of Indians between reservations (Massachusetts State Archives 1751:228). Several documents refer to Mattakeeset, where, like Titicut, Indians wished to either sell or rent their lands to Whites (Massashusetts State Archives 1755:675; 1757:767).

The Fall River Indians were granted a permanent Indian plantation, thanks to the efforts of Benjamin Church in 1707. According to Speck (1928:83), this group does not reappear in the records until 1747 when the Reverend Silas Brett administered to their spiritual needs. At that time, the Fall River Indians had a combination meetinghouse and school in one building. In 1763 the Indians there requested that their reservation lands be divided in severalty. Several years later, a census was taken which listed fifty-nine Indians on the reservation. Speck (1928:83) noted that most of the names on both the request and census were English names adopted from "white families friendly to them."

Mashpee's history is well-documented, thanks to Gideon Hawley, who administered to the Mashpee's spiritual needs.[6] He wrote comprehensive accounts of his activities which can be used to help illuminate the general cultural milieu of the Wampanoag in lieu of either extensive or specific information.

Early eighteenth-century Mashpee was organized as a "plantation," and, in this sense, it was similar to most other New England proprietary towns with undivided or common lands, individual home lots, and planting lands (Hutchins 1979: 69-71). Unlike the colonists' land policy, however, Mashpee's included inheritable use rights which descended in individual families (Hawley Papers: 1802b). Mashpee's eighteenth-century policy was similar to their aboriginal one: both were based upon usufruct land rights. If a man cleared land, he claimed the rights to it only for as long as he continued to work it (Campisi 1984: 65-66; Weinstein 1983b: 71-72).

Mashpee did well until the Massachusetts Bay Colony passed the 1746-1747 law to regulate the Indian plantations (Campisi 1984:66-67). The guardians were given the authority to lease surplus plantation land to Whites. Mashpee proprietors were upset—they said that there was no surplus land in Mashpee and that untilled land was used for grazing (Hutchins 1979:72). The Mashpee, therefore, petitioned the General Court of the Commonwealth not to alienate their lands and to remove the guardians. Other petitions followed, including one to the King of England (Campisi 1984:68). Because of these complaints, a committee was appointed to look into the matter, whereupon the Indians claimed that "we be incorporated . . . electing five persons for Overseers three of whom may be Indians [instead of guardians]" (Hawley Papers 1761). Their request was granted, and in 1763 Mashpee became an "incorporated district" (Campisi 1984:68). This status was subsequently modified, and Mashpee returned to a plantation in 1788-1789 (Campisi 1984:73).

Mashpee's racial history is indicative of the Wampanoag's opendoor policy in terms of allowing non-Whites to live with them.[7] It also suggests why Mashpee retained its vitality throughout the centuries. The 1761 petition (Hawley Papers 1761) included a clause which stated "that we may be allowed to vote on and receive any other Indians or mulatoes to share with us in our privileges or properties. But that any English or white man be expressly debarred settling or living [in Mashpee]." Hawley lamented that by 1788 the "Black Inhabitants upon these lands are about four hundred who are greatly and variously mixed as we have now only twenty and five males and about one hundred and ten females, who are truly originals and not mixed" (Hawley Papers 1788).

Wampanoag culture was undergoing important changes during the eighteenth century. Obviously, some changes included adjusting to the wealth of regulations imposed by the White world on Indian society. Other problems involved balancing old and new ways.

Mashpee's dialogue with the White world, via their petitions (usually written and signed by Hawley), is also indicative of the Wampanoags' eighteenth-century social conditions. The 1761 petition (Hawley Papers 1761) describes numerous problems, including: debts ("as we and other Indians have greatly suffered by being too largely credited and prosecuted for Debt"); intra-Indian quarreling ("many of us greatly suffered by going into a course of law for the settlement of our little petty quarrels"); and boundary disputes between English and Indians ("we pray the Line between us and the English may be perambulated").

The Wampanoag supplied the White world with a pool of cheap labor. Whalers, for example, often visited Mashpee and persuaded the Indians to work for them (Hutchins 1979:62-63). Sometimes the sailors resorted to treachery when they plied the Indians with liquor and then ordered the drunken Indians to work in compensation for their liquor debts (Hutchins 1979:62).

This problem, however, went beyond the whaling industry and proved to be so pervasive that the courts passed protective legislation against it. The 1725-1726 Act for Regulation of the Indians (Acts and Resolves 1874 [1725-1726]:363-65) included these provisions: "That no married Indian shall bind him- or herself a servant. . . . That no indenture of any Indian, whatsoever, shall be good or valid unless approbated by two justices of the peace. . . . That no bill, bond or book-debt be allowed and approved of by the court." The act also limited Indian indenture in the fishing industry to a period of not more than two years.

The 1746-1747 Act (Act and Resolves 1878 [1746-1747]:307) included a section on Indian fines: "That no action shall be brought against any of the said Indians for any debt hereafter to be by them contracted with any English persons, for any sum exceeding ten shillings."

In spite of these financial difficulties, the Wampanoag were able to survive. They maintained many of their traditional arts alongside European importations, as Gideon Hawley observed in 1802 (Hawley Papers 1802b): "Our Indian females are many of them good spinsters, combers and weavers," and "Our females are some of them very good wives and cloth[e] themselves and husbands in every-day-homespun." In another letter (Hawley Papers 1802a), Hawley wrote: "Many of our squaws make brooms and baskets."

Increasingly, more Indians opted for the European shingled house in lieu of the wigwam during the eighteenth century; however, many individuals were reluctant to give up their traditional home. In 1767 a majority of the houses were wigwams

(a few of these had brick fireplaces), but by 1776 there were forty-
two shingled houses to twenty-six wigwams (Hawley Papers 1776;
Hutchins 1979:68).

Although the Wampanoag were quick to adopt Christianity, they
never embraced it. Rather, they tailored it to fit their own needs.
Numerous quotations can be cited from Hawley where he reluc-
tantly tempered the progress he had made among his constituents
with information on their immorality or religious perversions. "It
appears . . . that my people encrease in wealth and numbers and I
wish they made the same progress in religion . . . the spirit of
religion is low among us" (Hawley Papers 1776). Hawley also
noted:

As to the state of morals and religion among the Indians, altho' we have
instances of great temperance and industry, I cannot say but that they are
too many of them overtaken at times with intoxication. Our females are
many of them temperate; but our young women are loose in their morals;
and wives have often been found with child when their husbands came
from their long voyages. (Hawley 1802b)

According to Kathleen Bragdon, the church was primarily a
source of community cohesion (1981:64). It provided a mainline
between distant communities where the renewal of both kinship
and friendship ties, and not the religious service per se, was the
focus of the sabbath meetings. Bragdon describes how the English
language and Christianity were interwoven into the fabric of Indian
culture. Literacy and religious instruction were learned simultaneously since "Puritan doctrine required wide personal knowledge
of scripture" (Bragdon 1981:50). Thus, reading and writing (in
both the Massachusett language and English) enhanced conversion.

Bragdon further notes that literacy promoted the differentiation
of Indian society along the lines of socioeconomic status (1981:59).
For example, many of those Indians who occupied positions of
authority as ministers or spokesmen on their own plantations were
literate. Leaders, such as the Indian minister Solomon Briant, who
shared the ministry with Gideon Hawley and preached in Massachusett while Hawley preached in English, and Reuben Cognehew,
who met with the King in 1760 to protest the institution of guardianship, were well versed in both English and Massachusett.
Literacy was a survival strategy which gave Indians an effective
tool in their dealings with White society.[8]

THE NINETEENTH CENTURY

The nineteenth century witnessed growing political strength among the Wampanoag. Whenever the White world impinged upon the Indians, they responded with political mobilization. In 1833, for instance, the Mashpee declared:

That we as a tribe will rule ourselves and have the rights so to do for all men are born free. . . . That we will not permit any white man to come upon our Plantation to cut . . . wood . . . hay or any other article. . . . That we will have our own Meeting House, and place in the pulpit whom we please. (Massachusetts Senate Document 1833, Doc. 14:5; Campisi 1984:85).

This resolution was sent to the governor of Massachusetts. It was drafted in response both to the state's failure to protect their Indians and their refusal to allow them to choose their own minister. The Mashpee then took over the Indian meetinghouse.[9] This coup forced the state to relinquish some of their control over the Indians, and in 1834 Mashpee was reincorporated as a district with power to choose their officers (Campisi 1984:85; Conkey et al. 1978:179).

Because of Mashpee's size (in terms of both its Indian population and acreage) and its access to valuable resources (woodland, cranberry bogs, and good hunting and fishing territory), the town had a unique political history. There was a constant give and take with the White world.

Another example of how Mashpee defended itself and its resources concerns the Indians' land policy. The newly elected President of Mashpee—Daniel Amos—together with Solomon Attaquin authorized the division of the tribe's common lands (Report of the Commissioners 1849:26; Massachusetts Commissioners 1861:48). Ten thousand of Mashpee's 12,000 acres were divided into lots of sixty acres, and each proprietor was given one of these lots. The division was intended not only to enable individuals to become financially stable, but also to protect the tribe's land-base from outsiders who were ever willing to take Mashpee land. The 1834 act prohibited alienation of lands to persons not belonging to the tribe (Report of the Commissioners 1849:26).

While the commissioners generally favored this new land policy,[10] they nevertheless cited some of its misfortunes (Report of the Commissioners 1849:38). For example, many Indians began to cut and sell the timber from their allotments. Unrestricted cutting destroyed the natural habitat for deer—one of the Mashpee's resources—and threw individuals "onto their own resources" (Report of the Commissioners 1849:27; see also Massachusetts Commissioner Report 1861:53).

Mashpee's land policy was revised periodically during the nineteenth century. At the heart of the revisions were the festering problems of how and to whom should the tribe's lands be divided, and what guarantees would there be to prevent its alienation to outsiders. The state of Massachusetts proposed its answer to the land problems. It called for the "enfranchisement of all Indians in Massachusetts," and accordingly, "Indians were to be granted citizenship and the entailment of their land removed" (Campisi 1984:100). Furthermore, the State transformed Mashpee from Indian district to Indian town in 1870. This enactment was against the wishes of a majority of the Mashpee, and it resulted in the division of the group's common lands (Campisi 1984:100). The revision of the Indians' land policy resulted in the transfer of many valuable cranberry bogs and shorefront properties to Whites.

Other Wampanoag Indian communities were not as controversial as Mashpee in their relations with the White world. Herring Pond, betwen Plymouth and Sandwich, numbered between forty-nine and sixty-two natives between 1849 and 1861 (Report of the Commissioner 1849:38; Massachusetts Commissioners 1861:68). The Commissioners noted that Herring Pond Indians fared better than the Mashpee because their lands were tightly managed by a treasurer, who helped ensure that the groups' common lands would not be alienated to outsiders (Report of the Commissioner 1849:38).

The Troy or Fall River Wampanoag resided on the east shore of North Wattupa Pond. The population numbered close to eighty individuals and controlled approximately 190 acres (Report of the Commissioner 1849:41; Massachusetts Commissioner 1861:78). The Fall River Indians shared a colorful history. The original Indian reservation formerly belonged to one person who was convicted in 1693 of "high misdemeanors." He fled to Rhode Island whereupon Captain Benjamin Church (of King Philip's War fame) submitted a petition to the General Court. The petition called for the Indian's lands in lieu of a fine. His lands were then transferred to Benjamin Church and "certain friendly Indians" (see Massachusetts Commissioner 1861:80) with the provision that the lands "not to be assigned or alienated, but continued forever, an Indian Plantation" (Massachusetts Commissioner 1861:80).

In spite of Fall River's legal guarantees, the Indians did not fare well according to the Commissioners. The Commissioner reported that the Indians lived in hovels, and little of the land was improved for farming (Massachusetts Commissioner 1861:82-83). Furthermore, these plantation Indians experienced "great poverty"; some received state aid while others lived in "advanced stages of pauperism" (Massachusetts Commissioner 1861:83).

The Commissioners cited Fall River's lack of a district and isolated community with strong local leadership as a major barrier to its progress. Unlike many of the other Indian communities, the Fall River Indians did not all live on the reservation lands. In fact, the Commissioners indicated that those who lived off the land found employment in the White world and were consequently much better off than their reservation brethren (Massachusetts Commissioner 1861:86-89).

Another group of Wampanoag lived in Yarmouth during the nineteenth century. The Yarmouth Indians were not politically organized and owned no land. They claimed that their lands had been previously illegally conveyed (Report of the Commissioners 1849:46). Because this group owned no land, they were largely "intermingled" with neighboring communities, and some had "merged" with the Herring Pond Indians (Massachusetts Commissioner 1861:109-10). Due to the high degree of intermarriage between Yarmouth Indians and the neighboring White communities, these Indians looked "White." They, therefore, enjoyed higher living standards than all other Indians and were "in possession of their civil rights . . . [and lived] in a condition of domestic ease and comfort" (Massachusetts Commissioner 1861:111).

The Dartmouth Indians were subdivided into the Acushnets, Acoaxets, and Aponegansets, by which names the several localities of their residences were still known in the nineteenth century (Massachusetts Commissioner 1861:112). Like the Yarmouth Indians, the Dartmouth Indians escaped the negative effects of being under White overseers as they had neither lands nor funds for the state to manage (Conkey et al 1978:180). Many of the Dartmouth Indians, in fact, were dispersed throughout the southeastern New England area, and some even emigrated to New York and Connecticut (Massachusetts Commissioner 1861:112).

The Namatakeeset or Manattakeesett originally inhabited the Monument ponds area in Pembroke (north of Plymouth). The council of War of Plymouth ordered them to Clarks Island in 1675, and thereafter they had no property remaining in either Pembroke or Clarks Island (Conkey et al 1978:180; Massachusetts Commissioner 1861:114). Their population numbered approximately twenty-five in the mid-nineteenth century, and all of them enjoyed citizenship and were integrated into the White community (Massachusetts Commissioner 1864:114-15).

The Tumpum Indians may have been interwoven with the Namatakeeset Indians since their former residence was cited as Pembroke (Massachusetts Commissioner 1864:115). The Commissioner (Massachusetts Commissioner 1864:115) traced the genealogies of some of these Indians to other southeastern Massachusetts Indian groups, including the Mashpee. The number of Tumpum remaining who were not intermarried with other Indian groups was only fifteen in the mid-nineteenth century, and they were all regarded as citizens of the state (Massachusetts Commissioner 1861:115).

One other relatively small Wampanoag group of the nineteenth century included the Middleboro Indians. This group was formerly located on Betty's Neck in Lakeville and numbered ten individuals. Some of these Indians became sailors; others moved to New Bedford. Even though the Middleboro Indians had no district organization and no lands in their possession, they nevertheless laid claim to a tract of land in Lakeville (Massachusetts Commissioner 1861:118).

Cultural Information

Gleaning cultural information from the Commissioners' reports and other documentary records is an enigmatic task, particularly since these data are biased—the White authorities seemed to be only interested in noting the "progress" Indians had made in becoming "White." Authorities were therefore keen to note if

Indians were receiving the gospel, going to school, and practicing English farming. One must try to read through these biases in order to see Indian culture.

The Wampanoag's economy was mixed during the nineteenth century. Indians adopted many of the European farming practices, such as raising potatoes and grains in addition to growing Indian corn. Indians also kept a variety of stock, including horses, cattle, swine, sheep, and fowls. Some Wampanoag rented out portions of their land to Whites to farm, or they sold wood to the neighboring White communities (Massachusetts Commissioners 1868:86;Conkey et al. 1978: 84-85). The practice of selling wood, however, occasionally led to problems in some areas like Mashpee where too much of the forest was cleared (Report of the Commissioners 1849:27).

Indians who did not farm, or who farmed very little, either worked as day laborers for Whites or took to the sea as whalers (Report of the Commissioners 1849; Massachusetts Commissioners 1869). These latter occupations led to high mobility among the Wampanoag. They became urban hunters and gatherers who exploited the White coastal towns for whatever temporary work they could find.

Material culture change went along with changes in the Wampanoag's economic system. By the early nineteenth century, wigwams had been almost totally replaced by framed houses (Hawley Papers 1802b: Conkey et al. 1978:185). In some areas (parts of Fall River and Mashpee), however, where Indians were too poor to either build a wigwam or a framed house, they lived in huts and hovels which the Commissioners reported as being very "filthy" (Report of the Commissioners 1849:25).

The Wampanoag adopted many European tools for both inside and outside work (Conkey et al. 1978:185). Indians also wore European dress and learned the English language (Conkey et al. 1978:185; Speck 1928). In spite of these changes, the Wampanoag still clung to many of their traditions. For example, several Mashpee leaders incorporated the Mashpee Manufacturing Company in 1867. The company produced native baskets, brooms, wooden wares, and other such objects (Campisi 1984:97).

As the information from the Mashpee and others suggests, the Wampanoag had a rather capricious political arrangement with the state of Massachusetts during the nineteenth century. According to Earle (Massachusetts Commisioners 1861:121), some of the group were Indians and their descendants who had never been under the special guardianship of the state, who had no reservations, and who were scattered and mingled with other populations. The Middleboro, Tumpum, Manattakeesett, Dartmouth, and Yarmouth Indians were examples of this status. Other Indians had reservations on which most of the native population resided. Furthermore, these distinct and isolated reservations were under the guardianship of the state (Massachusetts Commissioners 1861:121). The Mashpee and Herring Pond groups were examples of this second category. The last status, including the Fall River Indians, applied to those groups which had reservations and guardians. However the majority of the Indian residents moved off the reservation lands (Massachusetts Commissioners 1861:121).

Whenever Indians moved off their reservations and/or intermarried with Whites, they enjoyed U.S. citizenship, although it is questionable to what degree they were discriminated against because of their "Indianness" (Massachusetts Commissioners 1861:124). Indians under the auspices of guardians, overseers, and other White officials did not enjoy as much autonomy as did Indian citizens. Rather, the officials managed their lands, distributed state money to the tribe (for the poor, for construction of meetinghouses and churches, and so on), monitored and tried to enforce attendance at the schools and churches, and settled disputes between Indians and between Indians and Whites. Sometimes, as the history of Mashpee indicates, the White officials usurped too much of the Indians' power, and the Indians rebelled.

Religion and education were also strictly monitored by the state. Both the Society for the Propagation of the Gospel and the Williams Fund of Harvard College paid ministers to settle and preach among the Wampanoag. Both of these groups mainly supported Congregational ministers, such as Gideon Hawley and Phineas Fish—missionaries to the Mashpee and surrounding Indians during the eighteenth and nineteenth centuries. The Indians did not care much for either the ministers or Congregationalism. The 1833 declaration of tribal status was partially motivated by dissatisfaction with religious affairs.

The state's Indians were expected to attend either private (on the reservations) or public schools. Reports of the Massachusetts'

Indian commissioners (Massachusetts Commissioners 1861; Report of the Commissioner 1849) suggest that average attendance was 80 percent with children going to school eight months out of the year. All of these schools taught the English language at the expense of the Indians' native tongues and encouraged children to foresake all other aspects of their culture as well (Conkey et al. 1978:185; Speck 1928).

The Wampanoag's reaction to the various attacks upon their culture was both dramatic and subtle. Political mobilization provides an example of the former reaction, while disease and drunkenness are examples of the latter type of reaction. The Commissioners (Massachusetts Commissioners 1861) reported alarming rates of mortality of up to 33 percent or more among reservation Indians between 1849 and 1861 (the intervening years between the Commissioners' reports). Consumption, smallpox, a variety of infantile diseases, drowning, and old age were cited as the primary culprits for death (Massachusetts Commissioners 1861:69).

The Commissioners also cited with alarm the abuse of alcohol by the Indians: "no such liquors . . . are sold on any of the plantations, but there are groceries about their borders, kept by whites, and the laws are inefficient to prevent their introduction on the reservation" (Massachuetts Commissioners 1861:13).

THE CONTEMPORARY SCENE

Revitalization

The unity that one sees among the twentieth century Wampanoag is a combination of old and new. The new should not be regarded as a sign of non-Indianness; rather, it should be viewed in terms of its broader implications. The Wampanoag are going through a process of revitalization (Wallace 1972 [1956]) which has affected all aspects of their society from religion to sociopolitical integration. Revitalization is a:

deliberate, organized, conscious effort by members of a society to construct a more satisfying culture . . . [it is thus] a special kind of culture change phenomenon: the persons involved in the process of revitalization must perceive their culture, or some major areas of it, as a system . . . they must feel that this cultural system is unsatisfactory; and they must innovate not merely discrete items, but a new cultural system. (Wallace 1972:504).

According to Wallace's classic definition, a group need not have a prophet in order to initiate revitalization. Rather, revitalization can be a group effort to attempt to renew one's "mazeway" (Wallace 1972:507) before it threatens to disintegrate in the light of mounting tension and conflict.

Sociopolitical Organization

The twentieth century can be characterized as "Indian people working together" (Red Blanket 1985: personal communication). The Wampanoag have redefined their sociopolitical organization in order to revitalize their culture and thereby press for Indian rights. Revitalization is crucial to maintaining Indian identity in the face of widespread attempts to destroy it. This realization blossomed in 1928 with the birth of the Wampanoag Nation (Campisi 1985: personal communication).[11]

The contemporary Wampanoag sociopolitical organization is a reflection of the early twentieth-century movement. The group's leadership is subdivided among a variety of tribal organizations at both the regional and local levels. The regional institutions include the Grand Sachem, the Chief, and the Supreme Medicine Man. They are supported by local chiefs and tribal councils. The Grand Sachem, Ellsworth Oakley, is the titular head of all Massachusetts Indians. He works closely with the "traditional" leaders such as the chief, Early Mills, and the Medicine Man, John Peters. Mills, who has held his post for over twenty years, also helps to organize meetings and ceremonies (Oakley 1984: personal communication).

According to the Wampanoag, a true Medicine Man is one who is recognized as such by the spirit world (Pocknett 1984: personal communication). John Peters was appointed by Oakley some years ago to this position, and he currently divides his time between administering to the spiritual needs of the people and acting as Executive Director of the Commission on Indian Affairs for the state of Massachusetts.

The Wampanoag are subdivided into five regional "tribes" or bands, all of which are headed by separate chiefs who were elected by their people with Oakley's consent. These tribes include

Mashpee (Cape Cod), Gay Head (Martha's Vineyard)[12], Herring
Pond (from Wareham to Middleboro), Assonet (from New Bedford
to Rehoboth), and Nemasket (the Middleboro region) (Oakley
1984: personal communication). The appointment of the chiefs
began in 1975 when Oakley tried to "revive" the Wampanoag and
"bring back tributary tribes" (Oakley 1984: personal communication). He stated that the people "died out" in some areas or were
without leadership and organization (Oakley 1984: personal communication). Oakley added that the duties of all of the regional
chiefs include "getting everyone together" for meetings and
ceremonies and for providing leadership and inspiration to their
people. Oakley and Peters attend most of the regional meetings and
ceremonies and are therefore "always on the road" administering
to their people (Oakley 1984: personal communication). The Grand
Sachem also calls a "Council of Chiefs" meeting at which time the
chiefs discuss important issues facing them. Oakley's comments
about the regional bands are corroborated by evidence from some
of these groups' chiefs. Wind Song (Assonet), Alan Maxim (Herring Pond), and Red Blanket (Nemasket) all describe district activities. The Assonets and Nemaskets, for example, host a new year's
celebration in May to mark the earth's return to life after the long
winter. The Assonets also sponsor a King Philip ceremony (to com-
memorate the former sachem), a Green Corn festival (a thanks-
giving for the harvest), and various dinner and dancing socials
throughout the year (Wind Song 1985: personal communication).
Some of these ceremonies are described in greater detail in the
discussion of world view.

Maxim (1985: personal communication) spoke of his group's
spiritual and political needs as occasions for get-togethers. Name-
giving ceremonies, the sweat lodge, and ceremonies marking births
and deaths, all administer to the group's spiritual needs, while the
tribal council channels the group's political directions. Herring
Pond's tribal council, like all other regional tribal councils,
maintains the tribal roll call and other records, manages the
group's money, and meets regularly (Maxim 1985: personal communication).

While an individual may reside in one district, he or she is not
restricted to that area for either political[13] or ceremonial reasons.
Maxim indicates that there is much mobility between districts as
individuals seek jobs and mates and renew kinship ties. Such

mobility has led to a high degree of "interrelatedness via blood-lines" between all Wampanoag (Maxim 1985: personal communication).

While most of the bands have their own tribal councils, the most active and influential one is at Mashpee (Wind Song 1985: personal communication; Maxim 1985: personal communication). The Mashpee Council was founded in 1974 as a response to the renewed encroachment of Whites on Mashpee land.[14] The Indians needed to reorganize in order to defend their lands and develop their economic potential. "The next two years were marked by success in garnering federal grants for Indian cultural and economic projects, including one designed to develop the commercial potential of the Indians' traditional skill as shellfish gathers" (Hutchins 1979:167).

According to the Tribal Council Chairman, Vernon Pocknett (1984: personal communication), the Council is the governmental arm of the Wampanoag; it handles the "business" end of the tribe. Such business includes dealing with petitions for federal recognition and land suits, plus convening monthly and weekly meetings to handle a variety of issues facing the tribe.

The family is another source of revitalized Wampanoag unity and integration. Today's typical family is extended in two senses: On the one hand, the whole community is regarded as an extended family (Peters 1984: personal communication); and, on the other hand, the household group is usually extended to include parents, children, grandparents, and anyone else who happens to need a temporary place to stay. In this latter sense, the household's composition is constantly changing. Peters (1984: personal communication) notes that, ever since he can remember, his family always set five or six extra plates at dinnertime.

World View

World view, with its accompanying religious beliefs and ceremonies, is an integral part of any society's culture. For that reason, it has always been one of the primary sources of revitalization and cultural integration.[15]

World view is a peoples' "structure of reality" (Ortiz 1972:139) which classifies and orders the "really real" (Geertz 1972:175) in the universe. Part of that structure of reality includes concepts about the self and the group, plus axioms about the right way to live. Group ceremonies reinforce such concepts by mobilizing the community's religious moods and motivations and reifying its collective identity (Ortiz 1972:139).

For the Wampanoag, significant concepts about the self stress individuality, yet simultaneously emphasize the person's contribution to the whole. Ceremonies such as the non-public Unity Circles and Spiritual Gatherings and the public powwows give individuals the chance to express themselves. Expression might take the form of dancing, drumming, speaking one's mind to those assembled, and singing. The dances and songs are "personal prayers" to the spirit worlds (Pollard 1984: personal communication). The Wampanoag realize that individuals' spiritual directions are "different" (Peters 1984: personal communication); therefore, the prayers vary in form and content from one person to the next.

The ceremonials, however, also emphasize the group. The Unity Circles, as the name suggests, are probably the best examples of collective identity. Anyone can call a Unity Circle, and they can be held anywhere in New England, and even throughout the United States.[16] All Native Americans are invited to attend any one of these ceremonies, even though the Circles tend to draw the most participants from the area where they are held.

The Unity Circle's importance is not whether all Native Americans attend, but for those who do come, the purpose is to share a "likeness in mind and heart" (Pollard 1984: personal communication). Those who attend do not care about political matters such as federal recognition, per se; rather, they are there to express unity with the environment and with each other (Pollard 1984: personal communication). Besides drumming and singing, the Unity Circle gives participants ample opportunity for feasting and visitation—important ways to renew kin and friendship ties. Furthermore, it gives the people the chance to speak their minds. During one part of the ceremony, individuals sit in a circle, and pass around a "talking stick"; everyone has a turn. Usually, discussion centers on current problems—how to cope "with the area where you live" (Peters 1984: personal communication).

At the close of the ceremony, the ashes from the ceremonial fire are carefully preserved and are carried to the next Unity Circle. In this way, the fire is never allowed to be extinguished.

Other important Wampanoag ceremonies are the Spiritual Gatherings and powwows. The Spiritual Gatherings, like the Unity

Circles, are closed to non-Indians. Spiritual Gatherings are held throughout the year, and they usually coincide with the full moon. There are two major Gatherings either spring and fall or spring and summer to which many New England Indians come. Some Spiritual Gatherings include the Assonet-Nemasket new year's ceremony, the Assonet's King Philip ceremony, and the Green Corn festival. The rest of the Gatherings are smaller in size and tend to draw their participants from the Mashpee area. The tenor of the Spiritual Gatherings is more personal than that of either the Unity Circles or the powwows; individuals strive for "sovereignty within oneself" (Peters 1984: personal communication).

The public is invited to attend the annual Mashpee Powwow, which is scheduled to coincide with the July 4th holidays when Cape Cod is packed with tourists. Part of the reason for holding the ceremony then is to "cash-in" on the tourist trade and thereby increase the tribe's revenues. Another reason for holding the public powwows is to vividly demonstrate to non-Indians that the Wampanoag do indeed exist.

All of these ceremonies—the Unity Circles, the Spiritual Gatherings, and the powwows—emphasize the Wampanoag's lifeway. This lifeway includes beliefs in the "natural order of things" (Pollard 1984: personal communication). It recognizes that man is no better than any other creation, and that, consequently, all living beings must be treated reciprocally with utmost respect and thankfulness (Weinstein 1983b:42-44).

SUMMARY AND CONCLUSIONS

At the close of the seventeenth century, the Wampanoag's outlook appeared very bleak. Not only did they suffer defeat in King Philip's War, but they also suffered at the hands of the post-1675 colonial governments which passed restrictive and repressive legislation against the newly conquered Indians. The Wampanoag survived, however, in spite of the difficulties and much to the dismay of many skeptical Whites. Indeed, the vivacity of the contemporary Wampanoag belies their history. Their current political and social organization together with their ceremonial system, all point to the revitalization which this group has shared throughout their long history.

During the eighteenth century, the Wampanoag were dispersed

among a variety of reservations in the Massachusetts Bay Colony. The gospel was preached to them by missionaries such as Josiah Cotton and Gideon Hawley. Their sermons, however, were not widely appreciated as the evidence from Mashpee indicates. The Wampanoag learned to take both governmental and religious affairs into their own hands in order to protect their land-base from White guardians and debtors, and to protect their native beliefs from the attacks of ethnocentric missionaries.

Political mobilization was also integral to nineteenth- and twentieth-century Wampanoag culture, beginning with the Mashpee's 1833 statement of self-rule and continuing with the twentieth-century Wampanoag movement, which is still going strong today.

The Wampanoag learned ways of enriching their culture through the adoption of many White traits. Government, religion, and language were obviously three new adoptions. Other additions were in the economic sphere; Indians learned whaling and farming and sought work as day laborers for Whites.

Not all Wampanoag survived the centuries. Some of the groups mentioned by the nineteenth-century Commissioners "vanished," merged with other Indian communities, or "joined" the White world. Certainly, the Mashpee were the most successful of all of them, due in part to their political savvy. However, other smaller and less politically active groups continued to exist in Herring Pond, Assonet (New Bedford to Rehoboth), and Nemasket or Middleboro. These groups looked to Mashpee for strength—they were tied into Mashpee's government and ceremonial system.

If anyone should doubt the authenticity of the Wampanoag today, let them attend one of their ceremonies and experience the vitality of this group, for it is a vitality that speaks through the ages.

ACKNOWLEDGMENTS

The author is indebted to many individuals and institutions for their generous help in the preparation of this manuscript. Wampanoag Medicine Man John Peters; Tribal Council Chairman Vernon Pocknett; Grand Sachem Ellsworth Oakley; Tribal Historian Kenneth Coombs; regional chiefs Wind Song, Red Blanket, and Alan Maxim; and Mr. Tony Pollard and Eagle Hawk gave me invaluable insight into the contemporary Wampanoag scene. Dr. Jack Campisi was instrumental in directing me to sources and offering me his special ethnohistorical expertise. The Massachusetts Historical Society and the Massachusetts State Archives were kind enough to allow me to use their facilities. Finally, Dr. Frank Porter critiqued the paper and had the all-important faith in my work.

NOTES

1. Only the mainland southeastern Massachusetts and Cape Cod Wampanoag (or Nauset) are discussed in this chapter.

2. The tribal affiliations of the Cape Cod Indians is problematical. Speck (1928:118) ascribes them to a separate Nauset group. However, he notes that there are strong linguistic similarities as well as a great deal of intermarriage between the two groups (1928:120).

Further evidence of similarities between the Cape and mainland Indians is derived from the seventeenth century. Dutch official de Rasieres (1963 [1628]:78), writing in 1628 on native peoples of southern New England, indicated that "the tribes in their neighborhood [Plymouth] all have the same customs as already above described [meaning from the coastline of New York to Cape Cod]."

Englishman Daniel Gookin (1972 [1792]:8-9) included all of Cape Cod, the Vineyard, and Nantucket as the Pokanoket.

3. For more information on King Philip's War, see Leach 1966, Jennings 1975, Vaughan 1980, 1965.

4. Not all Wampanoag, however, see Mashpee as the center. Gay Head is one group that does not look to Mashpee for leadership. Another dissenting view is held by Red Blanket, chief of the Nemaskets (Red Blanket 1985: personal communication). While Red Blanket agrees that Mashpee is somewhat of the ceremonial and political center for many of the Wampanoag (because of its location, history, population size, and success in garnering federal grants), he thinks that the town's importance has been exaggerated. "If Mashpee is the center, it needs to recognize that it serves all the Wampanoag and not just Mashpee" (Red Blanket 1985: personal communication).

5. Josiah Cotton belonged to a long line of missionaries to the Plymouth area Indians. Josiah was the son of John Cotton, and he carried on his father's work by learning the Massachusett language and preaching to the Indians in their native tongue. Both men visited their Indian congregations approximately once a month (see Bragdon 1981:39-40 for more information about the Cottons).

6. Gideon Hawley's reports to the Governor, various governmental committees, and his colleagues at the Society for the Propagation of the Gospel vacillate between optimism and over-selling the progress he had made among them, to pessimism and feelings that the Mashpee were failures. Hawley's pessimism was in part fueled by racism—he believed the Mashpee's open-door policy was wrong and had enabled too many Blacks to reside there (Hawley Papers 1792). Hawley also chided the "Indian Chiefs, who act as Overseers" for "giving away for *Rum* their Land" (Hawley Papers 1792).

7. Contemporary Wampanoag refer to both the present and past time periods and indicate that there has always been a great deal of mobility and intermarriage between the local Wampanoag groups.

8. See, for example, Weinstein 1983a, 1983b for a discussion of how Indians learned to use the European legal system in their efforts to defend their territories.

9. After Hawley died at the turn of the century, Phineas Fish succeeded him. Fish, who was appointed by the state, was a graduate of Harvard and received a handsome salary from the William Fund (Hutchins 1979:100-101). After the Pequot Indian revivalist preacher William Apes exposed how Fish catered to White interests, the Mashpee turned against him. The Mashpee wished to "place in the pulpit whom we please . . ." (see Hutchins 1979:102-5). The Mashpee were able to persuade the Williams Fund to support the Indians' choices for both governmental and religious affairs. Such religious affairs included the establishment of a separate Baptist church in Mashpee (Campisi 1984:90).

10. In 1848 and 1861, the Commonwealth of Massachusetts ordered its Indian commissioners to report on the status of the state's Indian populations. The Commissioners visited with "all the tribes and parts of tribes . . . except perhaps a few scattered over the state . . . who are practically merged in the general community" (Report of the Commissioners 1849:4). These reports, sometimes referred to as the Bird (1849) and Earle (1861) reports, are the most extensive information we presently have on the Wampanoag of the nineteenth century.

11. Campisi (1985: personal communication) suggests that the name Wampanoag was a result of the tribe's revitalization and the organization of the Wampanoag Nation in 1928. Until that time, the southeastern Massachusett and island Indians were known by a variety of local or regional names. However, they all recognized common descent from King Philip and his Pokanoket.

12. The Gay Head Indians are separate from the rest of the Wampanoag although they are included by the rest of the Wampanoag as one of the tribe's five regional bands. Their autonomy is partially due to tension between the groups over land suits and federal recognition petitions

(Maxim 1985: personal communication; Red Blanket 1985: personal communication).

13. Band/tribal affiliation is particularly important to the federal government. Because of federal censuses and land and recognition petitions, individuals can be listed only on one band/tribal roll (Maxim 1985: personal communication).

14. During the 1960s and 1970s, increasingly more white tourists began to make Mashpee their permanent home. They began to monopolize both Mashpee's lands and the town's government. The Indians countered this White intrusion with political mobilization. They established a Tribal Council which helped the Mashpee press for federal recognition. Once federally recognized, the Mashpee would be in a favorable position to win their land suits against the state of Massachusetts for failure to protect the Indians' land. See Campisi 1984 and Hutchins 1979 for detailed discussions of the Mashpee's recent legal history.

15. For more discussion on the association of world view and religion in revitalization movements, see Mooney 1896 on the Ghost Dance; Slotkin 1972 on Peyote; and Wallace 1969 on the Long House Religion.

16. The discussion of the Wampanoags' sociopolitical organization and ceremonial system reveals the incorporation of new elements into their culture. The additions, such as the emphasis upon Pan-Indianism, are innovations which Wallace (1972:504) would say helps a society form a new cultural system.

REFERENCES

Acts and Resolves.
>1878   *Acts and Resolves of the Province of Massachusetts Bay.* Vol. III: 1742-1757. Boston: Albert and Wright (Archives of the Commonwealth).
>1874   *Acts and Resolves of the Province of Massachusetts Bay.* Vol. II: 1715-1742. Boston: Wright and Potters (Archives of the Commonwealth).
>1869   *Acts and Resolves of the Province of Massachusetts Bay.* Vol. I: 1692-1714. Boston: Wright and Potters (Archives of the Commonwealth).

Bradford, William.
>1620-1647   "Of Plymouth Plantation 1620-1647." *Collections of the Massachusetts Historical Society.* 4th ser., vol. 3.

Bragdon, Kathleen.
>1981   "Another Tongue Brought In: An Ethnohistorical Study of Native Writings in Massachusetts." Ph.D. diss., Brown University.

Campisi, Jack.
    1984   *Mashpee: Tribe On Trial*. In press.
    1985   Personal communication.
Conkey, L., et al.
    1978   "Indians of Southern New England, Late Period." In
            Northeast, Handbook of North American Indians, vol.
            15, edited by Bruce Trigger, pp. 177-189. (William
            Sturtevant, gen. ed.) Washington: Smithsonian.
Cook, Sherburne.
    1976   *The Indian Population of New England in the 17th
            Century*. University of California Press Publications in
            Anthropology, vol. 12. Berkeley: University of Califor-
            nia Press.
Cotton, Josiah.
    1716-1717   "Record of His Preaching to the Indians: Services
            Among the Indians 1716-1717." Massachusetts Historical
            Society.
de Rasieres, Isaak.
    1963   "Isaac de Rasieres" (1595-1669). In *Three Visitors to
            Early Plymouth*. Edited by Sydney James, pp. 63-79. Ply-
            mouth, Mass.: Plimoth Plantation.
Geertz, Clifford.
    1972   "Religion as a Cultural System." In *Reader in
            Comparative Religion: An Anthropological Approach*.
            Edited by William Lessa and Evan Vogt, pp. 167-177.
            New York: Harper and Row.
Goddard, Ives.
    1978   "Eastern Algonkian Languages." In *Northeast,
            Handbook of North American Indians*, vol. 15, edited
            by Bruce Trigger, pp. 70-77. (William Sturtevant, gen.
            ed.) Washington: Smithsonian.
Gookin, Daniel.
    1972   *Historical Collections of the Indians of New England*.
            New York: Arno Press. (Orig. ed., 1792, Boston:
            Belknap and Hall).
Hawley Papers.
    1761   "Gideon Hawley to William Brattle," August 13, 1761.
            Massachusetts Historical Society.
    1776   "Gideon Hawley to Thomas Cushing," June 24, 1776.
            Massachusetts Historical Society.
    1788   "Gideon Hawley to Shearjashub Bourne," December
            15, 1788. Massachusetts Historical Society.
    1792   "Gideon Hawley to ?, "April 4, 1792. Massachusetts
            Historical Society.

| | 1802a | "Gideon Hawley to R. D. S.," August 1802. Massachusetts Historical Society. |

1802a   "Gideon Hawley to R. D. S.," August 1802. Massachusetts Historical Society.

1802b   "Gideon Hawley to Rev. James Freeman," November 2, 1802. Massachusetts Historical Society.

Hutchins, F. G.

1979   *Mashpee: The Story of Cape Cod's Indian Town.* West Franklin, New Hampshire: Amarata Press.

Jennings, Francis.

1975   *The Invasion of America.* New York: W. W. Norton and Co.

Langdon, George Jr.

1966   *Pilgrim Colony: A History of New Plymouth 1620-1691.* New Haven: Yale University Press.

Leach, Douglas.

1966   *Flintlock and Tomahawk: New England in King Philips War.* New York: W. W. Norton and Co.

Massachusetts Commissioners.

1861   *Masssachusetts Commissioners to Examine Into the Conditions of the Indians of the Commonwealth.* Report to the Governor and Council Concerning the Indians of the Commonwealth. Massachusetts Senate Document No. 96. Boston: William White.

Massachusetts Historical Commission.

1982   "Historical and Archaeological Resources of Southeastern Massachusetts." Boston: Massachusetts Historical Commission Office of the Secretary of State.

Massachusetts Senate Document.

1834   *Document Relative to the Mashpee Indians.* No. 14:1-43.

Massachusetts State Archives.

1755   "Mattakeeset Indians," September 24, 1755. *Massachusetts State Archives,* vol. 32:675.

1754   "Titicut Indians," March 27, 1754. *Massachusetts State Archives,* vol. 32:494.

1751   "Plymouth Indians," November 15, 1751. *Massachusetts State Archives,* vol. 32:228.

1741   "Titicut Indians," Petition by Indians of Titicut to General Court, May 25, 1715. *Massachusetts State Archives,* vol. 31:21.

1703   "Titicut Indians," August 27, 1703. *Massachusetts State Archives,* vol. 31:17, 427-31a.

Maxim, Alan.

1985   Personal communication.

Mooney, James.
    1896   "The Ghost Dance Religion and the Sioux Outbreak of
            1890," *Annual Report of the Bureau of American
            Ethnology, 1892-93*. Part 2. Washington, D.C.
Morison, Samuel.
    1956   *The Story of the Old Colony of New Plymouth*. New
            York: Alfred A. Knopf.
Oakley, Ellsworth.
    1984   Personal communication.
Ortiz, Alfonso.
    1972   "Ritual Drama and the Pueblo World View," in *New
            Perspectives on the Pueblos*. Edited by Alfonso Ortiz,
            pp. 135-62. Albuquerque: University of New Mexico
            Press.
Peters, John.
    1984   Personal communication.
Pocknett, Vernon.
    1984   Personal communication.
Pollard, Tony.
    1984   Personal communication.
Red Blanket.
    1985   Personal communication.
Report of the Commissioners.
    1849   *Report of the Commissioners Relating to the Condition
            of the Indians in Massachusetts*. General Court House
            of Representatives. Doc. no. 46. Boston.

Salisbury, Neal.
    1982   *Manitou and Providence: Indians, Europeans, and the
            Making of New England 1500-1643*. New York: Oxford
            University Press.
Salwen, Bert.
    1978   "Indians of Southern New England and Long Island:
            Early Period." In *Northeast, Handbook of North
            American Indians*, vol. 15, edited by Bruce Trigger, pp.
            160-76. (William Sturtevant, gen. ed.) Washington:
            Smithsonian.
Slotkin, J. S.
    1972   "The Peyote Way." In *Reader in Comparative
            Religion: An Anthropological Approach*. Edited by
            William Lessa and Evon Vogt, pp. 519-22. (1955-1956).
Snow, Dean R.
    1980   *The Archeology of New England*. New York: Academic
            Press.

Speck, Frank.
       1928   "Territorial Subdivisions and Boundaries of the
                 Wampanoag, Massachusetts, and Nauset Indians." *Indi-
                 an Notes and Monographs.* Miscellaneous series no. 44.
                 New York: Museum of the American Indian Heye Foun-
                 dation.
Vaughan, Alden.
       1980   *New England Frontier: Puritans and Indians 1620-1675.*
                 Boston: W. W. Norton and Co.
       1965   *New England Frontier: Puritans and Indians 1620-1675.*
                 Boston: Little and Brown.
Wallace, A. F. C.
       1972   "Revitalization Movements." In *Reader in
                 Comparative Religion: An Anthropological Approach.*
                 Edited by William Lessa and Evan Vogt, pp. 503-12.
                 New York: Harper and Row (1956).
       1969   *The Death and Rebirth of the Seneca.* New York: Alfred
                 A. Knopf.
Weinstein, Laurie.
       1983a   "Survival Strategies: The 17th Century Wampanoag
                 and the European Legal System." *Man in the Northeast*
                 26:81-86.
       1983b   "Indian vs. Colonist: Competition for Land in 17th
                 Century Plymouth Colony." Ph.D. diss., Southern
                 Methodist University.
William, Roger.
       1936   *A Key Into the Language of America.* 5th ed.
                 Providence: The Rhode Island and Providence
                 Plantations Tercentenary Commission (1643).
Wind Song.
       1985   Personal communication.

4
TRI-RACIAL ISOLATES IN A
BI-RACIAL SOCIETY:
POOSPATUCK AMBIGUITY
AND CONFLICT
Ellice B. Gonzalez

INTRODUCTION

The concept of ethnicity is a continuing topic of theoretical debate
(Cohen 1978; Despres 1975; Royce 1982). For the Poospatuck of
Long Island, New York, a people whose origins include Native
American, African, and European ancestors, ethnicity and, in their
eyes, race, are topics grounded in the reality of their lives,
determining their social, cultural, and economic existence. While
many Native American groups are politically active in their fight to
enforce treaty obligations and to clarify territorial rights to land,
the Poospatuck are struggling, as individuals and as family groups,
to prove their identity as Poospatuck and ultimately their right to
reside on land which the state, but not the Federal government,
recognizes as a reservation. Their task is not made easier by their
invisibility in the historical and ethnographic record. Indeed, even
theoretically their position as an ethnic group is ambiguous. This
ambiguity also extends to their own perception of themselves and
results in severe schisms within the Poospatuck community. This
chapter examines these internal divisions and the Poospatuck's
current struggle with their ambiguous ethnic identity after

discussing the theoretical context of their position in the literature on race and ethnicity.

TRI-RACIAL ISOLATES AND ETHNICITY

Scattered throughout the southeastern and eastern Atlantic coastal plain are pockets of people whose ancestors were from Africa and Europe and were also native to the New World. They have been described as "tri-racial isolates" (Cahill 1965; Beale 1957; Greissman 1972; Pollitzer 1972); "mixed bloods" (Price 1950; 1953; Posey 1979); "mestizos" (Berry 1963:15); "quasi-Indian" (Berry 1963:15); "Indian survivals" (Porter 1980); and "marginal men" (Gist and Dworkin 1976). With few exceptions (Blu 1980; Gist and Dworkin 1976; Hicks and Kertzer 1972; Porter 1980), the social anthropological literature has ignored these small, isolated, and ethnically complex groups. Primarily physical anthropologists and social geographers were attracted to these populations, which they described in terms of common physical characteristics and geographical concentration rather than in terms of social and cultural markers.

It is frequently argued that the existence of such populations originated in the confluence of runaway Black slaves, indigenous Indian, and colonial European populations (Beale 1957:187; Price 1953:18; Stanton 1971:84). These populations remained in social and/or physical isolation for many years, marrying consanguineously and creating what one author describes as a "new racial element in society, living apart from other races" (Beale 1957:187). Phenotypic characteristics such as hair and skin as well as genotypic traits including blood type and rare recessive genes are used to identify these tri-racial populations (Beale 1957; Pollitzer 1972; Price 1953). These markers are discussed in terms of discrete boundaries rather than lines, implying that membership is clearly defined by physical characteristics. Geographical boundaries are also used to delimit these populations. Frequently, these groups are associated with rurally isolated areas, specifically living in areas of swamps, hollows, and inaccessible ridges (Beale 1957:188). Other factors marking their definition as tri-racial isolates are their numerical concentration and their proclivity to live within the aforementioned geographical boundaries.

This dependence on the fixed parameters of phenotypic and genotypic racial characteristics and physical association results in what Van den Berghe (1976:243) calls a "rigidity and invidiousness which makes them resemble caste groups more than ethnic groups." Although Van den Berghe may overstate the case, the inflexibility of these racially based definitions does prove problematic when discussing populations whose members adhere to some of the characteristics listed (geographical isolation, sharing common surnames), but not to others, and, indeed, could be phenotypically assigned to "White" or "Black" categories. Thus, although the authors discussing these populations from the perspective of race and geographical isolation, describe physical, geographical, and historical patterns, they perceive these groups as stable and static entities, only minimally acknowledging the social boundaries between these groups and the surrounding communities.

Social anthropologists, moving away from the type of theoretical and ethnographic inflexibility these quantitative definitions impose, developed another set of analytical constructs such as "ethnicity," "ethnic identity," "ethnic groups," and "ethnic category" (Cohen 1978:386; Royce 1982:17). These concepts have been criticized for being too rigid (Cohen 1978:387) as well as too loose (Blu 1980:221). For the purposes of this discussion, the critical factor is that this perspective analyzes tri-racial isolates not in terms of physical characteristics that set them apart from the rest of society, but through cultural symbols and values, which may be manipulated, and through social statuses, which are recognized by both the tri-racial group and the surrounding community as being different from that of the larger social context.

The ethnicity literature most germane to a study of tri-racial isolates is that which emphasizes flexibility of ethnic boundaries (Cohen 1978:397) and which discusses the behavioral aspect of ethnic identity, recognizing that people assume different ethnic identities "depending on what other identities and statuses the actor lays claim to" (Salamone and Swanson 1979:179). Rather than pursue a debate over how ethnicity is manifested and maintained and noting that "ethnic group" may be a term that is culture bound (Blu 1980:117), it would serve this discussion better to look at how ethnicity has been used to discuss tri-racial isolates.

The Lumbee of North Carolina (Blu 1980) and the pseudonymous Monhegan of southern New England (Hicks and Kertzer 1972) will provide the examples.

Both studies recognize the anomalous and ambiguous positions of these mixed groups. This ambiguity exists despite various symbols employed to mark one's ethnic identity: (1) physical appearance, (2) genealogical evidence, and (3) behavioral characteristics, including involvement in "tribal behaviors" (Hicks and Kertzer 1972:11). The absence of the first marker increases the emphasis on the latter two, yet there is a very real danger in this since "there is a fine line between a proud display of ethnic heritage and a performance that the public regards as ludicrous" (Hicks and Kertzer 1972:12). Blu (1980:231) likens this complexity and ambiguity to a "tangle, an irreducible, unorderly, intricate intertwining of strands." Cautioning against an ethnocentric perception of "tangle" as messy and disordered, Blu (1980:232) states:

When I say that the kind of ethnic identity the Lumbee have is best thought of as a tangle, I refer only to the form that identity takes. I do *not* mean to imply that either the Lumbee or their group identity is a mess, that Lumbees lead disordered lives or are confused people.

This ambiguity or tangle best describes the theoretical context in which the Poospatuck case can be understood. However, neither the works on race nor ethnicity include the Poospatuck as either a tri-racial isolate or ethnic group. Both Beale (1957:187) and Berry (1963:33) dismiss the Poospatuck along with the Shinnecock of Long Island, the Narragansett of Rhode Island, and the Pamunkey of Virginia from being termed mixed-bloods or mestizos, since "they cling tenaciously to their tribal identity, and guard their old Indian names as priceless possessions." Berry (1963:33) maintains this position despite the fact they "are all strongly suspected of having little Indian blood, and have retained almost nothing of their ancient language and customs." Because of their small population (203 in 1980), their varying phenotyic characteristics, their inability to substantiate genealogical evidence of their heritage, and their difficulty in manipulating cultural symbols, the

Poospatuck are not ethnically identifiable as a Native American group either by the surrounding community or in legal terms.

Who are the Poospatuck? They are not recognized as a tri-racial isolate and only as marginally having Native American ancestry. In their daily lives, they are constantly forced to make choices assuming one ethnic identity or another (White, Black, or Indian) depending upon a variety of factors including physical appearance, social situation, and place. To understand why the Poospatuck's contemporary ethnic identity is so ambiguous, it is first necessary to reflect on their history and their relationship with the Euro-American culture.

FROM UNKECHAUG TO POOSPATUCK

Long Island is neatly divided into thirteen tribal areas by local historians (Bolton 1975:46; Overton 1975); the Unkechaug were the group located on the eastern south shore between the Carmens (Connecticut) and Forge (Mastic) rivers. While it is clear that tribal affiliations in the anthropological sense did not exist at contact (Gonzalez 1979:8), there did seem to be a sense of territoriality corresponding to local dialects—a pattern common to many eastern Algonkian groups. The word Poospatuck or Poospaton was used as a place name in the colonial period to identify a specific parcel of land on Mastic Neck. It retained this meaning in later histories (Tooker 1911; Overton 1938), and also came to be known as the home of the Unkechaug chief (Beauchamp 1907:220). Neither in the early records nor in later histories did the word Poospatuck refer to a group of people. It referred to a place. Today the referent is to a group, and Unkechaug has all but vanished from usage, except for contemporary Poospatuck who frequently refer to themselves by that name. The transformation from Unkechaug to Poospatuck parallels the transition from a clearly Native American group to that of a multiethnic population.

One of the earliest records of the Unkechaug in European documents is their plea to the governor of New York, in 1677, complaining about the purchase of their land by Whites (O'Callaghan 1866:62). Despite the governor's assurances that their welfare would be protected, the land continued to be sold. The major land transaction, which encompassed an enormous territory and shaped the lives of Unkechaug descendants for years to come, was the patent granted to Colonel William Smith in 1693. Smith wished to develop an estate in the area between the Connecticut and Mastic rivers and requested a search be made of the area by the governor's office. Governor Benjamin Fletcher authorized a survey of the area by the Surveyor General, Augustine Graham, who ascertained that three tracts of land in the area were already granted through patents issued by a former Governor Dongan and that meadowland had been purchased by Brookhaven Town. However, the lands already allocated were a very small part of the area requested by Smith (Pelletreau 1903:265). Upon completion of the survey, Colonel Smith petitioned the court in October 1693 for a grant of land "being in compass about five miles, [to] be erected into a manor by the name of St. George's Manor." In his petition, Smith noted that the lands requested were purchased from the Indians (O'Callaghan 1866:236). Since those deeds remain in the hands of the Smith family and are unavailable for examination, the exact terms of Smith's purchases from the Indians remain unknown. Considering the rapidity with which the survey was made, the purchases occurred, and the patent was granted, actual sale of the lands by the Indians appears to have posed less of a concern for the English legal system than the granting of the patent to Colonel Smith. Governor Fletcher granted Smith the patent on October 9, 1693. The following document describes the area included in the patent, which encompassed the Unkechaug territory on its eastern boundary.

Bounded westard from the main sea or ocean to the west most banks of a certain river called East Coneticott and so along the banks of said river to a creek running out of said river called Yamphank, and so along the south west bank of ye said creek unto the head, the whole creek included, and soe in a direct north line until it comes to the banks of Coneticott river, and from there along the westermost banks of said river. [U]nto the said river head. [T]he whole river and all the branches thereof included. [A]nd from there along the west side of Conneticott Hollow to the Country road. Near the middle of the Island. [T]he whole hollow included. [A]nd so bounded north by the Country road to a marked tree five and a half miles. [A]nd so in a direct south line to a marked tree at the head of the main branch of Mastick river. [A]nd from thence along the easter most banks of Mastick river. [T]he whole river and all its branches included to the main sea. Also the small tracts of upland and meadow Lying east of Mastic river called Puncatone and Hoggs neck. [B]ounded eastward from the main sea to a river or creeke called Senekes river. [A]nd thence in a direct north line to the Country road. [A]nd bounded west by the lands aforesaid. (Pelletreau 1903:265)

Smith was a beneficent Lord of the Manor, giving to his English neighbors small plots of land to help them consolidate their holdings. Similarly, in 1700 he granted to the Unkechaug, who were still living in the area, rights to 175 acres of property in exchange for an annual rent of two ears of corn. The acreage was not contiguous, being split into four unequal parcels. The following deed is fascinating on several accounts. First, it restates Smith's right to the land; second, it lists a number of specific Indian names; finally, it conveys to the named Indians the right to live on and cultivate the assigned acres in perpetuity. In this last respect, it is no different from the grants that Smith conveyed to his English neighbors.

Whereass Seachemn Tobaguss deaceased Did in his Life Time with the other Indians Natives and possessors of Certaine tractes of Lande & Meddow on ye south side of ye Island of Nasaw Neare Vnquachock by severall Deeds under ther handes & seales & by posesshon Liverie and seanon given for Valuable Considerate. in sayd Deedes expressed Did Bargin sell alinate rattifi & Confirm Unto mee & my heires & assines to have holde & inioye for Ever all theire right titel:. . . . Bee it Knowne unto all men that to the intent sayd Indians there Children and posterryte maye Not Want suffesient Land to Plant on for Ever that I Doe here by grant for mee my Heires and assignes for Ever that Wisquosuck IoSen: wionconour Pataquam Steven Weramps Penaws Tapshana: Wepsha: Tacome: and Jacob Indian Natives of unquachocke there Children & ye Posterrite of there Children forever shall withoute any Mollestation from mee my Heires or assines shall and maye plant Sowe for Ever on the Conditions hereafter Expressed one hundred seventie and five Acres of Land part of the Lande so solde mee ass is a for sayd that is to saye one hundred Akers in mastick Neck fifty Acres at pospaton feftene acres at Constbles Neck and ten Akers at qualiecan & to burn under wood alwaies provided that ye sayd Indians there Children or posterrete have not any prevelej to sell Convaye Alinate or let this planting Right or any part thereof to any persun or persuns Whatsoever but this planting Rite shall Desende. to them & there Children for Ever and that ye herbidg is Reserved to mee and my Heires or a sines when there Croops are of & thaye yealdeing & payeing as: an acknowledgment to mee and my Heires for ever Two yellow Eares of Indian Corne in: Testimony Whereof I have to these present set my hande and seale at my Manner of St. Georges this second Daye of July: . . . 1700, Signed, Wm. Smith; [in presence of] Richard Woodhull; John Wood. (BTR 1880:358-59).

It is from this conveyance that today's Unkechaug descendants claim their rights. This deed also symbolizes the end of an era. The Unkechaug previously accommodated the English by selling or sharing their lands; the Smith deed conveys land *to* the Unkechaug. It clearly demonstrates that these Long Island natives were no longer in a position of accommodation, but were now forced to adapt to the dominant culture of English colonial society.

Unkechaug life in the seventeenth century changed in ways other than acceptance of their new neighbors. Like natives elsewhere, the Unkechaug turned to wage labor for subsistence due to a variety of complex reasons: (1) depopulation from disease with a consequent alteration of traditional division of labor, (2) new technology in the form of European iron and guns, (3) unavailability of lands in the face of colonial farming and settlements, and (4) the lure of European trade goods. On Long Island, wage labor was obtained by going to sea. The Town Records are filled with agreements made between White entrepreneurs and native fishermen to hire on for a season as whalers and fishermen. The following is a contract made between Mehane, an Unkechaug Indian, and Joseph Davies for a voyage in autumn 1683.

These pressents wittnesseth that I meheane unkechauk Ingen doth ingaege to goe to sea to help to Kill whate fish this next season for Joseph daves of brookhaven to begin there viege the ferst day of november next . . . and soe to continue tell the viege be don and if the saide mehene shall nott atend when there is sea wether I am contented to pay for every day soe misiing tenn shillens and to the true parformens of the same . . . 16 day of agust 1683; mahene is to goe half share and Joseph daves giues mehene a Iron pott and a shert as a free gift [signed] mahene; witnes tauknan, John Tooker. (BTR 1880:175)

These contracts reveal the variety of tasks that the native whalers were expected to perform, ranging from hunting the whale to preparing its various parts (e.g., blubber) for consumption. Some

Unkechaug hired out as individuals, others as a group. Payment for labor was the sharing of the catch. In some cases, the indentured were required to sell their share to the indenturer. The entrepreneur provided the boats and equipment, but the laborers had to compensate their employer if they did not work on any given day that the weather or tides allowed. Finally, these agreements suggest that Unkechaug men were peripherally becoming involved in the European economy.

Tangier Smith's account books reveal an indenture system whereby he hired Indians to whale for him and in exchange gave them clothing, corn, powder, leather, and so on. Frequently, he provided them with these goods in advance of the products, oil and whale bone, he hoped they would bring him. Often, "his Indians," as he called them, became sick or simply disappeared, not fulfilling their season's commitment. In one entry, dated 1707-1708, Smith commented: "he got nothing this season but went away; left the Beach like a villen, pretended he was sick and never came again" (Smith n.d.).

Simultaneously, it appears that the Unkechaug were experiencing difficulty pursuing their traditional subsistence fishing activities. The New York State records show that in May 1676 an order was issued "granting liberty to the Unchechaug Indians, to whale or fish on their own account" (O'Callaghan 1866:46). To remain economically self-sufficient while pursuing subsistence activities was increasingly problematic for these people toward the end of the seventeenth century.

In the eighteenth century, land continued to change hands between colonists, marking the intensification of settlement among the White population. The land originally purchased from the native population by William Smith and then granted to him by Governor Fletcher as St. George's Manor was gradually broken into smaller sections and bought by other English settlers. On May 7, 1718, Smith sold to Richard Floyd "in consideration of a reasonable sum of good and Lawfull money from England" the following property:

[B]eginning att the mouth of Mastick river from thence along the s:d river to the head of same, from thence due north to the middle of the Island, then due west one english mile, then due south till the head of Mastick bears due east; from thence southerly on a strate line to the head of pattersquash Creek, and from thence as the land of the s:d William Smith doth extend to the place [where] it first began. (Floyd Papers, deed 148)

It was this section of land which contained the 175 acres Smith deeded to the Poospatuck in 1700, forever, for two yellow ears of corn.

Through a series of exchanges, the Floyd family purchased from the Unkechaug all but approximately sixty acres of the original 175 acres. The first of these transfers occurred in 1730, when Nicoll Floyd traded "twenty Dutch blankets, four barrels of syder and . . . three pounds current money" for 100 acres (Floyd Papers, deed 125). Over fifty years later, Nicoll Floyd's son, William, drew up an agreement with the descendants of the Unkechaug who had signed the 1730 deed. This conveyance reaffirmed the transfer of the 100 acres on Mastic Neck to the Floyd family, and also included the sale of fifteen acres of Constable's Neck (Floyd Papers, deed 102). The following year, William Floyd negotiated with Sarah Solomon for rights to property on Poospatuck Neck (Floyd Papers, deed 106). This transaction suggests that the Floyds were treating the property deeded communally to the Unkechaug by Smith as individually owned property. Thus, negotiations were with separate individuals for specific plots of land.

At the conclusion of the eighteenth century, the land remaining to the Unkechaug consisted of approximately fifty acres at Poospaton. The one hundred acres at Mastic Neck were sold to Nicoll Floyd in 1730; that land plus the fifteen acres of Constable's Neck was regarded as belonging to William Floyd in the 1789 deed. Subsequent negotiations with individuals living on Poospatuck eroded the remaining fifty acres at Poospaton. No longer did Unkechaug have access to woodlands, meadows, and shorelines to practice their subsistence hunting, gathering, and fishing. The only land the Unkechaug held in common as a band group was the less than fifty acres called Poospaton, and even this claim was weakened by the transaction between them and the Floyds in the late eighteenth century.

While the Unkechaug community was contracting geographically, it was simultaneously adopting aspects of Euro-American culture. The indenture deeds and land transfers imply the growing dependence upon European material goods. Another element of European culture gaining major acceptance was that of Christianity. Azariah Horton (1741), missionary to the Indians on Long Island and an employee of The Society in Scotland for Propagating Christian Knowledge, began making regular visits to the Poospatuck in the mid-eighteenth century. The missionary noted that there were about "four hundred Indians upon Long Island, old and young." His journal indicates that from January 1741 through March 1744, he made a regular circuit of the Moriches-Mastic area. On April 5, 1741 he preached at Poospatuck, commenting that "Indians are almost universally desirous of instruction." He also noted that a great deal of death and disease had occurred among this population.

Elsewhere in Unkechaug culture, the fabric of their Native American way of life was eroding. Their most famous visitor in the eighteenth century was Thomas Jefferson, who visited General Floyd in June 1791. Jefferson took the opportunity to interview some elderly Unkechaug to obtain samples of their language. Jefferson's preamble to his "Vocabulary of the language of the Unquachog Indians" (1791) states that "this language is a dialect differing a little from that of the Indians settled near Southampton (Long Island) called Shinicocks, and also from those of Montuak or Montock, called Montocks, the three tribes can barely understand each other." He observed that only three people could speak Unquachog or Puspatuck, and they were old women; a young woman appeared to know something about the language. The list Jefferson obtained included European words such as "sheeps" and "hog," indicating the absence of such words for European domesticated farm animals in the Unkechaug vocabulary. Jefferson's dictionary had implications far beyond its linguistic value for it suggests the Unkechaug had all but abandoned speaking and using their language and had adopted English as their common tongue. Also, for the first time in European records, Unkechaug was equated with Poospatuck which is symbolic of their transformation from one cultural world to another—a transformation which would be completed in the following century.

It is not until the nineteenth century that there are indications that the Unkechaug were becoming Poospatuck in more than name. The Unkechaug's closest neighbors, the Floyds, commented in a variety of contexts on their changing ethnic identity: "Martha was given her freedom in [the] early 1850's . . . half Indian and half Negro . . ." (Floyd Papers, CFN, II, 95). Another family member recalled her memories of the Poospatuck settlement: "Blacks and Indians together raised their mongrel breed of children and corn on the same small patch of land. The Indians and darkeys had married and intermarried" (Turner n.d.:100). Upon his death at Poospatuck, Daniel Bradley was described as "a mixture of Indian and negro, his mother being an Indian and his father an African slave" (Floyd Papers, newspaper clipping). A visitor to the area in the late nineteenth century described the Poospatuck village:

On a short excursion trip which I made in September, 1875 to the southern coast of Long Island, I visited, south of the village of west Moriches, the western bank of the large Moriches Inlet, also called Moriches Creek. There I met the farming and fishing remains of the Poospatuck tribe, who at the present time number about twenty families, and are to some extent intermarried with negroes (Anon. 1877:257).

Census enumerators of the nineteenth century were perplexed with the ambiguous ethnicity of these people. The 1840 census lists one family, the Bradleys, as M for mulatto; however, a line crosses out the M designations, and it was replaced with an IN for Indian. Remaining community members, the Caesars, Wards, Mains, and Hawkins are all listed as Indian. Twenty years later, the enumerator chose to list the same families as either M for mulatto or B for Black (U.S. Census 1860; 1880).

Genetically and phenotypically, it is very difficult to speak of separate Unkechaug and Black populations living at Poospaton after the mid-nineteenth century. Marriage patterns initiated in the seventeenth century had created, by the nineteenth century, a multiethnic population. Culturally, however, the pattern was even more complex. Daily life for these people mirrored that of other marginal ethnic groups, especially other Native Americans in the Northeast. Their relationship with the White population, as the Floyd family papers indicate, placed them in a position of former slaves, emphasizing the response made to their Afro-American heritage. And, finally, the cultural identity which these people retained was not Afro-American but Native American. For these reasons, Unkechaug will be referred to as Poospatuck in the remainder of this paper, and no distinction will be made as to genotypic origin, since culturally the Poospatuck did, and still do, perceive themselves as Native Americans.

The phenotypic and ancestral changes noted by neighbor and vistor alike were accompanied by social and cultural changes. Subsistence hunting, fishing, and gathering along with barter were not sufficient to enable the Poospatuck to survive. Economically, they were dependent upon the Floyds and other White families for work. In a thinly disguised fictitious account of life on Mastic Neck, Katherine Floyd Dana described such relationships.

Jes' [when you] think you're gwine to spar' a dollar or two fer an ap'on or a pair o'shoes, and it's all gone. . . . I ben a-plottin' and a-plannin' these three days and nights. I *must* contrive to airn a little somethin' myself, or I dunno what we will come to. . . . Reckon mebbe Mis' Calvert would let me wash and iron this summer, or help Aunt Dolly in the kitchen. (Dana 1889:109-10)

Another way to earn money was the giving of "pay-parties" in which people would be invited to a gathering and be expected to make cash donations. Marty, preparing for such an occasion, requested from Mrs. Calvert "a little butter and flour and sugar and that big dish of beans and bacon" (Dana 1889:139). Elderly Poospatuck men and women were given material assistance by the Floyd family. Economic stability in the nineteenth century became tied to the Poospatucks' relationship with the Floyds.

Participation in White society by the former Unkechaug included adherence to the legal, religious, and political as well as economic system of the dominant culture. Residents of Mastic Neck even fought in the American wars of the nineteenth century. William Cooper, a "Poospatuck Indian Chief," died in the War of 1812 (Pennypacker n.d.). Abraham Edwin Enos fought in the Civil War in the navy (Hallock 1976:232). A Methodist church was established on Poospatuck land in 1812. A Sunday school often staffed by neighboring White women, such as the Floyds, and a state school, which was assigned a teacher, completed the formal structures imposed by the White culture. Despite these external symbols of participation in White culture and the pressure which forced the Poospatuck to conform to this cultural mode, elements of Unkechaug life were preserved, albeit adapted, in the nineteenth century. These elements took two forms: (1) the development of a tribal structure with a tendency toward matrilineality and (2) the celebration of the June meeting.

As noted above, the Poospatuck did not originally adhere to a tribal structure of political organization, but, in response to external pressure to have a spokesperson for the group and in an attempt to consolidate and preserve their identity, a pattern of "chieftainships" arose in the nineteenth century. The first chief mentioned in the ethnohistorical records is William Cooper, the War of 1812 casualty. Elizabeth Joe or Job, who died in 1832, is also named as the female sachem (Furman 1874:47; Hodge 1912: 281). Caroline Hannibal, alive during the mid-nineteenth century and one of the Floyd family servants, followed Elizabeth as Queen of the Poospatuck. Toward the end of the nineteenth century, two individuals, Martha Hill, queen, and Richard Ward, chief, were the leaders of the Poospatuck. Upon Ward's death, Mesh Bradley was elected to the position of chief.

At the conclusion of the nineteenth century, a structured tribal institution was in place among the Poospatuck. In addition to the chief's position there were three trustees. The chief was frequently the first deacon of the church, and the second deacon was the most likely person to inherit the position of chief. Leadership also followed along family lines. Jake Ward was eventually made chief, after his father's immediate successors. Selection of tribal leaders was based on a combination of lineage affiliation and personal achievement as a solid member of the Poospatuck community (*New York Herald* 1902).

Both positions of chief and queen represented the Poospatuck to the outside world. The chief and queen also served as judges within the Poospatuck community, settling internal disputes. Individuals who attained these statuses were respected for their wisdom and were often models of Christian training.

[Richard Ward] although not able to read himself, [urged] upon the authorities the necessity of supplying the reservation with a suitable school

house and a competent white [teacher]. It was he who built the Church and
insisted that every man, woman and child of the reservation [attend]. In
later years, led by religious enthusiasm, when preachers from distant points
were kept away by the inclemency of weather or other cause, Chief Ward
took the pulpit and preached with . . . fervor. (*New York Herald* 1902)

Poospatuck leadership conformed to the dominant culture's idea
of Indian sociopolitical organization: it was hierarchical; it was
represented by one individual, and succession was based in part on
communal vote. Individuals who were elected to the post conformed to Christian and American values. However, the tribal
structure also gave the Poospatuck a clear ethnic identity and
enabled them to interact with the White culture's political and legal
systems.

Another element in Poospatuck culture, the June meetings, also
provided a symbolic statement of ethnic identity and adherence to
past traditions. The meetings served as a forum to discuss and
decide tribal affairs, a social gathering, and a clear statement to the
dominant culture of differences with that culture. The annual
meeting took place in early June. Its time and function had echoes
of the Green Corn ceremony, which for Iroquoian and Algonkian
alike in the prehistoric and protohistoric periods celebrated the
coming harvest. The historic purpose of these meetings is best
articulated by Poospatuckers themselves:

Every June we have a reunion and sometimes our "brothers" from other
tribes join us. Last June was the farewell of my father to his people, for he
foresaw his end and bade one and all goodbye. It was a very affecting scene
and will long remain in the memory of the younger generation. This coming
June we will have another reunion and elect our chief. Thus is our tribal
interest kept up and our people held together. (Jacob Ward, *New York
Herald*, late nineteenth century)

I suppose, said Waters, that outsiders regard us as Negroes, but we find
something in these meetings and especially in the association of this spot
that is very sacred to us. It is the poetry of the thing. It takes only a little
imagination to hear again the soft tread of the mocassin. Many of us who
know the history of our Indian forefathers are very proud to be known as
their descendent because many of them were noble men. (James E. Waters,
New York Herald 1907)

The meetings, which were held throughout the nineteenth century and into the twentieth, contained elements of a religious ceremony, political caucus, and family reunion. The church ceremony remembering the dead began the day, but was quickly followed by a social gathering described by one White as "an occasion of much Sabbath profanation, and indecorum of conduct to multitudes of young people, who from motives of curiosity, or baser principles attend from a distance of twenty or thirty miles around. Its present moral influence on the surrounding country is, at least questionable" (Prime 1845:233). Indeed, people from all around the area, Shinnecock as well as non-Native Americans, attended the June meetings which, by the late nineteenth century, were a popular social outing.

Yet, although outsiders joined Poospatuckers on their day of religious, tribal, and social celebration, it remained a Native American celebration. It was no longer the Green Corn ceremony, but rather a festival that the Poospatuck, who were no longer Unkechaug, had created. It contained, like the Poospatuck themselves, elements of White culture and it also reflected, like its creators, the flexibility and adaptability of an indigenous culture in the face of the eradication of that culture.

Residents of Poospatuck began moving off the reservation in the early twentieth century in search of viable employment and adequate education. Patterns of emigration followed those of other centers of underdevelopment; many moved closer to urban centers, settling in Nassau County. Population estimates for the mid-1930s suggest the presence of only about sixty individuals on Poospatuck land. Only nine children attended the reservation school at this time (*New York Herald Tribune* 1935:16). After World War II, children of former residents began to drift back to Poospatuck, and by 1970 there were 160 residents; in 1980 there were 203.

Out-migration was prompted by two factors: the search for employment and better education for their children. Movement away from the reservation, though exacerbated by the Depression, preceded those difficult years. Men were employed in a variety of occupations off the reservation, usually performing manual labor. The Depression years proved difficult for Poospatuck families. Some men refused to return to the reservation during this time, because of its lack of adequate educational facilities and managed to survive with a variety of jobs. Others spent part of the year on the reservation (summer and fall) doing subsistence hunting and fishing and returned to urban centers for wage employment the remainder of the year. Although many moved away from Poospatuck, at no time was the reservation abandoned. A handful remained, eking out an existence composed of subsistence activities and local employment possibilities. Men worked as farm laborers, gardeners, and handymen. Women were employed as domestic servants, working in White households as well as specializing in specific tasks, such as taking in laundry. Informants describe the period preceding World War II as a peaceful one, in which the half dozen resident families lived in mutual cooperation.

During this period, characterized by isolation and contraction of the reservation population, the Poospatuck experienced the first of two major legal battles which inextricably altered Poospatuck life in the twentieth century. In 1935, the New York State Department of Education chose to close the one-room schoolhouse which had been present on Poospatuck land for fifty years. Funds were not appropriated for the school because the land was "not regarded as an Indian reservation and because the persons living there are not Indians" (*New York Times* 1935). Ultimately, through pressure from the Poospatuck themselves, as well as from influential White community members, they were able to retain the school. Yet, the questions about Poospatuck ethnicity and residential rights were raised. Very quickly following this attack, two Poospatuck families were sent eviction notices by William Dana, who had purchased the property from his Floyd relatives in 1927 and who was ostensibly paying taxes on the parcel. His claim to the land followed the same reasoning as that of the State Board of Education: The Poospatuck were no longer Indian and therefore did not have rights to live on the land. The case was resolved in spring 1936. The Suffolk County judge argued that historically the Poospatuck were given rights to the property by William Smith in 1700 and had continued to live on the land for over 200 years. Further, the judge found that the plaintiffs, as well as their parents, were born on the reservation and "that they have the blood of the same Poospatuck Indians who are named in the deed of Col. William Smith. . . . The fact that they

are not full-blooded Indians, would not . . . bar them such rights''
(Suffolk Co. Court Proceedings 1936:8). Since the 1936 court
ruling in favor of the Poospatuck, New York State refers to
Poospatuck land as a reservation and the Poospatuck as a tribe.

The conclusion of the controversy returned Poospatuck residents
to the quiet life they had experienced since the turn of the century,
but the advent of World War II heralded economic and social
changes which were to continue until the present time. With the
onset of the war, Poospatuck men were employed in the armed
services as well as the civilian work force. The post-war years were
ones of growth for Eastern Long Island. This expansion brought
with it increased opportunity for Poospatuck participation in wage
labor near the reservation. Gradually, relatives of Poospatuck
residents filtered back onto the reservation. Tribal education took
place in the public schools off the reservation, enabling Poospatuck
families to give their children the same standard of education as
elsewhere on Long Island. Poospatuck residents were employed in
a variety of occupations as skilled mechanics, artisans, and security
officers. Wage labor replaced barter; subsistence hunting,
gathering, and fishing; and reliance on one source of material
sustenance, the Floyd family, in the late twentieth century.

However, returnees found that reservation life did not enable
them to participate fully in Long Island's economic expansion.
Because the land is communally owned, yet not a Federal reservation, money for its improvement is difficult to obtain. Individuals
cannot apply for conventional home mortgages because, as
individuals, they do not own the property. Consequently, despite
efforts of Poospatuckers, who moved off the reservation to
improve their economic futures and then returned, as well as those
who remained and struggled, a reasonable housing structure
remains a sought after, but often unattainable dream.

Traditional elements of Poospatuck culture were minimized
during this post-war period of assimilation. The Methodist Church,
which was the focus of Poospatuck religious life throughout the
eighteenth, nineteenth, and early twentieth centuries shared the
allegiances of Poospatuckers with a Baptist Church, which was
established during the last two decades. Eventually, the older
church lost most of its membership to the newer congregation. The

June meeting, a regular feature of nineteenth-century Poospatuck life, disappeared during the course of the following century. During the 1970s, a form of the festival was revived and named the "Annual Corn Festival," but the religious elements along with the political purpose of the early festival were abandoned. The contemporary celebration is a social event for both Indian and non-Indian, although some members of the tribe recognized the sense of cultural continuity and adhesion that such a rite instills in its participants. The tribal structure, which emerged in the nineteenth century, remained in place during the twentieth, and, after experiencing difficulty, emerged greatly strengthened in the last few years.

The second legal confrontation that the Poospatuck experienced in the twentieth century arose not from external causes as did the first, but from internal conflicts. Although the 1936 court ruling clearly gave the Poospatuck rights to their reservation land and declared them a New York State tribe, questions of ancestry, rights to land, and ethnic identity continue to plague contemporary Poospatuck. Since 1977, controversy has existed over who can legally live on the fifty remaining acres. As more members returned to the site, conflicts arose over who had access to living space on the reservation. Added to this was a question of who would control the Federal funds which were made available to the Poospatuck in the mid-1970s for community projects. From these pressures, two factions emerged representing the two major family groups living on the reservation. In 1979 one faction challenged that year's elected council, arguing the incumbents were selected improperly and brought the controversy to the state court system. The court ordered that each member of the reservation be certified a Poospatuck before voting in the election; certification would be proved by presenting written documents attesting to Poospatuck ancestry. A third faction, people living off the reservation but claiming Poospatuck ancestry, entered the arena in 1980. Two years later, the court dissolved the tribal council, requesting that all Poospatuck, both on and off the Reservation, submit appropriate documentation. Out of 300 applicants, thirty-five were deemed acceptable by the court. An election was called in August 1983, and a new chief and council were elected by twenty-six out of the thirty-five eligible voters. People who continue to claim Poospatuck identity, but have not been recognized by the court, must now bring their case before the tribal council.

The issues at stake in this complex legal tangle reflect the ethnic ambiguity of the Poospatuck. The American legal system as well as the Poospatuck themselves find it difficult to determine who is a Poospatuck. While this conflict involves very real concerns about land, power, and money, these concerns are couched in terms of ethnicity, and it is to that problem which we now turn.

WHO IS A POOSPATUCK?

Poospatuck ethnic ambiguity is reflected on multiple levels: internally among themselves, externally among their neighbors, legally, and theoretically in the social science literature. Internal strife has led to protracted court battles. Each of the three factions has accused the other two of not being descended from true Poospatuck stock, being invited at a relatively late date to live on Poospatuck land, and being Black, not Indian.

The Poospatuck's neighbors perceive them as a pocket of Black population in white suburbia. Poospatuck children are offered educational programs which discuss Afro-American heritage. A smaller percentage of Poospatuck, especially those living off of the reservation, are perceived of as White through phenotypic characteristics and only by using outward symbols, such as hair style and clothing, claim their Indian heritage. The legal system, disregarding phenotypic characteristics, relies on documentary evidence to prove "Indianness," ignoring the difficulty of such a task for a group of people whose documentary records are incomplete and whose ethnic descriptions reflect ambiguity even in the ethnohistorical record.

Finally, the social science literature does not define them as a tri-racial isolate because they have maintained a continued identification as a Native American group. Yet, they are not recognized as a distinct Native American group because of their blurred lines of ancestry. This theoretical ambiguity is reproduced and replicated in Poospatuck lives.

In sum, the Poospatuck find themselves forced to identify their ethnic origins clearly with few tools to assist them. Etically, they are perceived usually as Black, less commonly as White, and rarely as Native Americans; emically, they perceive of themselves as Native Americans. The legal system attempts to support this position but ironically through etically applied criteria. Individual Poospatuck struggle to identify themselves as Native Americans in a bi-racial society, which defines group membership as either Black or White. While the concept of race has very real limitations in explaining the institutions and structures of social groups, it is a concept adhered to by the popular mind; a view the Poospatuck, in their fight to prove their preeminent right to reservation land, succumb to among themselves when discussing the "others."

As individuals and as group members, the Poospatuck find themselves forced to conform to a bi-racial model although they perceive of themselves as a tri-racial group, emphasizing one aspect of their heritage. The resulting tension not only affects individual Poospatuck lives, but also creates schisms among the Poospatuck themselves. While the concept of ethnicity may serve to explain how the Poospatuck seek to maintain and accentuate their Native American identity, through the manipulation of symbols and adherence to particular values, it is the concept of race and its perpetuation in the minds of Poospatuck and non-Poospatuck alike which explains the ambiguity and conflicts existing in contemporary Poospatuck lives.

ACKNOWLEDGMENTS

Funds for the ethnohistorical and ethnographic research on this project were provided by the National Park Service, Eastern National Park and Monument Association. Earlier versions of this paper were presented at the Northeastern Anthropology Association Meetings in March 1983 at Syracuse University and at the Conference of Native American Studies in May 1983 at the University of Oklahoma, Stillwater. The section entitled "From Unkechaug to Poospatuck" is taken from a larger manuscript of the same name prepared for the National Park Service, Eastern National Park and Monument Association. I would like to thank Dr. Frank W. Porter III for his very constructive editorial comments and suggestions. Dr. Steven Kesselman, National Park Service historian, was very instrumental in the completion of this project both with his continual support and with his generous sharing of the Floyd family papers. My greatest debt is, of course, to the individual Poospatuck who shared with me their time, memories, and lives.

REFERENCES

Anonymous.
        1877   "Queries." *The Magazine of American History,* with notes and queries 1(1):257.
Beale, Calvin L.
        1957   "American Triracial Isolates." *Eugenics Quarterly* 4(4):187-96.
Beauchamp, William.
        1907   *Aboriginal Place Names of New York.* New York State Museum Bulletin, 108, New York State Education Department.
Berry, Brewton.
        1963   *Almost White.* New York: Macmillan.
Blu, Karen I.
        1980   *The Lumbee Problem: The Making of an American Indian People.* New York: Cambridge University Press.
Bolton, R. P.
        1975   *New York City in Indian Possession.* Museum of the American Indian, Heye Foundation. Indian notes and monographs, 2(7), 2d. ed.
BTR (Brookhaven Town Records).
        1880   Brookhaven Town Records, Book B, 1679-1756. Patchogue, New York.
Cahill, Eugene E.
        1965   "Occupational Mobility in a Tri-Racial Isolate." *Dissertation Abstracts International* 26(4):4880-81.
Cohen, Ronald.
        1978   "Ethnicity: Problems and Focus in Anthropology." *Annual Review of Anthropology* 7:379-403.
Dana, Katherin Floyd.
        1889   *Our Phil and Other Stories.* New York: Houghton, Mifflin and Company.
Despres, Leo A., ed.
        1975   *Ethnicity and Resource Competition in Plural Societies.* The Hague: Mouton Publishers.

Floyd Papers.
> n.d.   Manuscript documents of the Floyd family, eighteenth to twentieth century. Mastic, New York: William Floyd Estate, National Park Service.

Furman, Gabriel.
> 1874   *Antiquities of Long Island.* edited by Frank Moore. Reprinted 1968. Port Washington, N.Y.: Ira J. Friedman.

Gist, Noel P., and Anthony G. Dworkin.
> 1976   "Introduction." *The Blending of Races: Marginality and Identity in World Perspective,* pp. 1-23. New York: John Wiley and Sons.

Gonzalez, Ellice B.
> 1979   *A Cultural Resources Inventory of Suffolk County, New York.* Stony Brook, N.Y.: Suffolk County Archaeological Association.

Greissman, B. Eugene.
> 1972   "The American Isolates." *American Anthropologist* 74(1):693-94.

Hallock, John.
> 1976   "John Hallock's Diary, 1876." *Long Island Forum* 39(10):232.

Hicks, George L., and David I. Kertzer.
> 1972   "Making a Middle Way: Problems of Monhegan Identity." *Southwestern Journal of Anthropology* 28(1):1-24.

Hodge, Frederick Webb, ed.
> 1912   *Handbook of American Indians North of Mexico,* part II. Smithsonian Institution Bureau of American Ethnology, Bulletin 30. Reprinted 1968. St. Claire Shores, Mich.: Scholarly Press.

Horton, Azariah.
> 1741   "Abstracts of the Journal of Mr. Azariah Horton, Missionary to the Indians on Long Island in the Employ of The Society of Scotland for Propagation of Christian Knowledge." *The Christian Monthly History.* Edinburgh, Scotland.

Jefferson, Thomas.
> 1791   "Vocabulary of Unquachog or Puspatuck." Manuscript, American Philosophical Society Library, Philadelphia.

136   Strategies for Survival

New York Herald.
        1902   "Lost Glory of Long Island Indian." February 16, 1902.
        1907   "Indian Tribe Has Thirty-fifth Feast." June 10, 1907.
New York Herald Tribune.
        1935   "Indians Face Eviction Threat on Long Island." October 5, 1935.
New York Times.
        1935   "State Denies Aid to Poospatuck School; Negroes cause it to lose its Indian Status." May 4, 1935.
O'Callaghan, E. B., ed.
        1866   *Calendar of Historical Manuscripts in the Office of the Secretary of State, Albany, New York.* Reprinted 1968, Gregg Press, Inc.
Overton, Jacqueline.
        1975   Indian Life on Long Island. Port Washington: Kennikat Press.
Pelletreau, William S.
        1903   *A History of Long Island,* vol. II. New York: Lewis Publishing Company.
Pennypacker, Morton.
        n.d.   "Poospatuck Indians Fought and Bled in Freedom's Cause." Manuscript collection, East Hampton Library, Long Island Collection.
Pollitzer, William S.
        1972   "The Physical Anthropology and Genetics of Marginal People of the Southeastern United States." *American Anthropologist* 74:719-34.
Porter, Frank W.
        1980   "Behind the Frontier: Indian Survivals in Maryland." *Maryland Historical Magazine* 75(1):42-54.
Posey, Darrell A.
        1979   "Origin, Development and Maintenance of a Louisiana Mixed-Blood Community: The Ethnohistory of the Freejacks of the First Ward Settlement." *Ethnohistory* 26(2):177-92.
Price, Edward T.
        1950   "Mixed Blood Populations of Eastern United States as to Origins, Localizations and Persistence." Ph.D. diss., University of California.
        1953   "A Geographical Analysis of White-Negro-Indian Racial Mixtures in Eastern United States." *Annals of the Association of American Geographers* 43:138-56.

Prime, Edward T.
1845   *A History of Long Island from its First Settlement by Europeans to the Year 1845, with Special Reference to its Ecclesiastical Concerns.* New York: Robert Carter.
Royce, Anya Peterson.
1982   *Ethnic Identity: Strategies of Diversity.* Bloomington: Indiana University Press.
Salamone, Frank A., and Charles H. Swanson.
1979   "Identity and Ethnicity: Ethnic Groups and Interactions in a Multi-ethnic Society." *Ethnic Groups* 2:167-83.
Smith, Tangier.
n.d.   Account book. Manuscript (1699-170?), Bellport Historical Society, Bellport, New York.
Stanton, Max E.
1971   "A Remnant Indian Community: The Houma of Southern Louisiana." In *The Not So Solid South: Anthropological Studies in a Regional Subculture,* pp. 82-92. Southern Anthropological Society Proceedings, 4.
Suffolk County Court.
1936   *William Sheperd Dana vs. Luther Maynes, Frances Maynes, Edward Gales, Elaine Gales.*
Tooker, William W.
1911   *Indian Place Names.* Reprinted 1975. Port Washington, N.Y.: Ira J. Friedman, Inc.
Turner, Sarah Floyd.
n.d.   Sunny memories of Mastic. Manuscript, William Floyd House, Mastic, New York.
United States Census.
1860   Eighth census of the United States; National Archives.
1880   Tenth census of the United States; National Archives.
Van den Berghe, Pierre L.
1976   "Ethnic Pluralism in Industrial Societies: A Special Case." *Ethnicity* 3:242-55.

5
THE NANTICOKE INDIANS IN
A HOSTILE WORLD
Frank W. Porter III

INTRODUCTION

The survival of Indian culture east of the Appalachian Mountains is notable for its rarity. In view of the extensive toll of the aboriginal population caused by disease, massacres, expulsion, and discrimination, the survival of any tribal unit in this grisly context is a remarkable achievement (Crosby 1972). These Indian survivals especially intrigue geographers who visualize them as small spatial islands amidst an alien White culture (Price 1953). Morton H. Fried (1952) suggests that these residual groups survived because of a combination of land tenure, geography, and ecology. The key to their survival has been indeed the adoption of White land tenure systems and the protection of marginal environments, but the strategies for survival—as is illustrated by the specific case of the Nanticokes of Maryland and Delaware—are far more complex than has been recognized. Their travail of three centuries is a heroic epic

This chapter is a revised version of "Strategies for Survival: The Nanticoke Indians in a Hostile World" which appeared in *Ethnohistory* 26 (Winter 1979):325-345. I would like to thank the American Society for Ethnohistory for permission to use this material.

of purposeful action, conscious choice, and willful resistance to tribal destruction.

After their initial contact with western civilization, the Nanticoke Indians attempted to accommodate the continued presence of an intruding culture in several fashions. This chapter attempts to discern and analyze the strategies whereby the Nanticokes were able to survive and maintain their Indian identity. Two of the major contentions are (1) the Nanticokes purposely selected a marginal environment as their habitat to prevent the continued encroachment of their land by Whites and to reduce the contact between the two cultures and (2) perceived as mixed-bloods or mulattoes, the Nanticokes experienced the same cultural and spatial segregation and treatment accorded the Negroes, which resulted in the formation of a distinct community.

IDENTIFICATION OF NANTICOKE

The identification of the Nanticokes has been somewhat obscured by the generic application of the term to all tribes residing on the Eastern Shore of Maryland and by their presumed affiliation with the Delaware Indians. John Heckewelder, in his *History, Manners, and Customs of the Indian Tribes,* stated that the Nanticokes referred to themselves as Nentego, a variant of the Delaware Unechtgo, meaning Tidewater people. C. A. Weslager has clarified this confusion by demonstrating that the Unalachtigo were not the Nanticoke known to modern Delawares as the Winetok. Furthermore, the colonial authorities of Maryland readily distinguished as separate entities the Nanticokes, Choptanks, Assateagues, and other tribes (Weslager 1942, 1944, 1975). The Nanticoke proper occupied the territory bounding the drainage system of the Nanticoke River.

SEASONAL SUBSISTENCE STRATEGIES
AND SETTLEMENT

In their adaptation to the natural environment of the Eastern Shore, the Nanticokes had devised a pattern of human settlement dependent on seasonal migration to food resources. The subsistence strategy of the Nanticokes and other Algonkian tribes reflected an economic adjustment to differing ecological niches. Ronald A. Thomas and Daniel R. Griffith, in analyzing the Indians' environmental adaptation to Delaware's coastal plain, identify six microenvironments: (1) poorly drained woodlands, (2) transitional woodlands, (3) well-drained woodlands, (4) tidal marsh and estuarine, (5) permanent fresh water, and (6) saltwater bays and ocean (Thomas et al. 1975; Griffith 1976). After the associated flora and fauna used as a foodstuff and their seasonal fluctuations were determined, Griffith, employing archaeological data, postulated four possible types of settlement required to exploit these ecological niches: (1) seasonal camps, (2) permanent camps, (3) semipermanent camps, and (4) transient camps. Early visitors to the environs of the Chesapeake Bay region noted this specific pattern of seasonal movement to food resources. Sir Richard Greeneville, who visited Virginia from 1585 to 1586, observed that "the Savages disband into small groups and disperse to different places to live upon shell fish. Other places afford fishing and hunting while their fields are being prepared for the planting of corn" (Greeneville 1965). Captain John Smith (Arber 1910) vividly described this seasonal subsistence strategy.

In March and April they live much upon their fishing, wearers; and feed on fish, Turkies and squirrels. In May and June they plant their fieldes; and live most of Acornes, walnuts, and fish. But to mend their diet, some disperse themselves in small companies, and live upon fish, beasts, crabs, oysters, land Torteyses, strawberries, mulberries, and such like. In June, July, and August, they feed upon the roots of Tocknough, berries, fish and green wheat.

The continued success of the Naticokes in their subsistence efforts depended entirely upon freedom of mobility and access to these microenvironments.

LAND ENCROACHMENT

A major problem which confronted the Nanticokes after their contact with Europeans was encroachment of their land. The prolific slaughter of fur-bearing animals and the constant clearing of woodland for agriculture created a shortage of plant and animal food sources so vital to the seasonal subsistence strategy of the Nanticokes. As a result, they became increasingly more dependent on European trade goods: food, clothing, utensils, and weapons. The colonial authorities of Maryland sought at an early date to protect the Indians by cautioning their inhabitants to respect the Indians' "Privileges" of hunting, fishing, and crabbing. Such admonitions went unheeded, and the early disturbance of the subsistence base of the Nanticokes can be evidenced by the numerous complaints registered against their killing and stealing domestic hogs and cattle. In 1666 an Indian named Mattagund appealed to Maryland officials to "Let us have no Quarrels for killing Hogs no more than for the Cows Eating the Indian corn. Your hogs & Cattle injure Us You come too near Us to live & Drive Us from place to place. We can fly no farther let us know where to live & how to be secured for the future from the Hogs & Cattle" (*Archives of Maryland* 1883, 2:15). A half-century later similar complaints were still reaching the Maryland Assembly.

ESTABLISHMENT OF RESERVATIONS

Exasperated by the loss of their land and as a means of accommodating the permanent presence of the White settlers, the Choptank, and later the Nanticoke Indians, requested the Maryland authorities to provide them with tracts of land legally established by a grant from Lord Baltimore, the Proprietor of Maryland. The Maryland Assembly responded with the establishment of the Choptank, Chicony, and Broad Creek reservations (see fig. 5). The provision of reservations, while serving to ease the difficulties arising from land encroachment, further undermined the seasonal subsistence strategy of the Nanticokes. Two critical problems emanated from permanent residence on the reservations: the disruption of the ecosystems of the Nanticokes' habitat and the misunderstanding associated with the clause, "so long as they shall occupy and live upon the same." In 1711, less than a decade after removing to the Chicony Reservation, the Nanticokes bitterly complained that their lands were worn out and insufficient for their use. They requested additional land, which was granted to them with the erection of Broad Creek Reservation. An equally grave

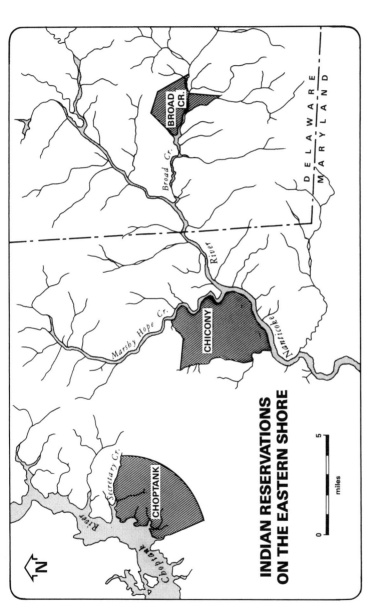

INDIAN RESERVATIONS
ON THE EASTERN SHORE

FIGURE 5

crisis, which continued to plague the Nanticokes, was the "repeated and excessive trespass" on their reservation land by the White settlers. Once again, the Maryland Assembly sought to stave off these offenses by assuring the Nanticokes of their "free and uninterrupted possession of the tract lying between the North Fork of the Nanticoke River and Chicucone Creek . . . so long as they or any them should think fit to use and not totally desert and quit the same." As a final precaution, the Nanticokes were prevented from the right to sell or lease their land (*Laws of Maryland* 1765; Kilty 1808; Hutchinson 1961).

Despite these protective measures, the abuse and disregard of the Nanticokes' right to occupy the reservations continued. In some instances, diverse "Trespassers and Wasters" destroyed Indian land "by falling, mauling, and carrying away the Timber off from such Land, and refus[ing] to pay and satisfy the said Indians for the same" (*Laws of Maryland* 1765). In complete violation of the laws passed by the Maryland Assembly, some people rented and settled on Indian land, and then failed to pay the agreed-upon rent. While certain individuals clandestinely purchased the land from the Indians and built farmsteads, others simply were squatters on the land and assumed ownership by right of occupancy. In 1759 a delegation of the remnants of several tribes assigned to reservations on the Eastern Shore informed Governor Horatio Sharpe of Maryland that they were severely reduced in number, suffering from a shortage of food, and being violently forced from their land. The Indians appealed to Sharpe to consider their "Pitiful Scituation and Condition" (*Archives of Maryland* 1883, 31:356). "There is but a Spot laid out for us not enough for Bread for us Indians," they complained, "and hard is our Condition if we cannot have the freedom and Privilege which we were allowed of in Antient Times." Although they tried to reside within the confines of the reservations, the Indians were thwarted in their efforts by land-hungry Whites. While venturing forth into the woods to hunt and build cabins for shelter, the Indians recounted, "some of the White People when we go out of them will set them on fire and burn them down to the ground and leave us Destitute of any Cover to Shelter us from the weather" (*Archives of Maryland* 1883, 31:356). The argument repeatedly advanced by the Europeans to justify their actions was that the Indian land appeared to be deserted and abandoned. The terms of the reservation grants stipulated that the land reverted to Maryland as soon as the Indians ceased to occupy it. In actuality, the Nanticokes had not abandoned the land but were merely following their traditional subsistence strategy of seasonal migration to food resources.

MIGRATION

Beginning in the early 1740s, several groups of Nanticokes abandoned their homes on the Eastern Shore and emigrated to Pennsylvania. An attempt by the French to unite the various tribes in Maryland and Pennsylvania in an uprising against the English settlers prompted the Nanticokes to leave the Eastern Shore. In 1742, after a century of abuse, hostility, and misunderstanding, the Nanticokes agreed to participate in this revolt. The Indians of the Eastern Shore congregated in a swamp called Winnasoccum along the Pocomoke River to join in a war dance. Fortunately for the Maryland settlers, a Choptank Indian informed the authorities of the pending uprising, and the plot came to an abrupt end. The Maryland Assembly severely reprimanded the Nanticokes for their part in the conspiracy and warned them that "We have it in our Power to take all your Lands from you, and use you as your ill Designs against Us have deserved. . . , but We are rather desirous to use you kindly like Brethren in hopes that it will beget the same kindness in You to Us." Unmoved by this empty overture of friendship, a delegation of Nanticoke Indians appeared in 1744 before the Maryland authorities and requested permission to leave the province and live among the Six Nations (*Archives of Maryland* 1883, 28:257-70, 338-39; Weslager 1948). By 1748 a majority of the Nanticokes had removed to the Juniata River and Wyoming Valley in Pennsylvania; another group had established a village at Chenango near present-day Binghamton, New York (fig. 6). Soon after constructing a village at Juniata, delegates from the Nanticokes and several other tribes complained to the governor and the Council of Pennsylvania that Whites "were Settling & design'd to Settle the Lands on the Branches of Juniata." The delegates insisted on their removal because this was the hunting ground of

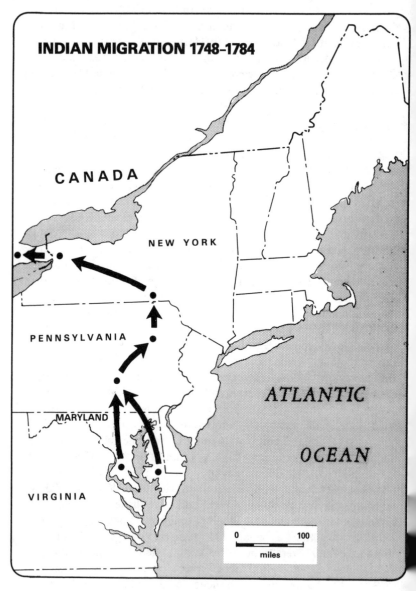

FIGURE 6

the Nanticokes and other Indians living along the Juniata. Within a short time the Nanticokes moved to Wyoming Valley, only to be forced out in 1755 with the outbreak of hostilities during the French and Indian War. By 1756 they temporarily resided at Oswego, Chugnut, and Chenango in New York. From New York the Nanticoke tribe settled in Canada and came completely under the dominance of the Six Nations, becoming virtually denationalized by the Iroquois (Johnston 1964:xi, 52, 203n, 281, 307; Speck 1927). Nanticoke efforts to accommodate the White settlers in Maryland had proven to be unsuccessful (Porter 1978).

SIGNIFICANCE OF FAMILY HUNTING TERRITORY SYSTEM

Although a majority of the Nanticokes had emigrated from the Eastern Shore, a small remnant group—estimated at thirty in number—remained behind and adopted specific strategies in order to survive and maintain their Indian identity in the presence of a numerically superior Euro-American culture. A significant key to understanding the successful survival and persistence of the remnant Nanticokes that chose to remain on the Eastern Shore lies in an analysis of the family hunting territory system. Frank G. Speck (1915) defined the family hunting group as a "kinship group composed of folks united by blood or marriage, having the right to hunt, trap, and fish in a certain inherited district bounded by some rivers, lakes, or other natural landmarks." The family hunting territory was often known by certain local names identified with the family itself. Equally significant, these territories had not only ties of kinship, but a community of land and interest. The long-established practice of small family hunting groups dispersing in the woods promoted "family isolation and a certain degree of permanency of residence in a particular territory" (Speck and Eiseley 1939).

Speck and Eiseley further argued that, for the Algonkian hunting territory system to function, there should be a highly localized and constant fauna to be exploited. Such a situation would limit the number of suitable sites available. Although much of Speck's data was derived from northeastern Algonkian tribes living in the

Eastern Sub-Arctic region, he contended, based on the assumption that the ethnically related Algonkian inhabiting southward into Virginia were organized similarly, that all of the Atlantic Coast tribes maintained the same institution (Speck and Eiseley 1939). William MacLeod (1922), utilizing primary sources in the form of land deeds, demonstrated "the positive existence of the hereditary Family Hunting Territory as the basis of social organization among the tribes of the Delaware River Valley." Leon de Valinger (1940) hinted of the presence of the family hunting territory in Delaware when he argued that the Indians exercised authority within the bounds of their kingdoms. C. A. Weslager, who was the editor of the *Bulletin of the Archaeological Society of Delaware* in which de Valinger's article appeared, suggested that these kingdoms were in fact family hunting territories. Weslager, reinterpreting de Valinger's data, extended the existence of the family hunting territory system southward into Kent and Sussex Counties (de Valinger 1941).

It is my contention that the disruption of the ecosystem of the habitat of the Nanticokes along the Nanticoke River jeopardized the food resource base of a number of the family units, and made impossible the continuation of their traditional subsistence strategy. While some Nanticokes could perhaps depend upon the generalized reciprocity of those families still able to subsist within their habitat, such a condition would have soon depleted the flora and fauna. In all probability, it was those family units whose hunting territory was disturbed that initially chose to migrate to Pennsylvania. That several individual Nanticoke families remained on the Eastern Shore in 1749 can be demonstrated. Representatives of the Six Nations of Iroquois, speaking on behalf of their "Couzins," the Nanticokes, informed Pennsylvania authorities that Maryland was preventing further removal of the remaining Nanticokes: "You know that on some differences between the People of Maryland & them we went for them & placed them at the Mouth of Juniata, where they now live; they came to Us while on our Journey & told us that there were three Settlements of their Tribe left in Maryland" (*Minutes of the Provincial Council of Pennsylvania,* 1851, vol. 5: 401-2). In 1761 spokesmen of the Nanticokes and Conoy again requested permission to remove some of their brethren still remaining in the province of Maryland (Stevens and Kent 1943:158, 161). A similar complaint was voiced in 1776 (Roger 1948:5).

DISPERSAL OF FAMILY UNITS

Although specific observations of the behavior of the Nanticokes during this critical period are lacking, several early references to Indians in Sussex County, Delaware and descriptions of comparable goups in Maryland and Virginia strongly suggest that these small family units did disperse to isolated and remote sites within or near their traditional habitats. The Reverend George Ross, who had been enjoined by the Methodist Church to preach to the Indians, complained bitterly of his task because "the Indians have their abodes a great way back in the Woods, so that we seldom see or converse with one another, unless it be when leaving their Winter Quarters they straggle up and down among the English plantations and villages to meet with a Chapman for their Burthen of Skins, or with a meal of Victuals" (Perry 1878: 21-22). In 1715, John Fontaine, while traveling from Williamsburg to the German colony on the Rappahannock, encountered a remnant of the once powerful Virginia Indians.

We see by the side of the road an Indian cabin built with posts put into the ground, the one by the other as close as they could stand, and about seven feet high, all of an equal length. It was built four-square, and a sort of roof upon it, covered with the bark of trees. They say it keeps out the rain very well. The Indian women were all naked, only a girdle they had tied around the waist, and about a yard of blanketing put between their legs, and fastened one end under the forepart of the girdle, and the other behind. Their beds were mats made of bulrushes, upon which they lie, and have one blanket to cover them. All the household goods was a pot. (Maury 1853:264)

The Reverend David Humphreys observed that the number of Indians in Sussex County "did not exceed 120, who had a small Settlement on the utmost Border of the Parish, where it adjoins to Maryland; they were extremely barbarous and obstinately ignorant'' (Humphreys 1730: 159-68). Lewis Evans, who wrote a brief account of Pennsylvania in 1753, remarked: "The Remnants of some Nations in Subjection to the six Nations & which they have not quite extirpated wander here & There for the Sake of making ordinary wicker Baskets & Basons, within a few miles of the Town, but have no Land of Their own or fixt habitations; What they get for their Work, they spend in Rum & their food They beg" (Evans 1753). In 1759, Andrew Burnaby observed a remnant group of Pamunkey Indians. His description illustrates the significant degree of acculturation experienced by these isolated family units.

A little below this place stands the Pamunkey Indian town; where at present are the few remains of that large tribe; the rest having dwindled away through intemperance and disease. They live in little wigwams or cabins upon the river; and have a very fine tract of land about 2,000 acres, which they are restrained from alienating by act of assembly. Their employment is chiefly hunting and fishing, for the neighboring gentry. They commonly dress like the Virginians, and I have sometimes mistaken them for the lower sort of that people. (Burnaby 1775:40-41)

In Bucks County, Pennsylvania, a small number of Delaware Indians left in 1775. Two of them, Indian Billey and his squaw Polly, were too old to go with them, and, as they had no children to care for them, they were left behind. William Worthing had on his property near Mill Creek below Wycombe an old house in which he furnished one room and made it comfortable for them to live in. They supported themselves in part by making baskets which they sold (Woodman 1917: 673-74). George H. Loskiel, in his *History of the Mission of the United Brethren Among the Indians in North America,* stated that these "detached Indian families living among the white people on the banks of rivers, and on that account called River-Indians, are generally a loose set of people, like our gypsies. They make baskets, brooms, wooden spoons, dishes, &c. and sell them to the white people for victuals and clothes." In 1797, an anonymous author of a "Description of the Cypress Swamps in Delaware and Maryland States," noted the vestiges of several Indian towns, and interviewed an old Indian who called himself Will Andrew. Andrew was a survivor of an unidentified tribe of Eastern Shore Indians.

I once owned all this land about here. Come, said he, I will shew you where my father lived: I walked with him about two hundred paces to an eminence about three hundred yards from a creek, where I saw a large quantity of shells. Here said he, stamping with his foot, is the very spot where my father lived. (Anonymous 1948-49:136-37).

Significantly, these observations indicate not only that small, dispersed groups of Indians had remained on the Eastern Shore, but also that they had adopted many of the outward accoutrements of the White society. Furthermore, they were quite accustomed to fishing, trapping, and hunting for their White neighbors, as well as manufacturing various domestic utensils to be sold. These changes in material culture help to explain the paucity of observations with regard to Indians on the Eastern Shore during the nineteenth century.

It would not have been a severe hardship for some Nanticokes to have elected to remain in their traditional habitat and maintain their family units. Once the natural resources which they depended upon became scarce, however, their only alternatives were either to emigrate to Pennsylvania and New York to join their relatives who had left earlier or to enter White society as landowners and farmers. In all likelihood, emigration no longer loomed as an attractive or viable solution to the intrusion of White society into Indian culture. The earlier difficulties confronting the Nanticokes as they moved from village to village throughout Pennsylvania, New York, and into Canada were known to their relatives who had remained in Maryland and Delaware. Migration had failed, and there was no guarantee of security on reservations.

MARGINAL ENVIRONMENT

Initially, these remnant Indians chose to reside in places of solitude, remoteness, and isolation—usually swamps, islands, or out-of-the-way necks of land. William B. Marye (1944:456) has demonstrated that such locations were quite similar to the sites chosen for quiackeson houses, structures which contained the bones of the dead Nanticokes. William H. Gilbert (1946, 1949), in his study of surviving Indian groups in the eastern United States, argues that these small local groups appeared to develop in areas with rather forboding environmental circumstances. After years of exposure to the harsh inroads of Euro-American culture, these remnant Indian groups would have inhabited sities that would afford them minimal contact with the outside world. These settlement sites would have been perceived by contemporary European standards as a marginal environment (unfit for large-scale commercial agriculture and lacking satisfactory transportation links with tidewater ports), but they offered the necessary resources to satisfy the basic needs of the Nanticokes. Descriptions of comparable locales tend to support their depiction as marginal environments. "Till the year seventeen hundred and fifty-nine," wrote the anonymous author of a "Description of the Cypress Swamps in Delaware and Maryland States," "it lay in a measure *unlocated* and was thought to be of little value" (Anonymous 1948-1949:135). Lewis Evans described the shores of Delaware Bay as "low, flat Marshes, void of Trees & lie mostly unimproved." Evans went on to describe much of the Eastern Shore as undesirable for habitation. Although he clearly exaggerated the question of actual occupation of the land, Evans pointed out several of the problems which plagued those families who attempted to establish residences on the Eastern Shore.

All the creeks on Delaware, the Verges of the Sounds, which extend along the Sea-coast, and some Creeks in Virginia, and towards the Head of Chesopeak on the West Side are bordered with Salt Marshes, some a Mile or two wide. The first Settlers of America, for the Sake of the Grass for the Winter Support of their Cattle, fixing their Habitations along these Places, were infested with Muskitoes and Intermitting Fevers, gave the Foundation for supposing America unhealthy . . . [and] were it not for the Scarcity of Fresh Water in some Parts of the Eastern Shore, would be as pleasant a Country as Imagination could well represent. (Evans 1753:161-62)

Weslager argues that the geographic position and physical environment of Kent and Sussex Counties were not attractive to the Swedes who made their first permanent settlement at Wilmington in 1638, nor to the Dutch who later obtained control of the Delaware Valley because the character of the terrain was low, flat, and in many places very marshy; fur-bearing animals were not numerous and beavers were rare; and the land served no strategic value (Weslager 1941:17). Those White settlers who did occupy the land exhibited a widely dispersed settlement pattern. John Oldmixon stated that "Sussex is not full of Townships, but like Kent, is inhabited by Planters, scattered up and down, as they thought best for their Convenience. The Inhabitants here live scattering generally at ½ a Mile or Miles distance from one another except in Lewes where 58 Families are settled together" (Hancock 1962).

CHANGE IN LAND TENURE

Between 1800 and 1830 the Nanticokes underwent a period of gradual change in land tenure. Unlike those western tribes who were confronted with the rapid changes stemming from the allotment system, the Nanticokes, by attempting to maintain their family units in their traditional habitats, were permitted as individuals to make free choices and slow adjustments as they entered American society. In making this transition, the Nanticokes initially were squatters who exercised their traditional means of exploiting the land for foodstuffs. The ability of the Nanticokes to subsist successfully as squatters diminished, however, as the number of White settlers increased and more land was cleared for agricultural use.

One of the first steps on the part of the Nanticokes in their move toward participating in the European form of land tenure was to become tenants on the land. In such a situation, William MacLeod contends, these remnant Indian groups scattered throughout the Eastern seaboard, ultimately becoming mixed-blood populations. "Many of them have absorbed considerable negro blood," he argued, because "Freed negroes found a haven of rest in these little islands, intermarried, and thus acquired land. Having been trained to labour, and in European agricultural methods, these ex-slaves and their mixed descendants made for intemperance and industry on the Indian reservations" (MacLeod 1928:391-92). William Byrd of Virginia, describing a mulatto family, depicted a similar but harsher situation. "We found time in the Evening to walk near half a Mile into the Woods," he stated, "There we came upon a Family of Mulattoes, that call'd themselves free, tho' by the Shyness of the Master of the House, who took care to keep least in Sight, their Freedom seemed a little Doubtful." Their "righteous Neighbors" failed to disclose their presence because they settled such fugitives on "some out-of-the-way corner of their Land, to raise Stocks for a mean and inconsiderable Share." Aware of their precarious situation, the mulattoes were compelled to submit to any terms (Bassett 1901:47). Unfortunately too many scholars have accepted without question that the Nanticokes became a tri-racial isolate (a presumed admixture of Indian-White-Negro blood), and have advanced cursory overviews to explain the manner in which they became a functioning segment of White society. Whether or not the Nanticokes are a tri-racial isolate is not the most important question to raise; instead, the focus should be on the means by which they formed a coherent community, thus preserving their identity.

ACQUISITION OF PRIVATE PROPERTY

One institution of White society which the Nanticokes could use to establish and preserve themselves as a community was private property obtained through the acquisition of legal title to land. This property afforded the Nanticokes a base upon which the community would later develop. In order to reconstruct the evolving system of land tenure which the survivors of the Nanticoke tribe participated in, the researcher is totally dependent on the data contained in the early land records, wills, inventories of estates, and real and personal tax lists. Several factors account for the paucity of evidence concerning the land tenure of the Nanticokes. Needless to say, these sources are incomplete; moreover, during the nineteenth century, no precise criteria existed for determining the racial status of the Nanticokes. The records fail to indicate a designation for Indian. Instead, local tax assessors, census takers, and other public officials classified the Nanticokes as being either mulattoes or "colored" people. In addition, many land transactions were oral agreements that were never recorded, and, presumably, most of the Nanticokes at this date were illiterate, which explains the absence of private papers. Fortunately, in the specific case of the Nanticokes, two men, Levin Sockum and Isaac Harman, were significant in the establishment of a new land-base. The records of the acquisition of land by these men is relatively complete, but more important is the fact that Harman and Sockum were the first Nanticokes to become landowners and, through their estates, they endowed parcels of land to their heirs, thus increasing through time the number of landholders. In addition to the land records, the wills and inventories provide some insight as to the gradual accumulation of the material wealth of these families.

ISAAC HARMAN AND LEVIN SOCKUM

Significantly, Isaac Harman and Levin Sockum were related by marriage. Harman's wife, Sarah, was the daughter of Levin and Eunice Sockum. Isaac and Sarah had eight children who reached adulthood; they are the descendants who inherited the Harman estate accumulated by their parents during the nineteenth century. While interviewing members of the Harman family, they informed me that, as a young man, Isaac earned his initial capital by going to sea in a sailing vessel. Isaac's brother, Charles Ephraim, was a boatman in Philadelphia and may have been instrumental in this decision. Isaac purchased his first land, a seventy-acre tract, for $250 in 1848. "He seemed to have an obsession for owning property," stated one member of the community, "it is told that he would drive his buggy to Georgetown barefooted in order to record the purchase of another parcel of land" (Pinkett: n.d.). Harman rapidly accumulated land and increased the assessment value of his real and personal property (fig. 7). In comparing the Assessment Lists of 1861 and 1872, it is evident that Harman's personal property was increasing along with his real estate. The 1861 assessment indicates that in addition to holding 147 acres of land Harman possessed an "old" horse, one pair of oxen, one cow, and five shoats. In the 1872 assessment, Harman had increased his landholdings to 357 acres, and owned a "mansion," one pair of mules, one yoke of oxen, two cows, one yearling, nine sheep, one sow, and shoats.[1] By 1872 Harman had become one of the largest landowners in Indian River Hundred. His estate included most of the land bordering on the northeast side of Indian River from Rosedale Beach to Riverdale. The bounds of his estate approximate the spatial limits of the Nanticoke community today.

Levin Sockum followed a similar pattern in the acquisition of land. In 1834 he had been assessed $307 for his personal property. By 1854 Sockum's real and personal property assessment had increased to $1174, placing him among the wealthiest men in Indian

River Hundred. In addition to his real estate, Sockum owned and operated a general store at the head of Long Neck on the north shore of Indian River. The 1861 Assessment List credited Sockum as owning 244 acres of land, and possessing two horses, one blind horse, one pair of oxen, four cows, seven yearlings, two sows, and six shoats.[2] Sockum, like his son-in-law Harman, experienced a steady increase in his real and personal property (fig. 7). Sockum's material wealth surely would have continued to increase, but shortly after 1861—because of his involvement in two court cases which questioned his racial status—he migrated to Gloucester, New Jersey.

Beginning in the early 1830s, through the gradual purchase and accumulation of a significant amount of land and personal property, the Nanticokes began to develop a community at Indian River. According to Beers' *Atlas of the State of Delaware,* in 1867 only two Nanticokes were landowners in Indian River Hundred: Ephraim and Isaac Harman (fig. 8). However, the Assessment Lists indicate that a substantial number of Nanticoke families, many of whom were related to both Levin Sockum and Isaac Harman, were in fact tenants and were amassing an impressive amount of personal property, most of which pointed toward agricultural activity. In time these families either inherited property or purchased land. The majority of these families resided in and later owned property within the confines of the current Nanticoke community (fig. 9).

RACIAL DISCRIMINATION BASED ON SKIN COLOR AND PHYSIOGNOMY

Despite their material success, a prejudicial attitude emerged toward the Indian River community based on their skin color and physiognomy. This external pressure further strengthened the social bonds of the community. During the nineteenth century, and perhaps earlier, some of the Nanticokes intermarried with individuals outside of their tribe and community. As such, the Nanticokes were labeled "colored persons" and/or mixed-bloods and were accorded the same treatment as Negroes. Consequently, they were segregated culturally and spatially from White society. This physical, cultural, and spatial separation from the broader White society allowed the Nanticokes during the nineteenth century

REAL AND PERSONAL PROPERTY OF LEVIN SOCKUM

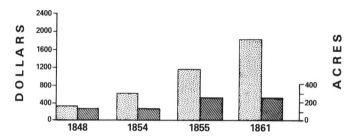

REAL AND PERSONAL PROPERTY OF ISAAC HARMAN

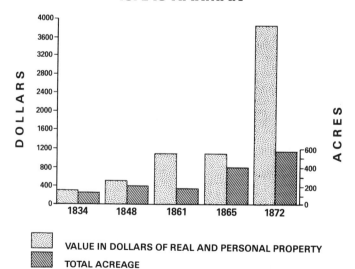

FIGURE 7

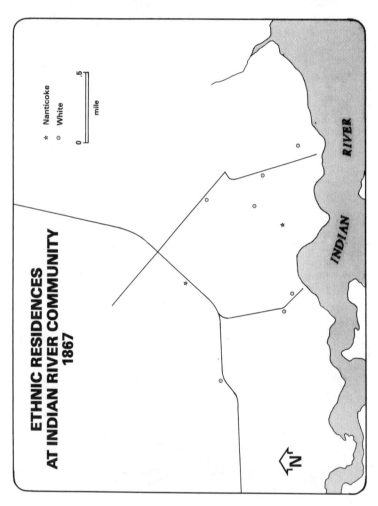

FIGURE 8

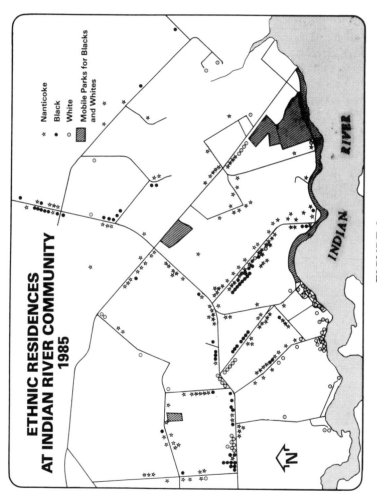

ETHNIC RESIDENCES
AT INDIAN RIVER COMMUNITY
1985

Nanticoke
Black
White
Mobile Parks for Blacks
and Whites

INDIAN RIVER

FIGURE 9

to acculturate gradually by selectively integrating specific new traits, material and non-material, into their changing aboriginal culture framework.

Harold R. Isaacs (1965) has poignantly stated: "Nothing marks a man's group identity more visibly or more permanently than the color of his skin and his physical characteristics." Although, in a period of relative social stability, attitudes toward race and physical traits are well-defined, during a time of flux and unrest these two factors become significantly more visible and assume a position of greater importance in individual perception and behavior between Whites and non-Whites. One critical issue involves the terms by which the two groups elect to reside within the same habitat.

SLAVE REVOLTS IN THE SOUTH

Prior to 1830 no overt signs of racial prejudice or hostility were evident specifically toward the remnant Indians in Delaware. In 1831, however, Nat Turner led a slave revolt in Virginia. Throughout the South, Whites feared that such incidents would lead to a violent confrontation with the non-White population. Many of the states invoked an unprecedented system of slave control by revamping the slave code, enacting repressive legislation to regulate the free Negro and slave population, and revitalizing the patrol.

In Delaware one particular event clearly depicts the phobia associated with the potential slave revolts. Shortly after the Southampton tragedy, most of the White population became extremely suspicious of the Blacks. "Rumor made herself exceedingly busy in spreading false alarms throughout the land, of plots and conspiracies, forming and in progress, and soon to break out against the White population," stated the editor of *The Delaware Register.* "While the public mind was in this feverish state of excitement, some mischievous persons, in cruel sport, laid a plan to bring it to its utmost height." A general election was scheduled for October 1831, the same day on which it had been previously reported the Blacks were to rise. A group of men assembled on the banks of the Nanticoke River, within sight of the town of Seaford. They divided into two parties. One contingent appeared to be firing on the others, some of whom fell, pretending to be shot. Others ran into Seaford and reported that the Negroes had landed, had killed several White men, and were preparing to march through the country for purposes of destruction. "Consternation for the moment seized upon all," exclaimed the editor. "The fearful ran and hid themselves in the woods, while the stout hearted flew to arms." A messenger was sent to Kent County who arrived at the nearest election ground just as they were tallying the votes. He shouted to the assembled crowd that fifteen hundred Negroes had landed on the Nanticoke River from Maryland, and were in full march up the country. This resulted in total confusion. The election was completely disrupted; and one of the clerks in his fright ran off with the ballet box, and was not found until the alarm had partially subsided the following day. Within hours it was discovered that all the reports were totally without foundation; yet, the people throughout Kent and Sussex counties acted exactly as if they had been accurate (Huffington 1838). When the legislature met the next January, a bill was introduced into the House of Representatives to disarm the free Negroes and mulattoes, to prevent their holding religious or other meetings unless under the direction of respectable White people, and to forbid non-resident free Negroes to preach or attempt to preach or to hold meetings for such purpose. Although the bill was not enacted, such uncontrolled fear resulted in stringent efforts to keep the Negroes "apart as a separate and distinct class of beings" (Huffington 1838:319).

Since a great deal of the racial prejudice directed at the Nanticokes stemmed from skin color, it is important to investigate this issue. In reviewing the contemporary literature—diaries, travel accounts, journals, and published histories—reference is continually made to the dark complexion of the Indians (Jordon 1968). Robert Beverley (1947:159), in his history of Virginia, states: "Their Colour, when they are grown up, is a Chestnut brown and tawny. Their Skin comes afterwards to harden and grow blacker." Loskiel (1794:12) described their skin as a "reddish color, nearly resembling copper, but in different shades. Some are of a brown yellow, not much differing from the mulattoes." Henry Ridgely of Delaware witnessed President Andrew Jackson's interview with Black Hawk and his Indian delegation. Ridgely expressed his disappointment because Black Hawk was "small, unimpressive except for a fine forehead, and reminded him of some elderly Negro (de Valinger and Shaw 1951:290). In 1840 Samuel J. Levick, a Quaker from Philadelphia, asked a chief of the Onondaga tribe, whose people were being forced to emigrate from New York, whether he preferred to come under the control of the British government or the U.S. government. The chief replied: "Americans treat Indians so bad. They hate Indians. White men think they got better color than Indians, so they want Indians away (Levick 1896:388).

TRIALS OF LEVIN SOCKUM AND ISAAC HARMAN

In Indian River Hundred, the remnant Nanticokes were considered by the Whites as a "class of colored people commonly called yellow men, and by many believed to be descendants of the Indians, which formerly inhabited this country. Others regard them as mulattoes and still others claim that they are of Moorish descent" (Scharf 1888:1270-71). Among the White population there clearly existed considerable confusion as to the origin and identity of the Nanticokes. One of the first episodes to draw attention to the status and identity of the Nanticoke community at Indian River materialized in 1855 when Levin Sockum, the successful landholder, was accused of violating a Delaware law which prohibited the sale or loan of firearms to a Negro or mulatto when he sold a quarter-pound of powder and shot to Isaac Harman. Because Sockum had admitted to selling the powder and shot to Harman, George P. Fisher, the prosecuting attorney, had to demonstrate that Harman was indeed a mulatto. It is significant to note that none of the court's witnesses were able to establish the ancestry of Harman. Fisher finally placed Lydia Clark, a blood relative of Harman, on the witness stand. Clark testified that before the American Revolution an Irish lady named Regua (a corruption of the name Ridgeway) purchased and later married a "very tall, shapely and muscular young fellow of dark ginger-bread color." The offspring of this union intermarried with the remnant of the Nanticoke tribe. This testimony established to the satisfaction of the court that Harman was a mulatto. Not only was Sockum found guilty and fined twenty dollars, he was brought into court on a second charge—possession of a gun. The court accepted testimony that Sockum was also a mulatto and fined him an additional twenty dollars (Fisher 1929). What seems incredible is that Fisher described Harman as a "young man, apparently about five and twenty years of age, of perfect Caucasian features, dark chestnut brown hair, rosy cheeks and hazel eyes." Furthermore, Fisher observed, "of all the men concerned in the trial he was the most perfect type of the pure Caucasian, and by odds the handsomest man in the court room, and yet he was alleged to be mulatto." It would appear, as Fisher himself later admitted, that "Sockum's case originated in the private spite of envious Caucasian neighbors" (Fisher 1929; Weslager 1943:31-37).

SEPARATE SOCIAL INSTITUTIONS

The verdicts rendered in the Harman and Sockum trials cemented the racial status and classification of the Nanticokes. In time, the White population came to regard the Indians in the same manner as the Negro in the Deep South, subjecting them to segregation in schooling, religious practices, residences, and social intercourse. Delaware history is replete with literature which focuses on the controversy over the origins of those individuals claiming Indian ancestry. At the state level, the presence of the Nanticoke has been reflected in the controversy over educational facilities for "colored" people (which included Negroes, mulattoes, Moors, and Indians) and Whites. Within the Indian River community, this resulted in the construction of separate school facilities for Negroes, Indians, and Whites. In 1875 the Legislature of Delaware enacted a law entitled "An Act to Tax Colored Persons for the Support of Their Schools." This legislation stipulated that an assessment of thirty cents on every one hundred dollars of property be levied on all Negroes for the erection and maintenance of separate schools for Negroes. Unwittingly, the legislators classified the Nanticokes as Negroes, thus legally requiring their children to attend school with Negroes. The Nanticoke resisted, organized, and hired a lawyer to exert pressure on local politicians to exempt them from this tax with the condition that they erect and maintain their own school. In 1881, the State legislature acquiesced and authorized them to construct and support two schools of their own: Harman School and Hollyville School. Johnson School was to be attended by Negroes. When Negroes began to attend the Harman School, despite assurances against such an event contained in the recent legislation, the Nanticoke withdrew their children. They erected at their own expense a one-room frame school, which became known as the Indian Mission School (Weslager 1943:112-27).

At the community level, this conflict between Indians and Negroes was also expressed in their division into separate churches. Prior to 1867 the Indians had attended their own church, but this building was destroyed by fire. A new church was built, and a white pastor was engaged. The congregation objected to this pastor and requested one of their own color. When a new minister was hired, part of the congregation withdrew, claiming that the man was a Negro. In 1888, the dissentors began holding services in private homes but soon constructed a new church. Today, this church is known as the Indian Mission Methodist Protestant Church. The church from which the dissentors withdrew became known as the Harmony African Methodist Episcopal Church. Both churches are still active within the community and continue to reflect the division between Indian and Negro (Weslager 1943:124-27; Porter 1977:2-3).

In Delaware, as elsewhere, draft boards and military administrative personnel found it difficult to classify young men claiming Indian descent. Several of the Nanticoke men who had been inducted had their Indian rights, provided by Delaware law and recognized by the Georgetown Draft Board, disregarded when they were identified as Negroes by military authorities. Two young men who had requested classification as Indians were stationed with colored troops in the South. C. A. Weslager, who had written several books about the Nanticoke and had become friends with many of the Nanticoke families, was called upon for assistance with this rather sensitive problem. Although officials in Delaware could classify the Nanticokes as Indian, there was no authority for such action on the part of the U.S. Army. W. Berl, state director of the Delaware selective service, informed Weslager that it would be "definitely up to the Army to determine the classification of these registrants" (W. Berl, Jr., to C. A. Weslager, May 22, 1942. Weslager manuscripts in possession of the author). On June 20, 1942, Weslager wrote to the Adjutant General of the U.S. Army about the status of the two young men from Indian River. Pursuing the matter, Weslager requested information from the National Headquarters of the selective service system as to the necessary procedures to transfer the two conscripts either to White or Indian units and what steps could be taken to ensure that future conscripts from Nanticoke families would have their Indian status preserved (C. A. Weslager to Adjutant General, U.S. Army, War Department, June 20, 1942). Two months later, on July 31, 1942, Weslager received an answer to his inquiries from Brigadier General H. B. Lewis, Acting General of the War Department.

With regard to race, there are two categories within the Army, white and colored. Members of the Negro race are assigned to colored units. All other distinct races are assigned to white units. Individuals of races with distinguishable Negro characteristices acquired through intermixture with that race are assigned to colored units. Under this policy, an Indian may be assigned as an individual to a white unit or he may be assigned to a company or regiment made up entirely of Indians, that company or regiment being a component part of a white regiment or division. (Brigadier General H. B. Lewis to C. A. Weslager, July 31, 1942)

As to the two men from Indian River, information obtained from the War Department revealed that the local draft board at Georgetown had classified them as colored. To allay any future mishaps with the local board, Weslager was informed by Major Morris S. Schwartz from the national headquarters of the selective service system that "the registrar will list the registrant as being the color which the registrant claims. In case the registrant is listed as being another color than that which he claims to be, the registrant may protest his listing and the matter should be referred to the state director for determination of race" (Morris S. Schwartz to C. A. Weslager, July 2, 1942). When a similar misunderstanding occurred the following year, the individual involved was immediately transferred out of the colored detachment and into a White organization (Brigadier General P. S. Gage to C. A. Weslager, September 4, 1943).

CONCLUSION

During the nineteenth century, the question of the identity of the Nanticoke has been brought to the fore on several occasions, forcing the Indian River community to identify itself officially or lose its separate identity forever. Their struggle for ethnic identity, in spite of repeated legal and other attempts to classify them as

Negroes, became more intense after the mid-nineteenth century. Through this period, their struggle for identity can be contrasted to their almost complete economic integration into the prevailing rural community of the period. The formation of the Indian River community was influenced by a complex set of internal and external forces. The internal forces were, in part, residual culture traits from an earlier aboriginal period. Specifically, the strong desire to remain in their traditional habitat and maintain close kinship ties, both affinal and consanguinal, served to keep the remnant Indian population socially and spatially intact. Fortuitous external pressures re-enforced this social cohesion. Primarily, the subjection of the Nanticokes to the social status and classification of Negro or colored people strengthened and further hastened the development of the Indian River community because of the resulting separation of residences, enforcement of preserving social distance with the White population, and creation of separate social institutions—particularly the church and school. The basic social institutions which were created during the middle decades of the nineteenth century have persisted, with the exception of the separate educational system, to the present (Porter 1978a).

NOTES

1. "List of Names of Taxables and Assessments of the Real and Personal Property in Sussex County, 1861"; "Assessment of the Real and Personal Property of Indian River Hundred, 1872." Hall of Records, Dover, Delaware.

2. "A List Containing the Names and Rates of the Several Hundreds of Sussex County for the Year 1834 for the Auditor of Accounts"; "Abstract of the Return of the Assessors of Sussex County, 1854"; "List of Names of the Taxables and Assessments of the Real and Personal Property in Sussex County, 1861"; and "Assessment of the Real and Personal Property of Indian River Hundred, 1861." Hall of Records, Dover, Delaware.

REFERENCES

Anonymous.
    1948-1949   "Description of the Cypress Swamps in Delaware and Maryland States." *Delaware History* 3:11-20.

Arber, Edward, ed.
    1910   *Travels and Works of Captain John Smith.* Edinburgh: John Grant.
Archives of Maryland.
    1883-   Baltimore: Maryland Historical Society.
Bassett, J. S., ed.
    1901   *The Writings of Colonel William Byrd of Westover in Virginia, Esqr.* New York: Doubleday, Page & Co.
Beers, D. G.
    1868   *Atlas of the State of Delaware.* Philadelphia: Pomeroy & Beers.
Beverley, Robert.
    1947   *The History and Present State of Virginia.* Edited with an Introduction by Louis B. Wright. Chapel Hill: University of North Carolina Press.
Burnaby, A.
    1775   *Travels Through the Middle Settlements in North-America.* London.
Crosby, A.
    1972   *The Columbian Exchange: Biological and Cultural Consequences of 1492.* Westport: Greenwood Press.
de Valinger, L.
    1940   "Indian Land Sales in Delaware." *Bulletin of the Archaeological Society of Delaware* 3:29-32.
    1941   *Indian Land Sales in Delaware with Addendum. A Discussion of the Family Hunting Territory Question in Delaware.* Wilmington: The Archaeological Society of Delaware.
de Valinger, L., and V. E. Shaw.
    1951   *A Calendar of Ridgely Family Letters 1742-1899 in the Delaware State Archives.* Dover: Hall of Records.
Evans, L.
    1753   *A Brief Description of the Province of Pennsylvania. 1753.* In L. H. Gipson, *Lewis Evans.* Philadelphia: Historical Society of Pennsylvania, 1939.
Fisher, G. P.
    1929   *The So-Called Moors of Delaware.* Dover: Archives Commission of Delaware.
Fried, M. H.
    1952   "Land Tenure, Geography and Ecology in the Contact of Cultures." *American Journal of Economics and Sociology* 11:391-412.

Gilbert, W. H.
      1946   "Memorandum Concerning the Characteristics of the Larger Mixed-Blood Racial Islands of the Eastern United States." *Social Forces* 24:438-47.
      1949   "Surviving Indian Groups of the Eastern United States." *Annual Report of the Smithsonian Institution for 1948*:407-38. Washington: Government Printing Office.

Greeneville, Richard.
      1965   "An Account of the Particularities of the imployments of the English men left in Virginia by Sir Richard Greeneville under the charge of Master Ralph Lane." In *The Principal Navigations Voyages Traffiques and Discoveries of the English Nation*. New York: AMS.

Griffith, D. R.
      1976   "Ecological Studies of Prehistory." In *Transactions of the Delaware Academy of Science*. Edited by J. C. Kraft, pp. 63-81. Newark: The Delaware Academy of Science.

Hancock, H.
      1962   "Description and Travel Accounts of Delaware." *Delaware History* 10:115-51.

Heckewelder, John.
      1876   *An Account of the History, Manners, and Customs of the Indian Nations Who Once Inhabited Pennsylvania and the Neighbouring States*. Philadelphia: Historical Society of Pennsylvania.

Huffington, W.
      1838   *The Delaware Register and Farmer's Magazine* 1:318-19.

Humphreys, D.
      1730   *An Historical Account of the Incorporated Society for the Propagation of the Gospel in Foreign Parts*. London.

Hutchinson, H. H.
      1961   "Indian Reservations of the Maryland Provincial Assembly on the Middle Delmarva Peninsula." *The Archeolog* 13:1-5.

Isaacs, H. R.
      1965   "Group Identity and Political Change: The Role of Color and Physical Characteristics." *Daedalus* 96:353-75.

Johnston, C. M., ed.
    1964   *The Valley of the Six Nations. A Collection of Documents on the Indian Lands of the Grand River.* Toronto: University of Toronto Press.
Jordan, W. D.
    1968   *White Over Black: American Attitudes Toward the Negro, 1550-1812.* Chapel Hill: University of North Carolina Press.
Kilty, J.
    1808   *The Land-holder's Assistant.* Baltimore: G. Dobbin and Murphy.
Laws of Maryland.
    1765   Annapolis: Jonas Green.
[Levick, S. J.]
    1896   *Life of Samuel J. Levick late of the City of Philadelphia.* Philadelphia: William H. Pile's Sons.
Loskiel, G.
    1794   *The History of the Mission of the United Brethren Among the Indians in North America.* London.
MacLeod, W.
    1922   "The Family Hunting Territory and Lenape Political Organization." *American Anthropologist* 24:448-63.
    1928   *The American Indian Frontier.* New York: Alfred A. Knopf.
Marye, William B.
    1944   "A Quiackeson House in Eastern Maryland." *American Antiquity* 9:456.
Maury, A.
    1853   *Memoirs of a Huguenot Family.* New York: George P. Putnam & Co.
Minutes of the Provincial Council of Pennsylvania Vol. 5
    1851   Harrisburg: Theo Fenn & Co.
Perry, W. S.
    1878   *Papers Relating to the History of the Church in Delaware, A.D. 1706-1782.* Privately printed.
Pinkett, S. D.
    n.d.   "Isaac Harman 1829-1900 and Sarah J. (Sockum) 1837-1908." *Indian Mission News* 3.
Porter, Frank W.
    1977   *A Photographic Survey of Indian River Community.* Millsboro: Indian Mission Church.
    1978a   "Anthropologists at Work: A Case Study of the

Nanticoke Indian Community.'' *American Indian Quarterly* 4:1-18.

1978b   "A Century of Accommodation: The Nanticokes in Colonial Maryland." *Maryland Historical Magazine* 74:175-92.

Price, Edward T.

1953   "A Geographic Analysis of White-Negro-Indian Racial Mixtures in the Eastern United States." *Annals of the Association of American Geographers,* 43:138-55.

Roger, T., ed.

1948   *Calendar of Maryland State Papers, No. 3, The Brown Books.* Annapolis: Hall of Records Commission.

Scharf, J. T.

1888   *History of Delaware.* Philadelphia.

Speck, F. G.

1915   "Family Hunting Band as the Basis of Algonkian Social Organization." *American Anthropologist* 17:289-305.

1927   *The Nanticoke and Conoy Indians with a Review of Linguistic Material from Manuscript and Living Sources.* Wilmington: Historical Society of Delaware.

Speck, F. G., and L. Eiseley.

1939   "Significance of Hunting Territory Systems of the Algonkian in Social Theory." *American Anthropologist* 41:269-80.

Stevens, S. K., and D. H. Kent, eds.

1943   *The Papers of Col. Henry Bouquet.* Harrisburg: The Pennsylvania Historical and Museum Commission.

Thomas, R. A., et al.

1975   "Environmental Adaptation on Delaware's Coastal Plain." *Archaeology of Eastern North America* 3:35-90.

Weslager, C. A.

1941   "A Discussion of the Family Hunting Territory Question in Delaware." In L. de Valinger, *Indian Land Sales in Delaware.* Wilmington: The Archaeological Society of Delaware.

1942   "Indian Tribes of the Delmarva Peninsula." *Bulletin of the Archaeological Society of Delaware* 3:23-56.

1943   *Delaware's Forgotten Folk: the Story of the Moors & Nanticokes.* Philadelphia: Univeristy of Pennsylvania Press.

1944   "Wynicaco—A Choptank Indian Chief." *Proceedings of the American Philosophical Society* 87:398-402.

1948   *The Nanticoke Indians: A Refugee Tribal Group of Pennsylvania.* Harrisburg: The Pennsylvania Historical and Museum Commission.

1975   "More About the Unalachtigo." *Pennsylvania Archaeologist* 45:40-44.

Woodman, L.

1917   "Last Delaware Indian in Bucks County." *A Collection of Papers Read Before the Bucks County Historical Society* 4:673-74.

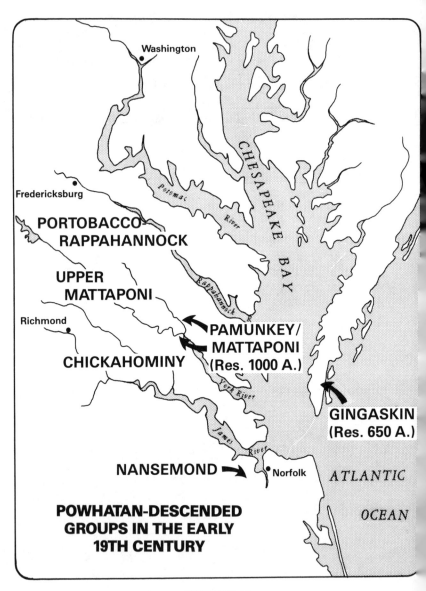

Washington

Fredericksburg

PORTOBACCO
RAPPAHANNOCK

UPPER
MATTAPONI

Richmond

CHICKAHOMINY

Potomac River

Rappahannock R.

CHESAPEAKE BAY

PAMUNKEY/
MATTAPONI
(Res. 1000 A.)

York River

GINGASKIN
(Res. 650 A.)

James River

NANSEMOND Norfolk

ATLANTIC

OCEAN

POWHATAN-DESCENDED
GROUPS IN THE EARLY
19TH CENTURY

FIGURE 10

6
ETHNICITY AMONG THE "CITIZEN" INDIANS OF TIDEWATER VIRGINIA, 1800-1930

Helen C. Rountree

INTRODUCTION

The Indian people with whom this chapter is concerned are certain descendents of the Algonkian-speaking Powhatan tribes who held eastern Virginia at the founding of Jamestown. For several decades their descendants have called themselves "citizen" Indians, in contrast with the "reservated" Indians who still hold reservation land. The term "citizen" is apt because today these Indian people live much as their non-Indian neighbors do. They own land in fee simple and pay taxes on it. Being no longer in a treaty relationship with Virginia, they are subject to the jurisdiction of the counties in which they live. And they are modern-dressing, English-speaking, television-watching Baptists. Yet, they are a people apart. They are modern Indians: not Indians who happen to live in the modern world, nor modern people who claim to be Indians. Their ancestors seem to have been modern Indians, too, for their times, though there are few records to prove it. The citizen Indians' ancestors are very hard to trace before 1850 because of poor record-keeping. Before 1900, they rarely said publicly that they were Indians; to do so would have been to invite derision at best and reprisals at worst. From the ancestors' first appearance in the surviving records, they seem to have been "people of colour" who were "different" from their free Negro neighbors in rural Virginia. This chapter will demonstrate that Virginia's citizen Indians between 1800 and 1930 can be viewed not only as a unique ethnic group but also as a specifically Indian ethnic group.

HISTORICAL BACKGROUND

When the English established Jamestown, there were thirty-odd tribes in eastern Virginia whom anthropologists call Powhatans after the father of Pocahontas. Powhatan had recently organized most of these tribes into an empire (not a true confederacy), but, in spite of sharing vassal status, language, and a Late Woodland type of culture, the tribes continued to retain their own names and a very strong sense of identity. This was especially true for the Chickahominy, whom Powhatan had never quite succeeded in conquering.

Within five decades a flood of Englishmen had washed over the tribes, leaving the dazed survivors high and dry on islands of tribal territory. The empire was broken up, and, though the English tried to keep it going to make administration easier, it was no longer a binding force on people who had never had time to internalize a supra-tribal identity. As the seventeenth century wore on, the Powhatan population decreased steadily: disease, violence, and assimilation into Anglo-Virginian society all took their toll. Tribes merged with each other as they lost people and land. The Woodland Indian way of life, however, was still followed in these tribal islands as long as enough people remained.

In English eyes, the character of the Powhatans changed greatly in the seventeenth century, and the Indians' rights under colonial law changed accordingly. Once "savages" to be conquered, the tribesmen became "poore, deprived Indyans" who were still expected to assimilate, albeit into ever lower levels of Anglo-Virginian society. Treaties and laws alike guaranteed Indian civil rights, but by the end of the century it was legal to enslave Indians who had been taken prisoner in war. That law was repealed in 1691, but in 1705 the guarantee of equal civil rights came to an end. A "black code" was passed, barring "negroes, mulattoes and Indians" from holding office, marrying Whites, testifying in court, or even striking a White person under any circumstances whatever

(Hening 1823, III:251, 298, 333, 449-50, 459). Another law passed
at the same time legalized squatters' hold on Indian reservation
land across any river from an Indian town (Hening 1823, III:466),
in spite of the fact that the Treaty of 1677 (Anonymous 1906) had
specifically granted land to the tribes within a three-mile radius of
their towns. Since these were Woodland Indians whose towns
nearly always fronted on a major stream (Smith ca. 1970 [1606]),
the law had the effect of taking away half of each tribe's land. The
English justified such behavior by pointing out that the Indians
were disappearing into the lower orders of society anyway.

The Powhatan tribes did indeed appear to be declining in the
early eighteenth century, and before long the survivors were rapidly
changing their lifeways. In 1705 there were only about a dozen
tribal reservations left (Beverley 1947 [1705]: 232-33). King William
County, between the Pamunkey and Mattaponi rivers, contained a
very large Pamunkey reservation (ancestor of today's Pamunkey
and Mattaponi reservations), on which lived the Pamunkey, the
Mattaponi (returned from the Rappahannock River basin after a
Seneca raid in 1683 [McIlwaine 1925, I:53; Nugent 1977:268]), and
probably other merged remnants from the York and James River
basin tribes. In the same county, far up the Mattaponi River, the
Chickahominy had a reservation. They had fled to join the
Pamunkey in 1646 (land patents on their old territory on the
Chickahominy River: Nugent 1934:162); in 1661 they formally
acquired a reservation of their own (Hening 1823, II:34). Most of
the Nansemond and Weyanoke had fled far south of the James
River in 1646, when the war following the 1644 massacre ended.
They disposed of their lands and merged much later with the
Iroquoian-speaking Nottoway (Rountree 1974.) Some Christianized
Nansemond went on living quietly without a reservation in Upper
Norfolk County (now in Portsmouth). The Appomattox had lost
their reservation on the river bearing their name and were living on
the lands of William Byrd. The tribes of the middle and upper
Rappahannock River basin were living under the names "Rappahannock" and "Portobacco" on a reservation in modern Caroline
County; the land had been staked out by English claimants since
1650 (Nugent 1934:200). The tribes of the lower Northern Neck,
between the Rappahannock and Potomac rivers, were reduced to
three old men living on a reservation as "Wiccocomicos." The

tribes of the lower Delmarva Peninsula lived as "Gingaskins" on a 650-acre reservation in Northampton County. Robert Beverley heard that there were nine more tiny tribal groups to the north, consisting of the Metomkin, Chincoteague, Kegotank, Matchapungo, Occohannock, Pungoteague, Onancock, Chesconnessex, and Nandua.

Within fifteen years only three reservations, Pamunkey/Mattaponi, Nansemond, and Gingaskin, remained in possession of the Indians. The end of the century would see the Pamunkey/Mattaponi reservation shrink into two small islands in a sea of Whites and the Nansemond reservation sold by its last five owners, who already lived with the Nottoway. The nine tiny groups in the mid-Delmarva Peninsula simply disappeared; they may not have been living on their own land in 1705. The Portobacco/Rappahannock apparently lost their dispute with the man who claimed the land, for Essex County deeds after 1705 show land within the "Indian boundary" being sold from White owner to White owner. The Wiccocomico reservation was sold in 1718 by the son of the last man to live there in the old style (Northumberland County: *Record Book* 1718-1726:95). The son still styled himself "King of Ye Wiccocomico Indians." The Chickahominy endured severe internal problems, prompted by a neighbor's desire for their land. Eventually an irresponsible leader sold out to the neighbor, who immediately asserted his claim. The bulk of the tribe complained to the colony's governor, who oversaw their affairs according to the Treaty of 1677. The Governor sent the case back to the King William County Court in 1718 (McIlwaine 1925, III:487). We do not know what action that court took, for the county courthouse burned in 1885. However, since the tribe appears by name in records concerning interpreters until 1726 (McIlwaine 1918:707) and interpreters for "the Indians" were employed until 1734 (Hening 1823, IV:461), it would seem that they held onto their land for a few more years before losing it.

Eighteenth- and nineteenth-century Virginia was thus left with three major Powhatan-descended groups lacking reservations: the Portobacco/Rappahannock, the Chickahominy, and part of the Nansemond in Norfolk County. They were people who preferred an Indian way of life but who no longer had any land-base on which to pursue it. Indian women went on doing domestic work, either for their husbands or for non-Indian employers. But the alternatives the men faced must have been distasteful to them: either to go to work for White landowners, in a status roughly analogous with slaves, or to become squatters on White-owned lands and turn to intensive farming (i.e., animal husbandry and plow agriculture) in order to survive. Neither occupation was suitable for men whose manhood was still symbolized by the hunt. But the second alternative was preferable to the first because it still allowed some freedom to hunt and fish.

John Peterson has pointed out that the Mississippi Choctaw, who went the same route for similar reasons, probably spent most of their lives during this period in relative isolation from non-Indians (1971:125-26). The same may have been true of the Powhatan enclaves. Their isolation, such as it was, did not prevent them from changing their own lifeways extensively at their own pace. Their language had already been fading due to their communities being too small to keep it up. By the early nineteenth century the Powhatan language was all but extinct. They slowly began adopting Anglo-Virginian modes of dress and housing.

It is impossible to say whether or not the people of these eighteenth century enclaves considered themselves "Indians" or "Indian descendants." Their reservation days were over, and yet the possession of a reservation and therefore of treaty rights were key requirements in everyone's definition of what an "Indian" was. There was little reason as yet for enclave members to try to change their own or others' definition of "Indian." Though the 1705 code was repressive, it actually interfered little in the lives of nonpolitical people who stayed out of court. There was no day-to-day disability involved in being identified with other non-Whites, so long as people possessed nothing that avaricious Whites might want. So the citizen Indians probably kept their opinions of themselves to themselves and allowed others to classify them as they would.

Sometime in the late eighteenth and early nineteenth century, according to twentiety-century oral tradition, the Chickahominy enclave in King William County split. As with many groups or families which develop some restless segments, some people left and some people stayed. The ones who left migrated southward through New Kent County and on to the high ground beyond the Chickahominy River, leaving families behind in New Kent (Stern 1952:193, 200). In 1899 James Mooney of the Bureau of American Ethnology found that these people considered themselves to be Chickahominy descendants who had returned to their homeland (Mooney 1889-1899). The people who stayed behind have since taken the name Upper Mattaponi. No tradition of movement exists today among the Rappahannock or the Nansemond remnants (Rountree fieldnotes).

The foregoing account of the eighteenth and early nineteenth centuries is largely a reconstruction. Few documents were ever made about the citizen Indians during that period, and few of these documents survive today. Once the tribes lost their reservation, they ceased to be the concern of the colonial (and later state) government. Consequently, they disappeared from that government's documents altogether. The county governments now had jurisdiction over citizen Indian people, and county records would be the place to expect to find any such documents. However, people did not get into the county records unless they bought land, made a will, got a marriage license, sued somebody, or got into trouble themselves. Many people in the lower strata of Virginia society did none of these things during their lifetimes. Even if citizen Indian people did occasionally enter the county records, there is no way for us to know about it, for most of the courthouses in the relevant counties were destroyed, either during the late campaigns of the Civil War or at a later time. County records therefore tell us practically nothing. Almost no private accounts of citizen Indians, such as diary entries or business accounts, have come to light from the 1720s onward (the exception is for the Nansemond), for the White population of Virginia was more concerned with its troubles with Britain than with obscure squatters in the backwoods. Finally, the citizen Indians of those days were illiterate and could leave us no accounts of themselves. In the records for the middle decades of their history, the citizen Indians were invisible. During that time, they changed so much that eventually outsiders had difficulty in distinguishing them from other small farmers, so that for a time they became invisible in another sense as well. But they seem not to have ceased to be Indians.

ETHNICITY AS APPLIED TO INDIAN PEOPLE

For most Americans, ethnicity is partly dependent upon genetic background, and in the case of "racial" ethnic groups like Indians, biology is all-important. A "real" Indian is a full-blood, in the popular stereotype: full-bloodedness supposedly carried with it a "typical" Indian profile, fluency in an Indian language, expertise in tracking and hunting (for men), and so on. Anyone who is less than a full-blood is less than fully "Indian" in culture; and the converse is often believed to be true as well: an Indian who lives in an Anglo-American style is probably not a full-blood. These are myths that persist in American minds. They survive and flourish in spite of numerous studies which have shown that physique and language and culture are not necessarily dependent upon one another.

"Blood" in the sense of "heredity" is a symbol of a person's physique and whole way of life, not a scientifically provable factor in determining those things. The symbolic quality of "blood" is deeply imbedded in our consciousness. "Expressions like 'royal blood' and 'flesh and blood' point to the mystical quality attributed to such connections. . . . Even when such definitions are demonstrated to be scientifically in error, if the person remains unconvinced, [then] his behavior will continue to rest upon his own version of reality" (Shibutani and Kwan 1965:39-41). The issue of blood had became paramount in defining social categories in Virginia by 1705, when the law began to classify non-White people socially according to their biological heredity and then to assign them fewer civil rights. Significantly, the laws of definition changed through time, particularly those involving Afro-Americans:

1705: [no definition of Indians or negroes] . . . the child of an Indian and the child, grand child, or great grand child, of a negro shall be deemed, accounted, held and taken to be a mulatto. (Hening 1823, IV:252).

1849: [no definition of Indians] Every person who had one-fourth part or more of negro blood shall be deemed a mulatto, and the word "negro" in any other section of this, or in any future statute, shall be construed to mean mulatto as well as negro. (Commonwealth of Virginia 1849: title 30, chap. 103, sec. 3).

1873: Every person having one-fourth or more of negro blood shall be deemed a colored person, and every person not a colored person having one-fourth or more of Indian blood shall be deemed an Indian. (Commonwealth of Virginia 1873: title 30, chap. 103, sec. 2).

1919: Every person having one-sixteenth or more of negro blood shall be deemed a colored person, and every person not a colored person having one-fourth or more of Indian blood shall be deemed an Indian. (Commonwealth of Virginia 1919: title 5, chap. 8, sec. 67).

1930: Every person in whom there is ascertainable any Negro blood shall be deemed and taken to be a colored person, and every person not a colored person having one-fourth or more of American Indian blood shall be deemed an Indian; except that members of Indian tribes living on reservations allotted them by the Commonwealth having one-fourth or more of Indian blood and less than one-sixteenth of Negro blood shall be deemed tribal Indians so long as they are domiciled on such reservations. (Commonwealth of Virginia 1930: sec. 67)

This remained the law until 1975, when all racial definitions were repealed from the Code of Virginia.

Two things about these laws are notable: first, it became increasingly easy after 1900 to be classified as a Negro, and second, the term "colored person" legally meant "Negro" only after 1873.

Exacting laws like Virginia's concerning racial and ethnic classification would logically presume a complete set of census, marriage, and birth records for each county, so that accurate classification based on genealogies could be carried out. Virginia has never had records that were adequate to that task. Even before so many courthouses were destroyed, few records were made concerning marriages and births. Only in 1853 did the state require every county to keep a register for births, marriages, and deaths. Before that, a few counties kept a register for marriage licenses, though the parents of each couple might or might not be listed. Colonial and state censuses were very rarely taken and tell us little. Even the Federal censuses, which began in 1790, do not list anything other than the head of household, number of dependents, and the race of household members until 1850. It is therefore impossible to construct complete genealogies for most Virginians, unless they are descended from the favored few who wrote in and then kept family Bibles, made wills, and bought tombstones for their dead. As Max Stanton has noted:

It would therefore be an injustice to demand a 'percentage pure' basis of one's genetic makeup to determine racial and ethnic affiliation. . . . Any arbitrary formula created by a state or federal agency will not suffice, especially in the case of a group such as the Houma [Indians of Louisiana, a tribe similar to Virginia's citizen Indians], because the social realities of the area often transcended known or presumed biological facts. (1979:93)

People were classified into "racial" categories according to "known or presumed biological facts," and in Virginia the latter kind of facts were generally used in the absence of documentation to prove the former kind. And yet what placed people in one category or another were the "social realities" with which they lived, i.e., the way that they and their real or presumed ancestry were viewed by Virginia society at large.

Demonstrating the long-term existence of an ethnic group ideally requires an examination of both the social factors that make them distinct and some evidence of biological continuity (not purity), although both social factors and biological makeup can change drastically over time without altering the fact that the group continues to exist. However, when the genealogical connections with long-dead group members cannot be verified, for whatever reason, then the group's long-term existence must be proved entirely by showing that varying social factors have set them well apart from other people during that time—far enough apart that the resulting pattern of social interaction will imply kinship ties that cannot be documented. Where documentation on social factors is lacking as well, then oral tradition and ethnographic analogy must be used. That is the way in which we must deal with the citizen Indians' ancestors. In the early nineteenth century, when documents about them are entirely lacking, we must use oral tradition and ethnographic analogy. Later in the century, their social and kinship patterns can be reconstructed from documents.

BEING A CITIZEN INDIAN IN VIRGINIA, 1800-1930

By 1800 the citizen Indians' culture had become almost entirely parallel with Anglo-Virginian culture. The lives of Indians living without reservations had become almost identical with that of non-Indian small farmers. They tilled the soil, and, according to the few surviving records, they later began slowly to purchase this land.

Their houses, furnishings, and clothing were identical with those of non-Indians of equal economic standing. They attended Baptist services along with their nearby non-Indian neighbors, for all three races worshipped together in those days. In the eyes of the law, there was supposed to be a social gap between Whites and free non-Whites, but the force of the law was not always felt among people of similar occupation and interests. Congeniality was more important than racial ideology among backwoodsmen. However, a recognizably Indian physical type remained. One Chickahominy woman who was born in 1815 was described in later years as having a "very bright complexion[,] straight hair[,] high cheekbones . . ." (Charles City County *Minute Book* 4:508). And a Rappahannock woman who was probably born about at the same time was described in her son's 1860 marriage license as being "of Indian extraction" (Essex County, *Marriage Register* 1:8, 22; the father is recorded as "a White man"). Other group members are given short shrift in the records, whether on the county level or in the Federal censuses. They are variously described as "persons of colour," "free negroes," or nothing at all (i.e., no racial designation). During these years of relative indifference to racial qualities, it is impossible to know exactly where the citizen Indian identity stood. It is likely that the people were content merely to be known by others as Indian-descended non-Whites and to continue to live quietly with their neighbors.

The racial situation in Virginia changed drastically after 1830. In particular, the Nat Turner Slave Insurrection of August 1831 roused the White population of the state to a high pitch of paranoia about not only their slaves but also all non-Whites. Free non-Whites who had previously been able to pursue their lives under moderate handicaps now found themselves subject to harsher laws. In April 1831, before the Insurrection, it was made illegal for "free negroes and mulattoes" to attend classes in any public place to learn to read and write (Commonwealth of Virginia 1830-1831: chap. 39). In March 1832, a law was passed prohibiting any "slave, free negro or mulatto" from holding any public meeting, religious or otherwise, for others and from attending such a meeting held by a non-White. Slaves could attend religious services held by Whites at night only if they got written permission in advance. The same law forbade non-Whites to buy slaves other than their own spouses or children and also prohibited them from owning firearms or dispensing liquor within a mile of any public meeting. And free Negroes and mulattoes were now denied a trial by jury, for the law stated that felony cases involving such people were to be tried in courts of oyer and terminer (by justices only), "in the same manner as slaves are" (Commonwealth of Virginia 1831-1832: chap. 22). The White people on the lower Delmarva Peninsula went even further, in a move that was subsequently imitated in other parts of the state. They had the state legislature authorize a committee of their number to divert county funds temporarily in order to underwrite a "humane" removal of all the county's "free people of colour"—a population which included the Gingaskin Indians, whose reservation had recently been broken up (Commonwealth of Virginia 1831-1832: chap. 23; Rountree 1973: 129-35; Rountree 1979: 30-32). That removal was never completed.

The social milieu in which the Indian descendants lived had changed radically. It was no longer tolerable to be considered merely a "free person of colour." One had to be able to prove *what kind* of non-White one was, in day-to-day life as well as on formal occasions at the courthouse. Otherwise, the full force of those discriminatory laws would come into play. The stage was set for the public reemergence of an "Indian" rather than "Indian-descended" identity among the citizen groups. Because of the extremely repressive conditions that non-Whites faced in Virginia, that reemergence took nearly a century to complete.

The Nansemond group in what is now Portsmouth had had good credibility all along; in the 1720s and again in 1742 some of them had gotten formal certification as people of Nansemond and English descent (certificates quoted in Bell 1961, Indian Section: 15). Now in 1833 the delegate from their county introduced a bill (Commonwealth of Virginia 1832-1833a:131) which was quickly passed by both houses of the General Assembly (Commonwealth of Virginia 1832-1833b: chap. 80). The new law stated that free non-Whites who were descended from Indians could get themselves certified as "persons of mixed blood, not being free negroes or mulattoes" if they got at least one White person to vouch for them before the county court. The Nansemond promptly visited the courthouse and got their certificates (Norfolk County *Minute Book* 24:27, 28, 43, 44).

There is no record of anyone in the other Indian-descended groups following suit. The Upper Mattaponi may have done so, but the Order Books of their county were entirely destroyed in 1885. The two counties with antebellum records that might have Rappahannock entries show none. And the only surviving Minute Books in the Chickahominy area show group members getting certified over a 30-year period as "free persons of colour" (Charles City *Minute Books* 2:75, 79, 92; 3:206; 4:104, 266, 338, 394, 396, 454, 497, 508, 617). All these Indian descendants may have failed to get certified as "persons of mixed blood" because they did not know of the law (they were, after all, illiterate), because they could find no sympathetic White friends to vouch for their Indianness, or because they simply did not qualify physically. The last reason does not apply to the Chickahominy, at least. Charles City County's "free negro register" gives fairly detailed descriptions of the persons certified: almost all the Chickahominy ancestors had "bright [pale]" or "very bright" skin, and one of the people certified was the decidedly Indian-looking woman mentioned earlier. It is probably that the Chickahominy registered as "born free in this county" (the actual wording of the record, there being no reference to race), while the Rappahannock did not register as anything at all, for economic reasons. These were rural people who had to do their shopping in market towns. The Rappahannock could shop in Fredericksburg, which is located in the county where they lived, while the Chickahominy had to cross a county boundary to reach Richmond, the market town nearest them. By law, free non-Whites who crossed county boundaries without carrying certificates of freedom could be arrested and jailed (Jackson 1971 [1942]:4).

Most of the Anglo-American pressure against Indian-descended non-Whites in those days was directed against the reservated Indians of the state, who were much more visible as a non-Negro race than were the citizen Indians. Since the Pamunkey and Mattaponi were officially "Indian" through their possession of reservation land, they could not conveniently be identified with "free persons of colour" for political reasons. They therefore stood in an awkward middle position in the increasingly polarized relations between "Whites" and "colored people." Naturally, the Whites wanted to simplify matters by eliminating that middle position. The citizen Indians might aspire at times, then or later, to acknowledged membership in that middle group, but for the group members themselves it was a very precarious position.

Not unexpectedly, pressure was brought to bear on the reservation people on racial grounds. A crisis point was reached in 1842-1843, when some Whites in King William County circulated a petition, which was later sent to the General Assembly in Richmond, alleging that because of marriage with Negroes the reservation people were no longer "real" Indians entitled to a special legal position. There were other charges, such as low moral character, of the sort that were regularly being made about free non-Whites at the time. But the intermarriage charge was a deadly serious one, considering the racial definition laws that were then on the books. The Pamunkey/Mattaponi wrote to Richmond in their own defense and persuaded the Assembly to reject the petition (Rountree 1973:141-47; 1979:34-36), but the experience left deep psychological scars on the people which are still apparent in their descendants (Rountree fieldnotes). The reservation people took steps then to strengthen their already stringent laws about marriage with outsiders. In 1894, the date of the first (and only) publication of the Pamunkeys' tribal laws (Pollard 1894:16-17), the marriage law was at the top of the list: "1st Res. No Member of the Pamunkey Indian Tribe shall intermarry with anny [sic] Nation except White or Indian under penalty of forfeiting their rights in Town [on the reservation]" (author's brackets).

The unorganized citizen Indian groups had no tribal councils to pass and enforce laws making a rigid ethnic boundary. As a result, they continued to have a substantial number of "fringe" families whose marriage patterns remained eclectic and who usually drifted eventually out of the group, but not before the surrounding non-Indian community had watched and concluded that all group members felt free to marry anyone. However, the actual rate of group endogamy seems to have been relatively high, if oral tradition can be trusted (since many citizen Indian surnames are shared with Whites and Blacks in the counties, it is necessary to check against tribal rolls in constructing genealogies from county records). This writer can only speak positively about the Chickahominy at present, for that tribe has been generous with its tribal rolls.

By the time that records become available for Chickahominy marriages, i.e., 1850, that group already showed a highly endogamous pattern. Chickahominy data indicate that an ethnic boundary was present, and very probably also a racial one. Figures proved almost impossible to get for in-marriage and out-marriage in any nineteenth century racial group (Schollaert 1984: personal communication). So instead, the Chickahominy data had to be tested against available data for a "clique." Many rural Virginians form cliques in which the members marry each other relatively frequently. Perhaps the Chickahominy were merely a clique within the larger non-White community? It happens that there is a published genealogy for a White clique in this writer's own home area, 50 miles from the Chickahominy. Since the Chickahominy data include only marriages solemnized within the people's home counties of Charles City and New Kent, the White clique's data had to be limited to marriages occurring within a 30-mile radius of the family's ancestral home in Gloucester County. The figures for in-marriage and out-marriage are summarized below:

MARRIAGES AMONG CHICKAHOMINY AND FAMILIES IN WHITE "CLIQUE"

| | Chickahominy | | Families in white clique | |
	In-marriages	Out-marriages	In-marriages	Out-marriages
1850–1869	10	7	1	12
1870–1889	25	22	6	16
1890–1909	21	22	5	21
1910–1929	41	13	6	33

To be absolutely certain that the figures were not due to coincidence, the two data sets were made proportional; a Chi-square test was run which yielded a value of 119.29, and, at the 3 degrees of freedom allowed in the calculations, that value is significant at least at the 0.000001 level. This means that the obviously much higher endogamy rate among the Chickahominy has only one chance in a million of being due to coincidence. The Chickahominy have deliberately practiced endogamy since at least 1850, in spite of pressures on them to merge with Blacks and in spite of the fact that there have long been congenial Whites who were willing to risk breaking the racial laws against intermarriage. Their endogamy may have been aimed at keeping their bloodlines pure, as their descendants still claim, but to a social scientist it is more significant as a measure of group solidarity. It is endogamous patterns like these that demographers like Calvin Beale look for when locating non-reservation population isolates with Indian ancestry (Beale 1973: personal communication).

The citizen Indians' lack of any formal organization was not unusual. They lived under very repressive conditions, and their lifeways were so similar to those of the dominant society that they needed no special services in order to survive as individuals. Recreating formal tribal organizations at that time would have served no essential functions (such as education and medical care) and might actually have been physically dangerous to attempt. Spicer (1971:795-800) has pointed out that ethnic identities can remain very strong under such conditions nevertheless, and Breton has described what the social life of such a community is like: it is "a community which consists essentially in a network of interpersonal relations; members of a certain ethnic group seek each other's companionship; friendship groups and cliques are formed. But beyond this informal network, no formal organization may exist."

The citizen Indians and their non-White neighbors shared many of the same social disabilities, but that did not necessarily make them sympathetic to one another. Indeed, it is probable that the Indians and the "negroes and mulattoes" they avoided were just as ready to stereotype each other—in the aggregate, at least—as they were to stereotype the condescending Whites. As Lyman and Douglass have noted:

it is very likely that in a plural society two actors of different ethnic groups, neither of which is dominant in the society, will possess very incomplete information concerning the nature of the other's ethnic heritage and the cultural nuances characteristic of the other's behavior. In lieu of these, such actors may resort to their own understanding of the larger society's stereotypes of each other's ethnic group. Plural societies are likely to be characterized by pluralistic ignorance. (1973:353)

After 1833, the legal advantages to be gained by aloofness toward Afro-Americans probably made for more separation, more stereo-typing, and more conflict between the citizen Indians and their non-White neighbors, though no contemporary documents exist to prove it.

The Indians' attitudes toward Whites must have been more complex. Alliances with individual Whites were politically desirable, but White ignorance and condescension toward Indian people must have made contact distasteful enough to both sides to be avoided much of the time. As Lyman and Douglass point out:

In a plural society characterized by an official culture and many racial groups in varying states of cultural and social distance from it, the interplay between the forces favoring the social contract [i.e., continued regulated interaction] and those favoring cultural and social apartheid often produces society instability and anguished personal ambivalence. (1973:346)

The conflicting forces operating on Whites and Indians in dealing with each other were operating on a much larger scale in White-Black relations, and the massive problems they created before and after the Civil War swept the Indians along in their wake. The Civil War was a bad time for the citizen Indians, for they were in danger of being forced to serve on the side that could not claim much of their loyalty. Many of the men kept such a low profile that no one bothered them. Some Chickahominy served with the Union forces, while others of their number simply fled the state and eventually came to rest for several years with the Ontario Ojibwa before returning home (Stern 1952:206). The U.S. Census of 1900 shows several Chickahominy as having been born in "western Canada."

Reconstruction was a traumatic time for everyone concerned, for Virginia society was in a state of flux. Before the war, White Southerners had proclaimed themselves to be members of a demo-cratic, egalitarian society and had simultaneously held some non-Whites in slavery while denying economic, social, and political equality to the rest. The flouting of America's ideals was done in standardized ways throughout the South. The Reconstruction period saw an attempt by Blacks to put idealistic norms into practice. The Whites, whose hegemony was thus threatened, eventually reasserted their power over the Blacks through segregation. However, physical segregation of Whites from non-Whites in public places did not arise solely for political reasons. There were social reasons as well, and that is why segregation—of all three races from each other in Virginia—predated the actual reclaiming of power by the Whites.

Pierre van den Berghe (1966) has set up two theoretical modes of race relations, and, although they do not tell the whole story of White-non-White relations in the South, they are useful paradigms to apply here. In a "paternalistic" system of race relations, represented by the Old South, there is a caste system that is rigid enough that members of the upper and lower castes may live at close quarters and interact frequently (using a prescribed etiquette, of course) without endangering the ascendancy of the upper group. In a system like that, people often live in large plantation communities, and they and their rural neighbors of all colors worship together, attend public meetings together, and so on. Social disruption or an increase in urbanism and industrialism causes a paternalistic system to evolve into a "competitive" one. Then there may be castes, as indeed there were in the postbellum South. But the status gap between them is much narrower because members of all castes can live in large, impersonal cities and may compete for the same jobs. Institutionalized evasion takes the form of informal discrimination rather than outright legal disabilities (Merton 1977 [1949]:27). For example, it was no longer illegal to educate Black children in late nineteenth-century Virginia, but for a number of reasons the schools provided for them did not stay open more than four or five months of the year, so that the children reached adulthood with less learning. In a competitive system, members of different castes no longer have close contact with each other, unequal or otherwise, in their private lives. The upper caste may withdraw from lower-castle people who have become "uppity," while the lower caste may find itself unwelcome in places and go off to form its own interest groups. In the South, separate Black churches were usually the first formal organizations to appear in those communities. Free public schools were imposed upon the Virginia counties a little later, and the counties further burdened themselves by setting up dual systems for Whites and non-Whites.

Virginia's Indians, reservated and citizen alike, watched the world change around them and pondered how to survive. The Pamunkey/Mattaponi reservation people decided early that separation from both Whites and Blacks in public places was desirable. In 1865, without waiting to see how the Whites felt at Colossee Baptist church where all the local Baptists had previously worshipped, they formed Pamunkey Indian Baptist Church. The Upper Mattaponi group then commuted nearly fifteen miles over dirt roads to worship with them. The Pamunkey Church remained the "Indian" church in King William County until the Mattaponi reservation people built their own church in 1932; the Upper Mattaponi did the same later on. Separate churches also came after the turn of the century for the Chickahominy and Rappahannock; the Nansemond attended various Baptist and Methodist churches with Whites. In the late nineteenth century, the Chickahominy attended Cedar Grove Baptist Church, a congregation within the geographical boundaries of their landholdings. When the church's membership gradually shifted from White to Black, the Indians moved over to the Samaria Baptist Church, which then disbanded in 1888. The Indian contingent continued to use the building and organized their congregation in 1901 as Samaria Indian Baptist Church. In 1910 they built the present church in the center of their enclave area (Stern 1952:208). Their pastor for many years after 1901 was the same man who served at the Pamunkeys' church (National Anthropological Archives MS. 112:6). Formal incorporation of the tribe had taken place in 1908 (*vide infra*). The Rappahannock attended St. Stephen's Baptist church, a multiracial congregation, until in 1964 part of the tribe bought an unused Episcopal church and established Rappahannock Indian Baptist Church (Rountree fieldnotes). Their tribe had been incorporated since the 1920s.

John Peterson has observed that in other parts of the South, separate Indian churches seem to have developed after separate Black churches did, all appearing after the Civil War (1971:127-29). He suggests that the Indians left it to the Blacks, a much larger and therefore less vulnerable minority than the tiny Indian one, to find successful ways of establishing their own institutions after the war ended. This practical solution was followed only by the citizen Indians in Virginia. The reserved tribes apparently felt secure enough in their state-recognized "Indian" status that they felt able to forge ahead and form their own congregation immediately.

Churches are an institution which most Christian Virginians, including Indian ones, feel they cannot do without. They may be said to be basic to the people's existence as "whole persons." Formal tribal organizations, on the other hand, are only secondarily basic to Indian people's survival, being the best but not the only public way of expressing one's Indianness. A church, in fact, can be an extremely effective way of expressing Indianness. Decades of study by cultural anthropologists have shown us that any religion is a focal point for the people's total values and aspirations for themselves. In a sense, religion is a summing-up of the people's lifeways and the place they feel they should occupy in the universe. (The cohesive value of an institution covering that much ground is obvious.) Virginia's Indian people in their tribal congregation considered themselves "Indian Christians" and saw no paradox in the combination of words; instead they disagreed violently with outsiders who did see a paradox. That kind of disagreement is not unusual in the history of ethnic relations, for "religion is frequently a way of asserting an ethnic or class or racial identity in a situation of intergroup conflict" (Wallace 1966:26). Christian churches were also legitimate places for group rituals to be held, according to Anglo-American ideals of religious freedom, while tribal group activities would be more suspect. Tribal churches thus performed a maximum number of useful functions: they formed an essential institution for the people; they expressed the Indians' sense of who they were; and they publicly asserted independence from and even conflict with other ethnic groups, particularly the other non-Whites with whom White society expected them to merge.

While the Indians were allowed by the dominate Whites to have separate churches, freedom of education was never guaranteed to the Indians or to anyone else. They were expected to take whatever was offered them. What they were offered was admission into the "colored" schools, an effort at assimilation that was intended to counteract the Indians' separatist tendencies. The Indians rejected the offer. Not only were the colored schools poor in quality (for a variety of reasons, few of which were the Black people's fault), but any Indian child who went to these schools became "Negro" by association. As long as non-Indians had their way, it was not possible to get a public school education and be an Indian at the same time.

The citizen Indians responded by forming their own schools at their own expense, while the reservations persuaded the state to set up a school on the Pamunkey reservation. These small schools had teachers who were either Whites or literate Indians, and their facilities consisted for years of the front parlor of someone's house. The Chickahominy managed to build a school before 1910, located near their new church building, and the county soon helped support their effort. The Upper Mattaponi did not get a schoolhouse from their county until 1919, and even then it was very grudgingly funded (Rountree fieldnotes; Coates 1971: personal communication). The Rappahannock never did succeed in coaxing a building out of any of the three counties in which they lived, probably because of the fact that they were scattered throughout three counties. Needless to say, the course work offered in these schools, public or private, reserved or citizen Indian, covered only the first few grades for many, many years. The Nansemond were far better off. Norfolk County accepted responsibility for their school, which became County School No. 9 with an Indian teacher, and the children were able to get high school course work with Whites (Rountree fieldnotes; Mooney Papers, MS. 2190; A. A. Bass letter of 1899, Mooney Papers).

Winning a third school system for citizen Indian children was exceedingly difficult, compared to establishing tribal churches. The existence of the churches depended only upon Indian people's feelings about themselves and their willingness to provide themselves with their own facilities, as everyone else did. Schools were another matter. County-supported schools were the norm, and entrance into them on one's own terms was an important status symbol. To get county-funded schools, the citizen Indians had to convince White officials that they were a third race, not merely another group of colored people (a term that now meant Black). Thus, they had to present their case in terms of Anglo-American racial ideology. As luck would have it, the citizen Indians had accepted that once-alien ideology themselves by this time in their history, so they were well prepared to take up the fight.

There are two ways for an ethnic group to try to establish a claim of the right kind of "blood." One way is to consult past records and establish genealogical connections with people known to have been full-bloods. That way was closed to Virginia's citizen Indians, as has already been shown. The other way is to emphasize how one—or one's relatives—bears a stereotypic "look" which can only have come from the "right" ancestry; for example, with copper skin, high cheekbones, and straight black hair. Lyman and Douglass identify these as "ethnic cues," or the relatively permanent aspects of one's appearance. Lyman and Douglass further contend that ethnic cues are rarely sufficient in themselves to get a stranger to identify a person positively as belonging to a certain group. It is therefore necessary to reinforce the ethnic cues with "ethnic clues," or consciously presented hints as to one's true identity (1973:361). The clues may be either visual or conversational.

It is hard to know what ethnic clues the citizen Indians presented to their non-Indian neighbors in the late nineteenth century in addition to the cues that we know they emphasized. Documentary evidence about their appearance and statements about themselves are few. The main source is James Mooney of the Bureau of American Ethnology, though he wrote only about ethnic appearance in general. Mooney visited the Chickahominy and Nansemond in 1899, making tribal censuses; only the Chickahominy one survives (Mooney Papers, MS. 2199). In his published account, Mooney stated that all the groups he actually saw were tri-racial, with Indian physical characteristics predominating (1907:145). He elaborated on this in the letter he wrote to his superior in Washington just after leaving Virginia: "I was surprised to find them so *Indian*, the Indian blood probably being nearly 3/4, the rest white, with a strain of negro. Some would pass unquestioned in any Western tribe" (Mooney Papers, Correspondence).

Neither Mooney's sketchy fieldnotes nor the photographs taken the same year by the Smithsonian's Delancy Gill (National Anthropological Archives *Photographic Negatives:*852, 855-65) show Chickahominy people giving "ethnic clues" in addition to their Indian physiognomy. It is not until 1905, after the organization of the tribal church and the still-informal organization of the tribe with a chief and councilmen (*vide infra*), that a photograph of the Chickahominy chief shows a citizen Indian with long hair (National Anthropological Archives *Photographic Negatives:* 852). By that time, the chief was ready to make a public statement by letting his hair grow, where before he had kept it short.

Beginning about 1900, White society in Virginia took steps to segregate itself further from non-Whites. De jure segregation in public places came in with a series of laws passed over a decade or more, until by 1919 the Code of Virginia provided for separate space for Whites and non-Whites in railroad coaches, streetcars, steamboats (an essential means of transportation in eastern Virginia until the county roads were paved in the 1930s), waiting rooms, and county land and personal property books (Commonwealth of Virginia 1919: passim). The definition of "colored person" was also expanded to include anyone with one-sixteenth or more of African ancestry, as noted earlier in this paper. The laws which affected the citizen Indians the most were probably those governing the county books: hereafter racial classification was to become a matter of law, not a matter of negotiation between clerks and Indians. The railroad coach law also had repercussions for the Chickahominy, who reached their market town of Richmond by rail at that time.

It was probably the latter pressure which led the Chickahominy, the largest and most compactly settled citizen Indian enclave, to take steps toward formal organization with the encouragement of the Pamunkey reservation people. In 1901 they officially established their religious congregation on a tribal basis (*vide supra*) and called the Pamunkey's White pastor, P. E. Throckmorton, to serve them as well. They also began to hold fish fries for themselves and sympathetic White friends—the ancestor of the Chickahominy Fall Festival, which is now held annually. One of their friends was Judge Isaac H. Christian, who saw to it that the Charles City and New Kent county records began to label them "Indian" instead of "colored" (National Anthropological Archives MS. 112: Throckmorton's affidavit; Charles City and New Kent counties: *Records*). The Chickahominy informally elected a chief and tribal officers in 1900 (*The* [Richmond] *Times* 1900a), and they began to issue tribal membership cards (copy of one in National Anthropological Archives MS. 112). The membership cards saved them the embarrassment of being sent to the "Jim Crow" coach, for the Pamunkey had won a ruling exempting Indians from riding there almost as soon as the coach law was passed (*The* [Richmond] *Times* 1900; *The* (Richmond) *Dispatch* 1900). In 1908 the Chickahominy achieved full incorporation as a tribe, with charter and bylaws.

Lacking the open support of the Pamunkey, the other citizen Indian groups took no action until another anthropologist appeared on the scene. Frank G. Speck of the University of Pennsylvania began to visit the Virginia tribes in 1919 and found the Upper Mattaponi and the Rappahannock extremely hesitant about organizing and thus exposing themselves to public derision (Speck's fieldnotes contain very few Nansemond references). One of the groups even asked him "if they were in danger of being killed by white people" for organizing (Speck Papers: Field Notebook 1). But with Speck's help and encouragement, they eventually overcame their fears and incorporated: the Rappahannock in 1921 and the Upper Mattaponi and Nansemond in 1923. Like the Chickahominy organization, all of the new "tribes" were Indian Associations, chartered under the Virginia State Corporation Commission and paying a nominal fee to that Commission annually. The Chickahominy and Rappahannock organizations have existed uninterruptedly ever since; the Upper Mattaponi charter lapsed during the 1950s and was renewed in 1976. The Nansemond charter lapsed in the 1930s and is now (in 1984) in the process of renewal.

The Chickahominy felt sure enough of themselves as a distinct, recognizable "racial" ethnic group that in the early 1920s, while Speck was helping the other groups to organize, they began collecting documents from reputable White friends in their community to use in a drive toward state recognition of the tribe as "Indians." Part of the tribe favored the purchase of a tract of land with tribal moneys; this would become their "reservation." The documents written by White friends all stated that the Chickahominy were genuine Indians and had always been so regarded (Coates Papers n.d.). There were, of course, other non-Indians who did not regard the Chickahominy as Indians and who later said so; the Chickahominy were still in many ways an ethnic "fringe" about whom outsiders disagreed, and thus they remained until the Anglo-Virginian definition of "real Indian" broadened. The movement of the 1920s did not last long, however, for the racial climate in Virginia became even colder.

In the same years that Speck was encouraging the citizen Indians to take on a publicly "Indian" identity, White society in Virginia was hardening further in its attitudes toward non-Whites. Since the late nineteenth century, "racial purity" and "eugenics" had been increasingly important issues to many people in the United States and abroad, and they were used to justify the colonial enterprises in which European and American Whites were engaged. In the 1920s and 1930s the attitudes even of educated Whites in Virginia were milder versions of Nazi attitudes after 1933. However, at that time, racial purity and eugenics had not become dirty words and a symbol of mass executions. Instead, a sort of "scientific racism" (Carr 1982: personal communication) prevailed. There was a sincerely held feeling among Whites that non-White blood was inferior and that the possessors of it should be kept in a sort of wardship position for their own and society's good. The evidence for non-White inferiority was supposedly the lesser accomplishments of non-Whites throughout history; little was known then of the early civilizations of sub-Saharan Africa, and the Egyptians were considered honorary "Whites." White people in the United States assured one another that mixing their blood with that of their "inferiors" was certain to bring the downfall of civilization as they knew it, just as the ancient Roman empire had supposedly fallen because of Romans marrying conquered people throughout the Mediterranean. Mixing with non-Whites must therefore be prevented. And non-Whites who refused to accept the "Negro" label and who were therefore obviously trying to join the privileged "White" group must be put back firmly into their place.

To Virginians, the way to keep everyone in his place was to classify everyone in the state, once and for all, according to race. The job fell to the Vital Statistics Bureau in 1923, after a Racial Integrity Law was passed. That law stated merely that everyone had to appear accurately classified (i.e., in accordance with the way the state labeled them) in the records of all public institutions. Somehow it was assumed that everyone's racial identity could be readily established and that racial purity could then be feasibly enforced. The identification of people, of course, was going to be made in spite of the absence of complete, detailed records of the Virginia population from colonial times onward.

The Vital Statistics Bureau's head, or Registrar, was only too glad to take the project on, and in so doing he became the force against which the citizen Indians had to fight the hardest. Walter Ashby Plecker, M.D. (1861-1946), came from the Piedmont of Virginia and spent almost his entire career in the South. An exceptionally able organizer, he joined the Bureau in 1912 and remodeled it into essentially its present-day form. He was a staunchly conservative Presbyterian (American Historical Society 1924), and his strongly held views on predestination had a great influence on both his racial opinions and his methods of dealing with people (Russell Booker, of the Vital Statistics Bureau, 1973: personal communication). He was, to put it politely, a hard-headed and preemptory man. People who wanted to flout the age-old, "God-given" racial barriers made him particularly angry—so angry and abusive, in fact, that a rumor began to circulate among his Indian victims in both the Tidewater and the Piedmont that his near-hatred of them stemmed from an unhappy love affair with some Indian woman (Rountree fieldnotes; Beale Papers).

Plecker insisted that all Indians and many Whites in Virginia should be classed as Negroes, which may well have been true according to the "ascertainable trace" definition of "Negro" that was then the law in Virginia. However, Plecker erred when he claimed that he could prove his contention conclusively through historical records (thereby establishing the grounds on which the new battle with the Indians would be fought). He had access in his Bureau to copies of the surviving county birth, marriage, and death records; and ancestor listed as "colored" in those records was enough for Plecker to label the descendants "Negro." Being a medical doctor, he did not take an historian's interest in the ways in which records were made or the changing meaning of "colored" in the nineteenth century, nor did he take a social scientist's interest in the reasons why that term was applied to certain people and not to others. A colored ancestor was always a Negro ancestor to Plecker. He therefore consulted the records and then began to make a list of Virginians descended from people described therein as colored who were then either claiming to be Indians or "passing" as White.

That list, together with copies of the old documents he worked from and the letters containing hearsay testimony from some of his sympathizers out in the counties, formed the bulk of his "Racial Integrity File," a collection that was destroyed only when a new registrar took over the Bureau in 1959. (It is understandable that the reservated and citizen Indians have been extremely skittish ever since about anyone's researching old records about them or compiling their genealogies. In their experience, non-Indians only collect such things to use against them.)

Armed with his File and backed by public (White) opinion, Plecker began to make increasingly strong statements against would-be non-Negroes in general and Indians in particular. The tone of his *Annual Reports of the Bureau* became more strident. The 1926 report called the eclectic wenching of frisky college boys "a great crime against their State and race" (Commonwealth of Virginia 1926). The culmination came in 1928 when Plecker wrote, "The Bureau of Vital Statistics has been maintaining alone and in silence the burden of maintaining a constant struggle to prevent these organized groups of mulattoes from securing the white classification which they are striving for as the climax of their life's ambition" (Commonwealth of Virginia 1928). Thereafter, Plecker broke his "silence," such as it had been, and spoke out at more public functions and in the newspapers. He wrote a pamphlet on eugenics which was published in 1924 by the Bureau (Plecker 1924) and sent it to all parents of children for whom birth certificates were being issued. The purpose of the pamphlet was to prevent "race deterioration" (Plecker's term) by warning people against race mixture and alerting them to the existence of suspicious mixed-bloods who were trying to be "White" (Plecker 1924:11, 15-16, 19-21, 332-33). The mixed-bloods were called "mongrels," a term Plecker used repeatedly in the years to come. In that same year, Plecker won legal permission to write on the backs of older birth certificates reading "Indian"—some of which he had signed himself at the time—that the person should in fact be classed as "colored." He had been writing a similar message there illegally for some time (Coates 1971: personal communication), but now that he was legally able, Plecker refined the procedure by attaching a long, printed "warning" notice which reflected his feeling that Indians were dangerous. For many years, any time an Indian person had to show a birth certificate to a public agency, there in photostat form would be both the birth certificate and the "warning" on the back which was legally part of it. That situation did not change until 1972 (Adkins Papers).

The anxiety and humiliation that Plecker caused among Virginia's Indians were tremendous. Here was as much "oppositional process" as Spicer could wish for. It was not enough to have tribal organizations and Indian schools and churches. Now the citizen Indians needed blatantly visible signs of Indianness, such as reservations and personal documents from public officials reading "Indian." Both could be extremely difficult to get. Local officials were rarely sympathetic. Rappahannock records continued to read colored, Chickahominy records reverted to reading colored, and only Upper Mattaponi records continued to read Indian, thanks to the presence of both of the reservations in the same county (Rountree fieldnotes). The only public record that Indian people could control was their marriage licenses: from 1924 until Plecker retired in 1946, few citizen Indian people got married in their home counties. They went elsewhere and married "Indians." Meanwhile, the Chickahominy movement for a reservation faltered. The idea had been favored mainly by tribal members living in New Kent County, i.e., the Chickahominy living closest to the Pamunkey reservation. However, the tribe became factionalized over the reservation issue, and the factions coincided with factions then arising in the church over religious issues. Thus, instead of binding the tribe together through cross-cutting disagreements, the conflict in the tribe became doubly strong between only two factions. The result was that the tribe had split apart by 1925. The Charles City County group became the Western Chickahominy, or Chickahominy proper, and the smaller, pro-reservation splinter group became the Eastern Chickahominy. Ironically, the latter had all they could do to organize their own church and tribal membership, and the reservation idea had to be dropped.

The pressures under which all the citizen Indians lived in the 1920s and 1930s (and, indeed, until the late 1960s) have been graphically described by Brewton Berry (1963). They were truly an ethnic fringe group: accepted by some and derided by others, never sure of their reception by strangers, and living under the force of laws that were openly antagonistic to them.

As the decade of the 1920s ended, the "Indian" battle in Virginia was forced upon the attention of the Federal government for the first, but by no means the last, time. In a sense, it was the beginning of the modern era for the citizen Indians, though it would be another fifty years before they began dealing directly with Federal agencies as Indians. The issue presented to Washington in the late 1920s concerned the Census Bureau (Beale Papers): How were the citizen Indians to be listed in the 1930 Census—as Indians or as colored people?

Registrar Plecker made the first move. In 1925 and 1926 he sent documents, some of which were inaccurately copied, and letters to the Census Bureau, stating that there were no "real" Indians in Virginia and urging that all claimants to the label be classified as colored. Census officials were polite but noncommittal. In 1929, the year before the enumerators went out on their interviews, real trouble came to Washington and stayed. Plecker resumed his correspondence, and now the Bureau heard as well from influential friends of the Indians such as Speck (no Indians seem to have written on their own behalf, though by now they had people capable of doing so). The Bureau, apparently unaware of the awful repercussions its listings could have on people's lives in a racially segregated state, kept on saying blandly to everyone that its data were being collected for "statistical purposes only." The other participants refused to be mollified, whether before the enumeration, during the interviews, or during the tabulation period that ended in mid-1931. The enumerators made either Plecker or the Indians mad no matter what they wrote for "race"; if they left "race" blank, they made the Bureau mad because it wanted to stay as far away from the combatants as possible. In the end, the result was a compromise that satisfied nobody: in the 1930 federal census, the Indians of Virginia were listed as "Indian*—the asterisk pointed to a footnote which stated that their classification as Indian was uncertain. Considerable time would pass before the citizen Indians felt that they had lived down that humiliation.

The pressures experienced by the citizen Indians in the 1920s and 1930s did not make them disappear. True, many of them left their kinsmen to find easier lives with more opportunity; some returned in later years; others stayed away permanently. But the ones who stayed became welded together to a degree not experienced before.

They valued the public statements of sympathic non-Indians (oral or written) more than ever, and they learned to seek those endorsements actively. They stepped up their visiting of one another and of other eastern Indians at Speck's urging, and for a time there was even talk of a new Powhatan Confederacy. Their tribal corporations, which remained perfectly legal under their State Corporation Commission charters, became a place of refuge and an even more important symbol of who they felt they were. The citizen Indians became more determined than ever that they had a right to call themselves "Indians."

SUMMARY

The experiences endured by the citizen Indians of Virginia in the nineteenth and early twentieth centuries would have been enough to mold them into an ethnic group even if they had not been one already. After they lost their reservations and, later, their language and much of their cultural distinctiveness, they became squatters and small farmers whose identity consisted in remembering who their ancestors had been and a preference for association and marriage within their own group. We know this not from records, for those were either destroyed or never made in the first place, but from analogy with other, better documented eastern Indian groups (Williams, 1979). When they first appear in the records again, the citizen Indians are in the same social position as those Indians in the analogy.

As time went on, the interests of the dominant society changed and so did the identity symbols of the citizen Indians. After 1830 White Virginians became more concerned about and repressive toward the free Negroes who were perceived as a threat to the system of slavery. It became desirable for Indian-descended people to emphasize the differences they had always felt between themselves and Negroes; since White society's definitions of people were made primarily on biological grounds, the Indians had to go that route, too. Oral tradition and hearsay were all that most people in Virginia had to prove who their distant ancestors were. When memories did not coincide, there was conflict, and the more powerful Whites usually won. In the social sphere, the citizen Indians remained in informal networks, partially because their way of life was so like their neighbors' that they did not need specialized institutions and partially because it was risky for non-Whites to try to create formal organizations among themselves in those days. They further cemented their idea of their uniqueness by marrying principally among themselves, as the surviving records indicate.

Virginia society changed considerably after the Civil War and so did the pressure put on Indians and the Indians' response to it. Where Whites and non-Whites had shared many institutions before the war, separate institutions now became the rule. Segregated churches and public schools became very important foci for community activities at the same time that Whites were gradually reestablishing themselves in power and relegating Blacks to a second-class position. Therefore it remained important to the citizen Indians to distinguish themselves from Blacks in the eyes of the Whites, and the logical way to do it was to set up Indian churches and schools. The churches were generally achieved first, since churches are private, voluntary organizations which are supposed to be free to all Americans. The schools came with much more difficulty; public moneys were involved, and non-Indian officials had to be convinced of the Indians' right to them.

The "Jim Crow" era was merely a time of intensification of racism and segregation in Virginia, as far as the citizen Indians were concerned. White people's attitudes toward both Blacks and suspected Blacks became even harsher than they had been, and de jure segregation laws were passed. The legal basis of racial classification remained biological, though the records of people's ancestors remained incomplete, and memory and hearsay had to count as evidence. The citizen Indians began to emphasize further their "Indian" physical characteristics, sometimes with the aid of "ethnic clues" such as long hair. They also formally organized themselves into "tribes"—actually incorporated tribal associations—and issued membership cards. The organization into tribes was an especially public way of announcing that they were Indians, and none of the groups undertook encouragement from "safe" sources: the Chickahominy had the Pamunkey, the Pamunkeys' minister, and several important local Whites behind them; the Upper Mattaponi, Rappahannock, and Nansemond organized later with the aid of Frank Speck.

The "racial integrity" movement in Virginia was a still more extreme pressure upon the citizen Indians to merge themselves with other non-Whites. As before, the pressure took the form of charges of non-Indian ancestry based on hearsay. As before, there were tacit charges that the people were not "real" Indians because they did not have their traditional language and culture anymore. The citizen Indians fought back as usual on biological grounds supported by hearsay; by so doing, they managed to hold their own during some very anxious times.

Neither the Indians, nor their friends or their enemies felt prepared to argue the Indians' distinctiveness on social grounds. Speck was interested in aboriginal survivals in technology rather than in the social organization of the people with whom he worked, judging by the fieldnotes and published accounts he left (Speck Papers; 1925; 1928). Social scientists in those days had not made serious studies of Indians or other groups over long periods of time, partly because social science was still a new arrival on the academic scene, and shunned by historians, and partly because everyone, except the Indians, assumed that the Indians would soon disappear, which made documentation of cultural survivals seem much more urgent than studies of whole modern ways of life.

Virginia's citizen Indians, with more aboriginal memories and an equally unique history, were also distinct from their neighbors for as long as the surviving records show and probably much longer. It was (and still is) patently unjust to expect them to prove biological purity, in view of the gaps in the historical record and the tendency of all ethnic groups to be more or less "impure." Yet, given the racial ideology that everyone believed in at the time and the primitiveness of historical method and social science techniques back then, it is hard to see any other ground on which the battle could have been fought. The Whites "had" to demand racial purity in the Indians, and the Indians "had" to deny the charges of biological impurity. Yet, when we look back and test the citizen Indian groups against the standards of modern social definitions of ethnicity, "racial" or otherwise, we find that they pass with flying colors. And when we test their history against the kind of history that other, better documented Indian people have had in relation to non-Indians, they still pass with flying colors. The citizen Indians of nineteenth- and twentieth-century Virginia can be shown today to have been decidedly "Indian," and they must now be recognized as such in the literature.

ACKNOWLEDGMENTS

I am indebted to the following people for their comments on an earlier draft of this paper: Warren Cook, Pamunkey; Michael Holmes, Western Chickahominy; Chief Marvin Bradby, Eastern Chickahominy; Malcolm Tuppence, Upper Mattaponi; my teacher, Nancy O. Lurie; and my colleague, Leslie G. Carr. Another colleague, Paul Schollaert, assisted me with the statistical material.

REFERENCES

Adkins, O. Oliver (Western Chickahominy Chief).
        Papers, family and tribal. In Mr. Adkins' possession.
American Historical Society.
        1924   *History of Virginia*. Vol. 5, *Virginia Biography*. New York.
Anonymous.
        1906   "Treaty between Virginia and the Indians, 1677." *Virginia Magazine of History and Biography* 14:289-96.
Bass, A. A.
        1899   Letter. In Mooney Papers, National Anthropological Archives.
Beale, Calvin L.
        Papers. In Mr. Beale's possession; xeroxed copy of Virginia-related papers in author's possession.
        1957   "American Triracial Isolates." *Eugenics Quarterly* 4:187-96.
        1972   "An Overview of the Phenomenon of Mixed Racial Isolates in the United States." *American Anthropologist* 74:704-10.
        1973   Personal Communication.
Bell, Albert D.
        1961   *Bass Families of the South*. Rocky Mount, N.C.: privately printed.
Berry, Brewton.
        1963   *Almost White. A Study of Certain Racial Hybrids in the Eastern United States*. New York: Macmillan Company.

Beverley, Robert.
  1947 [1705]   *The History and Present State of Virginia*. Edited by
                 Louis B. Wright. Chapel Hill: University of North
                 Carolina Press.
Blu, Karen I.
  1980   *The Lumbee Problem: The Making of an American
                 Indian People*. New York: Cambridge University Press.
Booker, Russell.
  1973   Personal Communication.
Breton, Raymond.
  1964   "Institutional Completeness of Ethnic Communities
                 and the Personal Relations of Immigrants." *American
                 Journal of Sociology* 70:193-205.
Burnaby, Andrew.
  1812 [1760]   "Travels Through the Middle Settlements in North
                 America, in the Years 1759 and 1760." In *Voyages and
                 Travels*. Edited by John Pinkerton, XIII: 701-52.
Caroline County, Virginia.
                 Records. Bowling Green Court House.
Carr, Leslie G.
  1982   Personal Communication.
Charles City County, Virginia.
                 Records. Charles City Court House.
Coates, James R.
                 Papers. In Mr. Coates' possession; xeroxed duplicate in
                 author's possession.
  1971   Personal Communication.
Commonwealth of Virginia.
  1830-1831   *Acts of Assembly*. Richmond.
  1831-1832   *Acts of Assembly*. Richmond.
  1832-1833a   *House* [of Delegates] *Journal and Documents*.
                 Richmond.
  1832-1833b   *Acts of Assembly*. Richmond.
  1849   *Code of Virginia*. Richmond.
  1873   *Code of Virginia*. Richmond.
  1919   *Code of Virginia*. Richmond.
  1926   *Annual Report of the Bureau of Vital Statistics*.
                 Richmond.
  1928   *Annual Report of the Bureau of Vital Statistics*.
                 Richmond.
  1930   *Code of Virginia*. Richmond.

The [Richmond] *Dispatch.*
   1900 Various articles on Indian status on railroads. August through November.
Essex County, Virginia.
     Records. Tappahannock Court House.
Hening, William Waller, comp.
   1823 *The Statutes at Large, Being a Collection of All the Laws of Virginia from the First Session of the Legislature.* 13 volumes. New York: R. and W. and G. Bartow.
Hodge, Frederick Webb.
   1907, 1910 *Handbook of American Indians,* parts 1 and 2. Bureau of American Ethnology, Bulletin 30. Washington, D.C.: Government Printing Office.
Isajiw, Wsevolod.
   1974 "Definitions of Ethnicity." *Ethnicity* 1:111-24.
Jackson, Luther Porter.
   1971 [1942] *Free Negro Land and Property Holding in Virginia, 1830-1860.* New York: Russell and Russell.
King and Queen County, Virginia.
     Records. King and Queen County Court House.
King William County, Virginia.
     Records. King William County Court House.
Lyman, Stanford M., and William A. Douglass.
   1973 "Ethnicity: Strategies of Collective and Individual Impression Management." *Social Research* 40:344-65.
McIlwaine, H. R., comp.
   1918 *Legislative Journals of the Council of Colonial Virginia.* Virginia State Library, Richmond.
   1925 *Executive Journals of the Council of Colonial Virginia.* Virginia State Library, Richmond.
Merton, Robert K.
   1977 [1949] "Discrimination and the American Creed." In *Race, Ethnicity and Social Change.* Edited by John Stone, pp. 26-44. North Scituate, Mass.: Duxbury.
Mooney, James.
   1889-1889 Papers. National Anthropological Archives.
   1907 "The Powhatan Confederacy, Past and Present." *American Anthropologist* n.s. 9:128-52.
National Anthropological Archives.
     Photographic negatives.
New Kent County, Virginia.
     Records. New Kent County Court House.

Norfolk County, Virginia.
　　　Records.
Northumberland County, Virginia.
　　　Record Books (colonial).
Nugent, Nell Marion, comp.
　　1934　　*Cavaliers and Pioneers: Abstracts of Virginia Land
　　　　　　Patents and Grants.* Vol. 1. Richmond: Dietz Printing
　　　　　　Company.
　　1977　　*Cavaliers and Pioneers: Abstracts of Virginia Land
　　　　　　Patents and Grants.* Vol. 2. Richmond: Virginia State
　　　　　　Library.
Paredes, J. Anthony.
　　1980　　"Kinship and Descent in the Ethnic Reassertion of the
　　　　　　Eastern Creek Indians." In *The Versatility of Kinship.*
　　　　　　Edited by Linda S. Cordell and Stephen Beckerman, pp.
　　　　　　165-94. New York: Academic Press.
Peterson, John H., Jr.
　　1971　　"The Indian in the Old South." In *Red, White and
　　　　　　Black.* Edited by Charles Hudson, pp. 116-33. Athens:
　　　　　　University of Georgia Press.
Plecker, Walter Ashby.
　　1924　　*Eugenics in Relation to the New Family and the Law on
　　　　　　Racial Integrity, Including a Paper Read Before the
　　　　　　American Public Health Association.* Richmond:
　　　　　　Superintendent of Public Printing.
Pollard, John Garland.
　　1894　　*The Pamunkey Indians of Virginia.* Bureau of American
　　　　　　Ethnology, Bulletin 17.
Rountree, Helen C.
　　1971-1985　Fieldnotes.
　　1973　　"Indian Land Loss in Virginia: A Prototype of Federal
　　　　　　Indian Policy." Ph.D. diss., University of Wisconsin-
　　　　　　Milwaukee. University Microfilms, Ann Arbor.
　　1974　　"The Termination and Dispersal of the Nottoway
　　　　　　Indians of Virginia." Department of Sociology and
　　　　　　Criminal Justice, Old Dominion University. Xeroxed.
　　1975　　"Change Came Slowly: The Case of the Powhatan
　　　　　　Indians of Virginia." *Journal of Ethnic Studies*
　　　　　　3(3):1-20.
　　1979　　"The Indians of Virginia: a Third Race in a Biracial
　　　　　　State." In *Southeastern Indians Since the Removal Era.*
　　　　　　Edited by Walter L. Williams, pp. 27-48. Athens:
　　　　　　University of Georgia Press.

208   Strategies for Survival

Schollaert, Paul.
 1982   Personal Communication.
Selden, Jefferson Sinclair, Jr.
 ca. 1963   *The Sinclair Family of Virginia: Descendants of Henry Sinclair . . . and Allied Families.* Hampton, Va.: privately printed.
Shibutani, Tamotsu, and Kian M. Kwan.
 1965   *Ethnic Stratification.* New York: Macmillan Company.
Smith, John.
 ca. 1970   *Virginia Discouered and Described by Captayn John*
 [1606]   *Smith.* Map. Richmond: Virginia State Library.
Speck, Frank G.
 1911-1950   Papers. American Philosophical Society Library, Philadelphia.
 1925   "The Rappahannock Indians of Virginia." *Indian Notes and Monographs.* Vol. 5, no. 3. New York: Heye Foundation.
 1928   "Chapters on the Ethnology of the Powhatan Tribes of Virginia." *Indian Notes and Monographs.* Vol. 1, no. 5. New York: Heye Foundation.
Spicer, Edward.
 1971   "Persistent Identity Systems." *Science* 174:795-800.
Stanton, Max.
 1979   "Southern Louisiana Survivors: The Houma Indians." In *Southeastern Indians Since the Removal Era.* Edited by Walter L. Williams, pp. 90-109. Athens: University of Georgia Press.
Stern, Theodore.
 1952   "Chickahominy: The Changing Culture of a Virginia Indian Community." *Proceedings of the American Philosophical Society* 96:157-225.
The [Richmond] *Times.*
 1900a   Article on election of Chickahominy chief and officers. July 15, p. 2.
 1900b   Various articles on Indian status on railroads. August through November.
van den Berghe, Pierre L.
 1966   "Paternalistic Versus Competitive Race Relations: An Ideal-type Approach." In *Racial and Ethnic Relations: Selected Readings.* Edited by Bernard E. Segal, 1st ed., pp. 53-69. New York: Thomas Y. Crowell.

Wallace, Anthony F. C.
      1966   *Religion: An Anthropological View.* New York: Random House.
Williams, Walter L., ed.
      1979   *Southeastern Indians Since the Removal Era.* Athens: University of Georgia Press.

7
CONCLUSION
Frank W. Porter III

"The Indian is virtually extinct in the eastern United States," Julian H. Steward concluded in 1945, and in "a matter of years the last survivors will disappear without leaving any important cultural or racial mark on the national population" (1945:28). In the years since this statement was made, a significant amount of research aptly demonstrates the error of Steward's prediction. D'Arcy McNickle (1962), Brewton Berry (1963), and Walter L. Williams (1979) have convincingly demonstrated that American Indians did survive ethnically and culturally in the eastern United States. "In the regions of earliest contact, viz., the Atlantic seaboard and the states fronting on the Gulf of Mexico, tribal territories were appropriated and the indigenous population was either destroyed or driven inland," McNickle admits, but "in recent times, from the swamps and coves and wooded mountains of those regions Indians appear in growing numbers, and it is apparent that extermination was never complete" (1962:2).

The persistence and survival of American Indians in the eastern United States occurred in part because certain tribes or remnants of tribes refused to migrate west after signing treaties of land cessions. Since treaties frequently did provide land allotments, individual

Indian families, bands, or parts of bands remained behind on these tracts. Others simply would not abide by the agreement and severed themselves from the tribe (Snyderman 1951). Under these circumstances, these groups of Indians became isolated populations in their traditional habitats. In the course of time, many were assimilated gradually into White society, ultimately forgetting their native language and losing much—if not all—of their aboriginal culture.

Many of these American Indians were assimilated into White society to such a degree that they became virtually indistinguishable from their counterparts of Euro-American ancestry. It has been suggested that the common pattern of acculturation among these groups was to borrow a great many Euro-American traits and institutions and "fit them into a context of the older covert Indian patterns of life (Thomas 1961; Wax 1971:178). Many anthropologists describe such a situatiuon as a survival of fragments, of incomplete entities. McNickle, criticizing such a narrow point of view, declared: "Any people at any time is a survival of fragments out of the past. The function of culture is always to reconstitute the fragments into a functioning whole. The Indians, for all that has been lost or rendered useless out of their ancient experience, remain a continuing ethnic and cultural enclave, with a stake in the future" (1962:6).

Edward P. Dozier, George E. Simpson, and J. Milton Yinger suggest that the "place of Indians in American society may be seen as one aspect of the question of the integration of minority groups into the social system" (1957:158). Most studies have sought to determine whether Indians have been assimilated or integrated into American society. It seems apparent that before we raise questions about the assimilation or integration of these groups into American society, an effort should be made to determine how these cultural systems have persisted to the present. As the essays in this volume demonstrate, the survival of American Indians in the eastern United States has been under extremely adverse conditions, complex social environments, and baffling political situations.

In this context, Edward H. Spicer has identified and described a persistent identity system as a people's belief in their personal affiliation with certain symbols (1971:456-57). Spicer makes several important points: (1) a given identity system at one time may have no genetic characteristics in common with people who believe in that same system at a later date; (2) the focus is on history as people believe it to have taken place, not as an objective outsider sees it; (3) there have always been differences, either imposed by those outside the community or insisted on and maintained by the people concerned; and (4) a territory once occupied by a given people may be lost without the breakdown of the identity system. The persistent identity system is in large measure a product of these factors. Eric R. Wolf has added another important dimension with reference to organized communal structure. Wolf characterizes this structure as a "corporate" community that maintains a bounded social system with clear-cut limits, in relation to both outsiders and insiders, and has structural identity over time (1957:456-57).

The maintenance of a persistent identity system and the development of an organized community structure have been essential to the survival of American Indians in the eastern United States. Each attempt in the past by Whites to question or eliminate their Indian identity—be it racial classification, separate educational facilities, separate churches, or social segregation—has served only to strengthen their social cohesion and reinforce their Indian identity. The future will certainly present new problems for these American Indian communities. Given the difficulties which they have overcome in the past, it is clear they will continue to survive as distinct ethnic groups and to assert their role in American society.

REFERENCES

Berry, Brewton.
    1963   *Almost White: A Study of Certain Racial Hybrids in the Eastern United States.* New York: MacMillan Company.
Dozier, Edward P., George E. Simpson, and J. Milton Yinger.
    1957   "The Integration of Americans of Indian Descent." *Annals of the American Academy of Political and Social Science* 311:158-65.
McNickle, D'Arcy.
    1962   *The Indian Tribes of the United States: Ethnic and Cultural Survival.* New York and London: University of Oxford Press.
Snyderman, George L.
    1951   "Concepts of Land Ownership Among the Iroquois and Their Neighbors." In *Symposium on Local Diversity in*

Iroquois Culture. Bureau of American Ethnology. Bulletin 149, pp. 15-34.

Spicer, Edward H.
    1971   "Persistent Cultural Systems: A Comparative Study of Identity Systems." *Science* 174:795-800.

Steward, Julian H.
    1945   The Changing American Indian. In *The Science of Man in the World Crisis.* Edited by Ralph Linton, pp. 282-305. New York: Columbia University Press.

Thomas, Robert K.
    1961   "Population Trends in American Indian Communities." Paper presented for the American Indian Chicago Conference, Chicago.

Wax, Murray L.
    1971   *Indian Americans. Unity and Diversity.* Englewood Cliffs: Prentice-Hall.

William, Walter L., ed.
    1979   *Southeastern Indians Since the Removal Era.* Athens: University of Georgia Press.

Wolf, Eric R.
    1955   "Types of Latin American Peasantry: A Preliminary Discussion." *American Anthropologist* 59:452-71.

BIBLIOGRAPHICAL ESSAY

In recent years there has been a significant increase in the volume of literature about American Indian tribes in the eastern United States. Many of these tribes are not officially recognized by the Federal government and, as a consequence, receive no services from the Bureau of Indian Affairs. Paradoxically, some of these studies were written by anthropologists working in the Bureau of Indian Affairs. Many of the publications are not widely known by students, professional scholars, or tribal historians. Most of the older literature has become antiquated, obsolete, and out of print. Both the published and unpublished material is uneven in quality.

During the nineteenth century, little attention was given to the belief that small enclaves of Indians remained in the eastern United States. "As a sizeable native minority they deserve more attention than the meager investigations which sociologists and anthropologists have hitherto made of their problem," observed William Harlan Gilbert in "Memorandum Concerning the Characteristics of the Larger Mixed-Blood Racial Islands of the Eastern United States," *Social Forces* 24 (May 1946):438. Beginning in the 1930s and continuing to the present, a number of social scientists have directed their research at several population groups of presumed tri-racial descent. Variously termed mulattoes, mestizos, mixed-bloods, and tri-racial isolates, the consensus was that they were a people of intermingled Indian, Caucasian, and Negro ancestry.

Although the myth of the vanishing Indian in the eastern United States was laid to rest, this particular line of research certainly created new problems and raised new questions. For the most part, the White population remained confused about the origin and status of these isolated communities. More recent studies have addressed these critical and sensitive issues, but, as B. Eugene Griessman has stressed in "The American Isolates," *American Anthropologist* 74 (1972):694, difficulties have confronted researchers involved with these communities.

In many ways a person who studies these peoples is like a surveyor who goes into an area where there has been a boundary dispute. Some of the principals would prefer that he stay away and "let matters be." The reason is that through the years boundaries have been formed and agreements have been reached. An investigator, even though careful and fair, can disturb or threaten these arrangements.

This brief bibliographical essay is representative of the literature available about nonrecognized American Indians in the eastern United States.

GENERAL STUDIES

The history of many of the nonrecognized tribes in the eastern United States has always been something of an enigma. In the absence of historical documentation, myths and legends surrounding their communities have flourished. Only a few of these communities have been the subject of scholarly research. In the 1940s, social scientists became extremely interested in geographically and culturally isolated settlements and communities of people who were deemed to be the products of miscegenation between Whites, Blacks, and Indians.

William Harland Gilbert became a leading authority on these groups. In "Memorandum Concerning the Characteristics of the Larger Mixed-Blood Racial Islands of the Eastern United States," *Social Forces* 24 (May 1946):438-47, Gilbert provides a general discussion of the primary characteristics of these "racial islands." Gilbert elaborated this study in *Synoptic Survey of Data on the Survival of Indian and Part Indian Blood in the Eastern United States* (Washington, D.C.: Library of Congress, Legislative Reference Service, 1947) and "Surviving Indian Groups of the Eastern United States," *Annual Report of the Board of Regents of the Smithsonian Institution for 1948* (Washington, D.C.: Government Printing Office, 1949). The material about these groups is presented by individual states in geographical order. Brewton Berry's *Almost White: A Study of Certain Racial Hybrids in the Eastern United States* (New York: Macmillan Company, 1963) remains the major work about the survival of Indians in the eastern United States. Berry examined in great detail the social dilemma which faced these communities because of their Indian, White, and Black ancestry.

In 1972, the *American Anthropologist* provided a special section about "The American Isolates," with B. Eugene Griessman as editor. The series included Calvin Beale's "An Overview of the Phenomenon of Mixed Racial Isolates in the United States." Lynwood Montell settled many of the myths surrounding the Coe Ridge Colony of Kentucky. Griessman and J. K. Dane, focusing on the Haliwa and Sampson County Indians of North Carolina, examined the conditions and forces that make for the collective identity within these isolated communities. Daniel F. Collins discussed the Jackson Whites (Ramapo Mountain Indians) of New Jersey. John Peterson demonstrated that the social position of the Choctaw in Mississippi is not based on miscegenation but on their being a third group in a local society which recognizes only two racial groups, White and non-White. William S. Pollitzer summarized the studies of the physical anthropology of these communities in the southeastern United States. Edgar T. Thompson proposed that these Indian communities are "little races," but Griessman suggests they be viewed as "marginal peoples."

Southeastern Indians Since the Removal Era, edited by Walter L. Williams (Athens: University of Georgia Press, 1979), presents an overview history of the American Indian groups remaining in the southeastern United States. The authors of this collection of essays discuss both nonrecognized and recognized tribal groups who remained behind after the removals.

ORIGINS

The origin of the American Indians has been questioned since the first Europeans set foot on the shores of North America. Brewton Berry, in "The Myth of the Vanishing Indian," *Phylon* 21 (Spring 1960):51-57, demonstrates that the fantastic and diverse answers put forth by the early explorers, missionaries, and settlers are no less final or consistent than the answers provided us today by scientists and scholars. There has been one perennial question, however, upon which there has been unanimous agreement. What is to become of the American Indian? Each generation of Whites has responded: They will disappear. Scattered throughout magazines and periodicals published in the nineteenth century in the eastern United States are articles about the "last" surviving Indian(s) of their state. C. S. Rafinesque (1832:128), for example, briefly discussed "The Last Indians of New Jersey," *Atlantic Journal* 1 (1832):128. Colonel D. Mead (1832:127-28) in the same issue of the *Atlantic Journal*, described "The Last Indians of Virginia" as a few individual Pamunkeys in 1822. Benson J. Lossing (1877:452), in his testimonial about "The Last of the Pequods," in *The Indian Miscellany*, edited by W. W. Beach, (Albany: J. Munsell, 1877, p. 452), offered a slightly different twist. "Art, history, and romance have touchingly depicted that rare, melancholy person, the last of *his* race or nation, but have yet failed to portray that rare, melancholy being, the last of *her* race of nation," observed Lossing as he recounted his visit with Eunice Mahwee—"the last of the Pequods." Nathan Lewis similarly described "The Last of the Narragansetts," *Proceedings of the Worchester Society of Antiquity* 16 (1897).

DETAILED HISTORIES

In recent years, detailed histories of a handful of the nonrecognized tribes in the eastern United States have resolved many misconceptions about their origin. Lynwood Montell's *The Saga of Coe Ridge: A Study in Oral History* (Knoxville: University of Tennessee Press, 1970) clearly demonstrated that the absence of written records need not be a deterrent in the study of isolated, rural communities. David S. Cohen's *The Ramapo Mountain People*

(New Brunswick: Rutger's University Press, 1974), conversely, challenged the oral traditions surrounding the origins of the Ramapo Mountain Indians through extensive research and documentation. Daniel Collins' "The Racially-mixed People of the Ramapos: Undoing the Jackson White Legends," *American Anthropologist* 74 (1972):1276-85 should also be consulted. C. A. Weslager's *The Nanticoke Indians* (Newark: University of Delaware Press, 1983) is an updated version of his earlier *Delaware's Forgotten People.* Weslager chronicles the history and survival of the Nanticoke who remained in Delaware after their tribe migrated northward. The cultural survival and community growth of Indians in Virginia are documented in Theodore Stern's "Chickahominy: the Changing Culture of a Virginia Indian Community," *Proceedings of the American Philosophical Society* 96 (April 1952):157-225 and Helen C. Rountree's "Change Came Slowly: The Case of the Powhatan Indians of Virginia," *Journal of Ethnic Studies* 3 (1975):1-20; "The Indians of Virginia: A Third Race in a Biracial State," in *Southeastern Indians Since the Removal Era,* pp. 27-48, edited by Walter L. Williams (Athens: University of Georgia Press, 1979); and "Powhatan's Descendants in the Modern World: Community Studies of Two Indian Reservations with Notes on Five Non-Reservation Enclaves," *The Chesopian* 10 (1975):62-96. Ethel Bossevain's "Narragansett Survival: A Study Through Adapted Traits," *Ethnohistory* 6 (Fall 1959):347-62 and "The Detribalization of the Narragansett Indians: A Case Study," *Ethnohistory* 3 (Summer 1956):225-45 discuss the processes whereby the Narragansett, who recently obtained Federal recognition, adapted to White society in order to survive.

RACIAL PREJUDICE IN SCHOOLS AND CHURCHES

The public school was the battleground for Indians in the eastern United States, for it was there that the question of their racial identity was explicitly challenged. In those states where Indians were most numerous, they were excluded from the White schools, and only under extreme duress would they attend schools for Blacks. In some communities, Indians constructed and maintained their own schools; elsewhere, missionaries provided education for them; special schools were established by some states; or they simply did not attend school at all.

The North Carolina Lumbee's struggle to have schools of their own became the foundation for their pride, dignity, and recognition as an identifiable race. Adolph L. Dial and David K. Eliades discuss the Lumbee's fight for education in *The Only Land I Know: A History of the Lumbee Indians* (San Francisco: Indian Historian Press, 1975). Dial and Eliades also provide the history of "The Lumbee Indians of North Carolina and Pembroke State University," *Indian Historian* 4 (Winter 1971):20-24. Weslager documents the Nanticoke's efforts to provide schools for their children in *The Nanticoke Indians* (Newark: University of Delaware Press, 1983).

The influence of the church in the development of eastern Indian communities has not been adequately studied. The church has served through time as a focus for group loyalty and identity. Thomas J. Harte has analyzed "The Integrative Role of Religion in the Brandywine Population," in *Research Plans in the Fields of Religion, Values, and Morality,* edited by Stuart W. Cook (New York: The Religious Education Association, 1962).

FAMILY AND COMMUNITY LIFE

The family and the community life of nonrecognized tribes have received very little treatment. There have been some studies of the demography of nonrecognized tribes. In an early study, Roland M. Harper suggested that the Lumbee Indians of North Carolina were "The Most Prolific People in the United States," *Eugenical News* 23 (March-April 1938):29-31. His data was drawn from "A Statistical Study of the Croatans," *Rural Sociology* 2 (December 1937):444-56. More recently, the students of Thomas J. Harte at The Catholic University of America extensively investigated the demography of the Brandywine community of southern Maryland, a group descended from the Piscataway. Sister Ellen Mary Desmond focused on "Mortality in the Brandywine Population of Southern Maryland," (Ph.D. diss., Catholic University of America, 1962). Sister Claire M. Sawyer discussed *Some Aspects of the Fertility of a Tri-Racial Isolate* (Washington, D.C.: Catholic University of America, 1961). And Angelita Q. Yap performed *A Study of a*

Kinship System: Its Structural Principles (Washington, D.C.: Catholic University of America, 1961). No other eastern Indian community has been so exhaustively studied as the Brandywine of southern Maryland.

URBAN INDIANS

In the mid-twentieth century, there was a prodigious exodus of nonrecognized Indians from their rural enclaves to urban centers. In the cities, they found jobs as construction workers, factory operatives, mechanics, carpenters, truck drivers, painters, and day laborers. The Lumbee Indians in Baltimore, Maryland have been studied quite thoroughly. Mohammed Amanullah's *The Lumbee Indians: Patterns of Adjustment* (Washington, D.C.: Government Printing Office, 1969) discusses the development of leadership within the group and concentrated assistance in obtaining available social, educational, and employment opportunities. Abraham Makofsky has examined "Tradition and Change in the Lumbee Indian Community of Baltimore," *Maryland Historical Magazine* 75 (March 1980):55-71 and with his son, David, has explored "Class Consciousness and Culture: Class Identifications in the Lumbee Indian Community of Baltimore," *Anthropological Quarterly* 46 (October 1973):261-77. John G. Peck's "Urban Station: Migration Patterns of the Lumbee Indians" (Ph.D. diss., University of North Carolina, 1972) discusses the movement of the Lumbee to various northern cities.

NON-RECOGNIZED TRIBES IN FICTION

The social life and economic life of non-recognized tribes have occasionally been portrayed in fiction. The "Brass Ankles" are the basis for Gertrude M. Shelby and Samuel G. Stoney's *"Po' Buckra* (New York: MacMillan Co., 1930) and DuBose Heyward's *Brass Ankle* (New York: Farrar and Rhinehart, 1931).

EASTERN INDIAN LAND CLAIMS

One of the most important issues to develop concerning Indian rights has been eastern Indian land claims. *Passamaquoddy Tribe v. Morton* is potentially the most complex litigation ever brought in the Federal courts. The origins of the eastern Indian land claims are discussed in Robert N. Clinton and Margaret Tobey Hotopp's "Judicial Enforcement of the Federal Restraints on Alienation of Indian Land: The Origins of the Eastern Land Claims," *Maine Law Review* 31 (1979):17-90. Reynold Nebel, Jr., analyzes the "Resolution of Eastern Indian Land Claims: A Proposal for Negotiated Settlements," *American University Law Review* 27 (Spring 1978):695-731. The events leading up to the Passamaquoddy case are carefully presented in Francis J. O'Toole and Thomas N. Tureen's "State Power and the Passamaquoddy Tribe: 'A Gross National Hypocrisy'?" *Maine Law Review* 23 (1971):1-39. Tim Vollman presents "A Survey of Eastern Indian Land Claims: 1970-1979," *Maine Law Review* 31 (1979):5-16. An excellent overview of eastern Indian land claims may be found in *Indian Tribes: A Continuing Quest for Survival,* a report prepared by the United States Commission on Civil Rights in 1981. Paul Brodeur's *Restitution: The Land Claims of the Mashpee, Passamaquoddy, and Penobscot Indians of New England* (Boston: Northeastern University Press, 1985) explains why the claims were made in the first place and how the cases were ultimately resolved.

NONRECOGNITION OF INDIANS IN THE EASTERN UNITED STATES

There is no commonly accepted definition of an Indian. Each agency of the Federal government uses different criteria to define who is an Indian. It should be obvious that the term "Indian" today has very little relation to racial purity. Berry, in "The Myth of the Vanishing Indian," *Phylon* 21 (Spring 1960):51-57, points out:

Under the effects of different laws the same individual may be counted as Indian for some purposes and non-Indian for others. Officially classified as Indians are many persons whose ancestry is largely that of other races. Individuals with as little as one two-hundred and fifty-sixth part Indian blood have been included in allotments of tribal lands. At the same time there are many whose degree of Indian blood is considerable, but who are going, by preference or otherwise, as either White or Negro (1960:55).

Because the definition of an Indian is quite complex, population figures leave much to be desired. Calvin L. Beale had detailed the "Census Problems of Racial Enumeration" in *Race: Individual and Collective Behavior,* edited by Edgar T. Thompson (New York: The Free Press, 1958), especially as it pertained to nonrecognized tribes. Anthony J. Paredes and Kaye Lenihan have analyzed "Native American Population in the Southeastern States, 1960-1970," *Florida Anthropologist* 26 (1973):45-46.

There has been, to date, very little literature about the phenomenon of nonrecognition of American Indian tribes. An excellent summary is provided by the American Indian Policy Review Commission's *Report on Terminated and Nonfederally Recognized Indians* (Washington, D.C.: Government Printing Office, 1976). *Nonrecognized American Indian Tribes: An Historical and Legal Perspective* (Chicago: The Newberry Library, 1983, edited by Frank W. Porter), examines the historical and legal precedents of nonrecognition. Terry Anderson's "Federal Recognition: The Vicious Myth," *American Indian Journal* 4 (May 1978):7-19 vividly points out the contradictions on the part of the Bureau of Indian Affairs in their dealings with nonrecognized tribes.

INDEX

ABOUT THE CONTRIBUTORS

MARSHALL BECKER received his Ph.D. in Anthropology from the University of Pennsylvania. He is Associate Professor of Anthropology at West Chester University in West Chester, Pennsylvania.

ELLICE B. GONZALEZ received her Ph.D. from the State University of New York at Stony Brook. She was formerly a member of the Sociology and Anthropology Departments at the University of New Hampshire and at Colgate University. Dr. Gonzalez is currently practicing anthropology in the business world. She is the founder of STRATEGIC SOLUTIONS, a marketing consulting firm serving small and medium-size businesses in the New York metropolitan area.

FRANK W. PORTER III received his Ph.D. in Geography from the University of Maryland. He is Director of the American Indian Research and Resource Institute at Gettysburg College in Gettysburg, Pennsylvania.

HELEN C. ROUNTREE received her Ph.D. in Anthropology at the University of Wisconsin-Milwaukee. She is Associate Professor of Anthropology at Old Dominion University in Norfolk, Virginia.

LAURIE WEINSTEIN received her Ph.D. in Anthropology at Southern Methodist University. She is Lecturer in Anthropology at Northeastern University in Boston, Massachusetts and Guest Curator at the Haffenreffer Museum of Anthropology at Brown University.